On Art and Literature

On Art and Literature

Critical Writings

José Martí

Edited, with an introduction and notes by
Philip S Foner

Translated by
Elinor Randall

With additional translations by
Luis A Baralt
Juan de Onís
Roslyn Held Foner

AAKAR

On Art and Literature: Critical Writings
José Martí

First Published in India 2011
Reprinted 2025

ISBN 978-93-5002-144-6

Published in agreement with Monthly Review Press, New York for publication and sale only in South Asia.

Published by
AAKAR BOOKS
28 E Pocket IV, Mayur Vihar Phase I
Delhi 110 091, India
www.aakarbooks.com

Printed at
D.K. Fine Art Press, Delhi

Contents

Preface 9
Introduction by Philip S. Foner 13

I
Art and Artists

Painting: Felipe Gutiérrez 35
A Visit to an Exhibition of Art 38
A Visit to an Exhibition of Art (Continued) 44
A Visit to an Exhibition of Art (Concluded) 49
Marat's Death 54
The Painter Carbó 63
Sculpture: Francisco Dumaine 66
Impulses of the Heart: A Play by Peón Contreras 69
The Metropolitan Museum 74
The Fifty-Fifth Exhibition in the National Academy of Design 80
Fromentin 83
The Runkle Collection 87
A Statue and a Sculptor 90
A Remarkable Mexican Painting 92
Fortuny 94
Edouard Detaille 97
The French Water-Colorists 101
Goya 106

Ancient American Man and His Primitive Arts 113
A New Exhibition of Impressionist Painters 118
The Munkacsy Christ 125
Exhibition of Paintings by the Russian Vereshchagin 135

II
Literature and Literary Figures

Emerson 149
Walt Whitman, the Poet 168
Longfellow 186
Mark Twain 190
Louisa May Alcott 197
Aboriginal American Authors 201
Modern French Novelists 205
Heredia 208
Francisco Sellén 225
Julián del Casal 242
Charles Darwin 245
Modern Spanish Poets 257
The Pampa 266
Flaubert's Last Work 278
Pushkin 284
Oscar Wilde 294
Literary Matters 305
The Poem of Niagara 308

III
José Martí's Literary Will and Testament

Letter to Gonzalo de Quesada 329

IV
Chronology of the Life of José Martí

Chronology 335
Index 343

On Art and Literature

Preface

The importance of José Martí as a critic is being increasingly recognized. Manuel Pedro González and Ivan Schulman consider him as "one of the most original and brilliant men writing in Spanish," and, in their opinion, no other in Spain or Hispanic-America equals him as a literary commentator.[1] The late Cuban literary giant, Juan Marinello, did not hesitate to proclaim José Martí the greatest critic of the Hispanic world.[2]

Martí's writings as a critic encompassed literature, plastic arts, theater, and music. But it is generally agreed that his writings in the first two categories are more important. He himself recognized this by suggesting that his collected works include material gathered under the name *letras*, *educación*, and *pinturas* (literature, education, and painting). We have published Martí's writings on education together with selections from his writings for children in *The Age of Gold* in the third volume in this series.[3] The present volume, the last in the series, includes Martí's essays on art and literature. We use the term essays, even though Martí himself did not give them this name, in keeping with the trend in modern criticism. I have also included one article by Martí dealing with the theater. This is his review of the play *Impulses of the Heart* by the Mexican playwright Peón Contreras, which, fortunately, includes several of Martí's most interesting comments on the theater.

Although Martí's remarkable studies of Ralph Waldo Emerson and Walt Whitman have been translated more than once into English,[4] none of his art criticism and few of his other literary essays have been made available to English-speaking readers. Hence the present volume in the comprehensive of the writings of José Martí in English is of special importance.

In this volume most of the translations are by Elinor Randall. However, the article on Longfellow has been translated by Luis A. Baralt and those on Charles Darwin and The Pampa by Juan de Onís. My wife, Roslyn Held Foner, translated excerpts from Martí's writings and by others in Spanish that are used in the introduction.

In the preparation of this volume I again had the good fortune to be able to discuss its contents during visits to Cuba and through correspondence with Roberto Fernández Retamar, director of Casa de las Americas and of the Centro de Estudios Martianos, and with Salvador Morales, the director of Sala Martí, Biblioteca Nacional in Havana. I wish to thank them for valuable suggestions. I also wish to thank Enrique Gaona Suárez and his charming and industrious wife, Esther Schumacher, for assisting me, through the organization they direct, CEHSMO of Mexico City, in obtaining copies of Martí's articles in *Revista Universal* of Mexico City.

Philip S. Foner

Professor Emeritus
Lincoln University, Pennsylvania
September, 1981

Notes

1. José Martí, *Literary Sketches: Selección*, preface, footnotes, and notes by Manuel Pedro González and Ivan Schulman (Mexico, 1961), p. 257.

2. Juan Marinello, "Estrada," *José Martí, Crítica Literaria* (Havana, 1960).

3. *On Education: Articles on Educational Theory and Pedagogy, and Writings for Children from The Age of Gold*, translated by Elinor Randall, edited by Philip S. Foner (New York, 1979).

4. Two other translations of the essay on Emerson are available in English: one by Juan de Onís *(The America of José Martí)*, another by Luis Baralt *(Martí on the U.S.A.)*. Four other translations of the essay on Whitman are available in English: one by Juan de Onís *(The America of José Martí)*; one by Luis Baralt *(Martí on the U.S.A.)*; one in Guy Wilson Allen, *Walt Whitman Abroad* (Syracuse, 1955); and one in *Homenaje a Walt Whitman: Homage to Walt Whitman*, trans. notes by Didier Tisdel Jaén (University of Alabama, 1969).

Introduction by Philip S. Foner

In April 1880, José Martí wrote to his friend Miguel Viandi in Havana: "If you could see me struggling to dominate this beautiful but rebellious English: Three or four months more and I shall open a way for myself."[1] Martí's first article in English testifies both to his remarkable ability to master the language as well as his insight as a critic of art. Written for the newly founded magazine *The Hour*, it was entitled "The Metropolitan Museum of Art."[2] Martí's appreciation for the leading art museum in the New World comes through clearly and vividly. Thus he wrote:

> New York may well be proud of its Metropolitan Museum of Art, of the precious ceramic collection and the highly interesting Japanese works to be found there. A well-arranged light adds to the real value of the objects accumulated. Old laces, ancient books, classic engravings, are placed side by side with the most remarkable products of Asiatic art. In the capacious halls everything looks clean and fresh; the mummies grin and the sarcaophagi recall memories of ancient history, not of death. Classification and division have been closely attended to, as if the director intended to prepare visitors for the study and not merely for the contemplation of treasures.[3]

Martí also wrote on art in French for the *New York Sun*. These were translated into English for publication. In whatever language he wrote, however, Martí as an art critic did not wander into unfamiliar fields. From his visits to the museums of Spain and France, he brought to his writings on art rapidly jotted notes, ideas, and his own sound judgment. In Madrid he had the opportunity to study modern Spanish paintings, especially those by Rosales and Madrago and the work of Fortuny. In Zaragoza, moreover, Martí became acquainted with the painter Pablo Gonzalvo. Through frequent visits to Gonzalvo's studio and discussions with him on art, Martí acquired ideas that were to influence his writings. Then too, he came to know the work of Goya whose paintings were well represented in Zaragoza. Years later Martí called Goya "one of my teachers," and exclaimed: "Here is a great philosopher—this painter—a great vindicator, a great demolisher of all the infamous and terrible."[4]

While in Mexico, Martí made the acquaintance of the Mexican painter Manuel Ocaranza, and he spent hours at his studio watching him paint and listening to discussions of art by Ocaranza and his artistic colleagues. It was a period of intense intellectual life in Mexico, and the discussion emphasized that Mexican art should be separated from European models in order to seek its own expression. Through Ocaranza, Martí became acquainted with the work of Mexican artists and the artists themselves.

In *Revista Universal*, published in Mexico City, Martí commented on contemporary Mexican art. Unlike many other critics, he did not praise that which was European and denigrate that which was American. He insisted, rather, that if they wished to go forward, the American artists had to forget European models and dig into their own roots.

Because these were their traditions, they were not artificial. Of course, this did not mean that they should ignore everything that Europe had accomplished, but it did mean that Europe should cease being the only model to be imitated.[5]

Here is an example of Martí's insight as an art critic, written when he was but eighteen years of age. Published in *Revista Universal* of August 24, 1875, Martí's article began:

In Mexico there is a prominent painter whose presence among us gladdens the few who know him, and pleases everyone who enjoys seeing the art of painting in strong and intelligent hands.

Felipe Gutiérrez paints with great brush strokes within great areas of shading. He does not dilute the light but disintegrates and contrasts it; he does not draw with lines but with experimental attacks of the brush. He does not use chiaroscuro but light and dark; a bold and luminous light and a dark filled with power and vigor. He opposes one to the other, does not reconcile them. His style is free and proper to a painter who has seen life in the canvases of Michelangelo, Ribera and Tintoretto. Gutiérrez paints rapidly, prolifically and very well. He has something of the imposing coldness of Rosales. The Spanish artist painted with nerves and muscles rather than with colors. Gutiérrez goes hurriedly down that path.

Or this in *Revista Universal* of December 31, 1875:

Art is a form of harmony. At times irregularity is artistic; but irregularity in painting must be logical in its fundamentals, as the whims of poetic fantasy must be logical and grouped in a unity. Monotony is a wild beast because it destroys everything, even the sanctity and customs of love. In painting, the parallel lines, symmetrical dots of color, uniform and alternating lines, geometrize the figure, vitiate the whole, and destroy the painting's grace and undulations with the harshness of straight lines. There is no beauty in rigidity: life is mobile, daring, abandoned, tender, active; the flesh has to be sensed and the nerves felt in an attitude of movement; if grief has been copied, tears must hang from the soft and silken eyelids; if fierceness has been imitated, angers must be collected upon the formidable furrowed brow. In painting, the simple is nonexistent: the first step is the beautiful, the next the sublime. A painter must not be said to be accurate, but proud, innovative, spirited and grand.[6]

Art, in Martí's view, was an enjoyment for mankind, but it must also serve as a link of unity among people. It must be at the service of truth, progress, and justice. "What is art," he observed, "but the shortest way of achieving the triumph of truth, and placing it at the same time, so that it will endure and shine in hearts and minds?" Art was "not a venal adornment of kings and pontiffs, where the face of genius is barely seen, but a divine accumulation of souls, where men of all the ages meet and congregate." The true artist had to be inspired by all that elevated mankind.[7]

Martí's art criticism reveals him to have been in advance of his time in appreciating the great contribution of the impressionists. He understood, moreover, how difficult it was for the avant-garde painters of nineteenth-century France to overcome the all-powerful domination of the academic painters, who opposed every innovation and fresh thought of the period, bringing misery and often penury to many of the great painters of the time—Courbet, Manet, Monet, Degas, Pissarro, and Renoir—who were so often penalized for their originality and daring. Through their control of official schools, exhibitions, and patronage, the academic painters relegated the real masters of nineteenth-century French painting to obscurity; Martí tried to break this influence, and called for recognition of the truly great painters of the period. True, he appreciated that the academicians were prodigious in their technical prowess, but he saw that the impressionists were bringing art to a new and more significant horizon and would influence the entire course of painting for centuries to come.[8]

Martí's comments on art in the United States are also significant. He observed that there were preparations for great artists of the future, but at the time he was writing, there was little or no North American art. Describing the "Fifty-Fifth Exhibition in the National Academy of Design," he noted the wealth of unfinished portraits, which tended to give the exhibition the appearance of a studio rather than a gallery. Upon close observation, it became evident that the important workers were not North American.

Yet, Martí observed, there was ample evidence to support the view that the United States was well on the way toward the development of its art. There were important galleries and there were the best of instructors. There were also numerous models to follow. Still as a comparatively new nation the United States had not had the time to develop a true North American art.[9]

How different was Martí's evaluation of North American writers. In an article written in 1889 for *El Partido Liberal*, Martí reviewed the book *Jonathan and His Continent* by Max O'Rell, the pen name for the French author Paul Blouet. In his review Martí dismissed the book as a superficial view of the United States. But he reserved his sharpest criticism for the French author-journalist's treatment of literature in the United States. After commenting on the book's overall superficiality, Martí wrote:

> And nowhere is this deficiency and lightness more evident than in what the author says about literature, which consists of a short list of names, without any attempt at classification or comment and without the type of passing sentence in which it is understood that the modesty of the critic belies his considerable knowledge of the subject. By listing Whitman he thinks he's said it all; without knowing who Thoreau was he declares that North America has no writers who depict nature, and since he is ignorant of Emerson to the point of omitting the name of America's foremost poet, he assures us that the U.S. has not yet produced a transcendental genius.[10]

Although, as we have seen in previous volumes, Martí took a keen interest in nearly every phase of American life, he was especially involved in understanding and evaluating the nation's literature. In his "literary testament," written only about a month before his death and directed to his disciple, Gonzalo de Quesada, the Cuban revolutionist revealed his concern that his writings about North American authors be well represented in the collection of his works for posterity.

These writings include seven articles or essays that deal at length with a single United States author: Ralph Waldo Emerson, Walt Whitman, Henry Wadsworth Longfellow, John Greenleaf Whittier, Amos Bronson Alcott, Louisa May Alcott, and Mark Twain. But Martí also discussed Edgar Allan Poe, James Russell Lowell, Washington Irving, Henry David Thoreau, Nathaniel Hawthorne, Fitz-Greene Halleck, Harriet Beecher Stowe, Helen Hunt Jackson, and William Dean Howells. As José Antonio Portuondo, the distinguished Cuban literary critic, has pointed out: "Neither before nor after him has there been a writer of our language who has judged North American literature in such quantity and with greater awareness."[11]

In *Martí Escritor*, published in 1945, Andrés Iduarte rates Martí's essay on Ralph Waldo Emerson one of the best Spanish-language essays of the nineteenth century and the "clue to the depth and form of Martí."[12] Others, like Esther Elise Shuler, argue that Martí is so wrapped up in his subject, and is so enthusiastically identified with Emerson, that it is difficult to know where what refers to Emerson ends and what pertains to Martí begins.[13] Felix Lizaso, the Martí critic, points out that the discovery of Emerson was a turning point in Martí's life.[14] And, indeed, among Martí's notes, we find the following passage:

> I have journeyed through much of my life and partaken of its various pleasures, but the greatest pleasure, the only absolutely pure pleasure which I have experienced up to this point, was the one I felt that afternoon when I looked out from my room to the prostrate city and envisioned the future, thinking about Emerson.[15]

The Emerson essay was written shortly after Emerson's death in Concord on April 27, 1882. Yet this was only the most extended treatment of Martí devoted to Emerson. The number of other tributes, comments in his notebooks,[16] references in many of his articles, and translations of several poems[17] and fragments of verse by Emerson, reveal that Martí devoted more time, effort, and interest to Emerson than to any other North American author. Just when Martí began to take an interest in Emerson is difficult to establish. There are no references to

Emerson in his writings until 1881, that is, until Martí was a resident in the United States. Lizaso has suggested that Martí may have had knowledge of the sage of Concord prior to that time.[18] But it is evident that Martí was convinced that to anyone interested in the life and mind and imagination of America, Ralph Waldo Emerson is indispensable.

Ivan Schulman, a specialist in Martí's use of symbols, points out that Martí employed his loftiest symbols in writing of Emerson. Emerson is likened to a mountain, the symbol of a superior being. Or he is typified by the words "eagle" and "pine," two symbols which represent color and greatness. "Star" is used as a symbol of ideal human qualities in Emerson, and "butterfly of fire" is used to represent the free flight of Emerson's artistic inspiration. The poet's verses are symbolized with "wings of gold." Schulman also notes that Martí was like Emerson in his implicit preference for symbols of nature. He points to light, sun, and stars as three major symbols used by both Emerson and Martí. There is even evidence, according to Schulman, of Emerson's concept of analogies in nature being incorporated into Martí's thinking.[19]

To Martí, Emerson was a monarch, a noble lion, a giant in the realm of ideas. Reading Emerson filled one's mind with light, set one's soul ablaze. His pages were radiant. For Martí, Emerson embodied purity and virtue; his works were lucid and pure. When Emerson said, "The soul is the perceiver and revealer of truth," Martí viewed it as the utterance of a seer. He did not consider Emerson a member of the Transcendentalist group of New England, but a lone prophet rising in America to teach mankind. Emerson was a man who saw the essence of the human spirit as evident in all peoples, a man whose spirit would serve as a salvation for the selfish interests at work in the United States.[20]

What Martí admired most in Emerson was his complete independence of mind from the chains of the past and established institutions. He read with joy how Emerson boldly attacked tradition, institutions, public opinion—all the external authorities other Americans were concerned to establish—which impeded the development of the individual imagination and with it republican virtue. That which so shocked the Harvard ministry was noble to Martí. He could heartily agree with Emerson's observations in the "Divinity School Address": "Wherever a man comes, there comes revolution. The old is for slaves. When a man comes, all books are legible, all things transparent, all religions are forms. He is religious. Man is the wonderworker." Such doctrines challenged the basic religious and social beliefs of conservative New England Unitarians, but they thrilled Martí. Even before John Dewey, Martí heralded Emerson as "the Philosopher of Democracy."[21]

Then too, Martí considered Emerson as justifying his own theory that man was glorified by being allowed to partake of the universal truth. Emerson's concept of the Over-Soul appealed to Martí who was a religious man by nature but anticlerical in opinion. Both believed in an impersonal God. Martí accepted Emerson's formulation of the Over-Soul as the cornerstone of his philosophy. Emerson defined God as "the soul of the world whole, the wise science; the universal beauty, to which every part and particle is equally related, the eternal one," a definition that Martí accepted. He accepted, too, Emerson's assertion of the divinity of nature, the morality of the universe, and his celebration of the individual who stood in primary relations to the world and refused to take life secondhand.[22]

One aspect of Emerson's thought that appears to have had particular appeal for Martí was the idea that the poet might discover truth before the scientist did. Martí did not denigrate the role of science; indeed, as is made abundantly clear in the volume of his writings on education, he insisted that science be incorporated into the educational curriculum beginning with elementary school.[23] But he believed that the universe presented a challenge for both men of science and men of letters, and that the latter were often more understanding of the former. "When the cycle of science is complete and it knows all there is to know, it will not know more than the spirit knows today," he wrote. In a June, 1883 article in *La America*, Martí mentioned Emerson's contribution to Tyndall's thinking as an example of the insight into the reality of nature which a poet might provide. How the poet might even anticipate the scientist was pointed to by Martí when he cited the following lines, which prefaced the second edition of *Nature*, as evidence of Emerson anticipating the theory of evolution: "And striving to be man, the worm/ mounts through all the spires of form." In *La Nación* of October 22, 1890, describing the various types of learning that Chautauqua offered, Martí mentioned an instance where a man stood up to say: "In my town we've always said the poets see the truth before anyone else and this conversation proves it because men are no more than grown worms, which is what Emerson said before Darwin, when he said that in his struggle to be man the worm rises from form to form. . . ."[24]

But perhaps Martí was most deeply impressed by the fact that Emerson never critically capitulated to the worshipers of science and technology, and he could agree wholeheartedly with Emerson's observation in *Nature* that "the use of commodity, regarded by itself, is mean and squalid . . . a thing is good only so far as it serves." Here again Martí was overjoyed as he read Emerson's bold assertion in his lecture "The Poet" that it was the poet who had the power to control technology, integrating expanding technology with the natural world by the force of the creative imagination. In one of his many references to Emerson in his notebooks, Martí cites this comment about critics from Emerson's "Poetry and Imagination": "The critic destroys; the poet says nothing but what helps somebody."[25]

Martí's famous essay on Emerson begins with the writer tremulous with excitement and apprehension at the prospect of discussing such a great man—a man who embodied the characteristics Martí valued most: integrity, humanity, independence, morality, and idealism. It closes with a discussion of Emerson's death. Martí called it "victorious," and wrote that Emerson's hearse was like a "triumphal Chariot." Emerson's death was surrounded by symbols of the victorious warrior: palms strewn below and swords raised on high. Emerson's death was a return of the finite to the infinite. Death was not frightening to one who had lived nobly. "He will be immortal who deserves to be." Hence Martí saw Emerson's death as a victory and not a loss to mankind.[26]

Martí made Emerson part of nearly all his work, and because of him, Emerson became a living person in Latin America. Through Martí, the current of Emerson's transcendental and universal thought was spread to Spanish America.[27]

José Martí was the first to reveal to Hispanic America the figure of Walt Whitman, America's "Poet of Democracy." Rubén Darío, the Nicaraguan poet and undisputed leader of "modernismo" in Spanish-American poetry, pointed out that Martí "made you see a prestigious, patriarchal Walt Whitman, the biblical author of *Leaves of Grass*, long before France knew him through Sarrazin." While Darío may have overlooked critics like Mme. Benitzon, Louis Etienne, Jules La Forgue, whose work preceded Sarrazin's writings on Whitman, he was correct in noting that Martí was the first to write in Spanish about the "good grey poet."[28]

Beginning as early as 1881, Martí featured brief comments on Whitman in his journalistic articles. But it was his 1887 essay honoring the American poet that is Martí's most important contribution to the study of Whitman. Published in both *El Partido Liberal* and *La Nación*, it was later reprinted by other periodicals in Latin America. The essay was written following Whitman's lecture on Abraham Lincoln in New York City which Martí attended. In developing his essay, Martí used the Lincoln lecture at several points. However, the first work by Whitman Martí mentioned is *Leaves of Grass*, which is not listed by name but merely introduced by the notice that this "astonishing book" was prohibited. Noting that in 1887 Whitman's greatness was still unappreciated in the United States, Martí observed that natural greatness is overlooked because people seek out the petty differences among themselves, rather than recognizing the essential and eternal elements held in common. Because modern education failed to teach how to distinguish among the teachings of different philosophical schools, when the public came face to face with a sincere individual like Walt Whitman, they refused to recognize that here was a superior human being. Martí emphasized Whitman's lone stand by comparing it to Gladstone's stand in Parliament when he rose to ask for a more just government for Ireland. Both men, he notes, resembled an invincible mastiff surrounded by a crowd of dogs.

Martí emphasized that Whitman stood far above the petty philosophers, the formula poets ("puny poets"), and the literary mannequins. He wrote a poetry fit for the new life in a new continent—a poetry to match the vigor of his land. He was a "natural" man who lived out in the open, a "true, sonorous and loving" man because he lived by his belief that men are brothers, and who sang the glories of the world and of man. In spite of the lack of good taste he often displayed, Whitman merited study and the widest reading because he was the most daring, inclusive, and free poet of his time.[29]

In the writing of Whitman's poem "Calamus," Martí defended the forceful, direct, and corporal language and chided those who saw in this poetry the reflection of a homosexual love. He believed Whitman was singing the glory of comradeship and exalting the love of friendship.[30] He did not find the language lascivious, but saw it as an earthly form to express the ideal. Pointing to "Children of Adam," with its exaltation of the love of man for woman, Martí noted that Whitman was not brutal; on the contrary, he was one of those few men who could combine virility and tenderness. Again, in discussing the love poems in "By the Roadside," Martí observed that in superior men extreme virility and a feminine tenderness are found united.

To readers in Latin America unfamiliar with Whitman's poetry, Martí sought to explain its novelty of form and structure. He noted that the rhythm in Whitman's poetry was not in rhymes and accents, but in the strophes themselves, where Whitman distributed his ideas in great musical groups. Martí added that this was the natural poetic form for a people who built not stone by stone, but by tremendous blocks. In short, Whitman did not use rhyme because the subject would not allow such limitations. His metre was irregular because he was trying to reproduce what he saw and felt in nature. Whitman's method was to reproduce the various elements of his composition in the same "disorder" in which they appeared in nature. He denied Whitman's apparent lack of rhythm. He compared Whitman's language to a patriarchal song, to a row of beef carcasses hung up in a butcher's shop, to a brutal kiss, to the sound of a dry hide bursting open in the sun, but observed that his verses always had the rhythmic movement of the sea wave.[31]

Martí's most specific comment on Whitman's style and method came in regard to "When Lilacs Last in the Dooryard Bloom'd," the song of mourning composed by Whitman for Lincoln, which he considered to be perhaps one of the most beautiful productions of contemporary poetry. Martí interpreted the meaning of this "mystical threnody" as the mystery of death and the sublimity of love, and he agreed with Whitman's concept of death as a redemption, the "strong delivress." Martí showed how the clouds, the stars and moon, and the solitary bird in the marsh all contributed to the melancholy mood of the poem, how nature accompanied the journey of the coffin, and how the whole earth seemed to join in the mourning.[32] Martí compared the poem to "The Raven" by Edgar Allan Poe, and concluded that Whitman's "mystical threnody" was more beautiful, strange, and profound.[33]

Martí's essay is significant in a way that goes beyond his attempt to place Whitman in literature. For in doing so, he gave his own theory of poetry and literature. He believed Whitman was representative of the qualities and tendencies of his age. He noted his own agreement with Whitman's theory that a poet must be commensurate with society, must, moreover, have an ethical purpose. To Martí, poetry was a social force vastly more important than industry to humankind, since the latter gives people the manner of subsisting, while the former gives the desire and strength for life.[34]

Whitman's fervent love for humankind, his respect for the heroic, his scorn for cowardice and envy, his identification with every person regardless of race, creed, color, or social standing,[35] certainly influenced Martí's high regard for the poet. ". . . I love men like Walt Whitman. . . ," he rhapsodized.[36] Martí saw Whitman as the poet of democracy in the United States, but he also viewed him as the poet of the world and the future—a future of a new, just, and democratic era. Martí appreciated values in Whitman that were disapproved even by many North American critics of the times, and saw him as one of America's greatest writers. José Antonio Portuondo notes that Martí probably read the critical chapter on Whitman by Clarence Day in his 1885 *Poets of America*, and that in his essay, Martí may have been answering some of Stedman's objections to the poet.[37] In any event, Martí's essay on Walt Whitman is of singular importance, and there are few contemporary evaluations as valuable. Martí introduced Whitman to Spanish Americans, and in so doing, was to exert an important influence on the Modernist movement in poetry. For not only was Martí's essay the first written in Spanish about Whitman, but it remained the undisputed source of reference for many years for the Modernist poets.[38]

Just as Martí introduced Emerson and Whitman to Spanish America, it was he, as Ivan Schulman notes, "who first popularized the literary productions of Samuel L. Clemens throughout the Spanish-speaking world."[39] In the whole span of Martí's writings about the United States (1880–1890), there is a growing appreciation for the works of Mark Twain. Four of Twain's books (*A Tramp Abroad*, *Innocents Abroad*, *Roughing It*, and *A Connecticut Yankee in King Arthur's Court)* are mentioned by Martí at various times, and there were notes about three of them. Martí gave a plot summary of *A Connecticut Yankee*, described several of the episodes, and offered his interpretation of the book. He described a passage from *A Tramp Abroad*, and also one from *The Innocents Abroad*, and gave a short sketch of Twain's varied and active life as a steamboat pilot, miner, and printer, described him as a public speaker, and made several references to him in his notes. In one place, Martí wrote in his notebook: "Mark Twain—*humorista americano, descriptor del Oeste* (American humorist, describer of the West)—*autor del 'Mighty Dollar' (teatro)* (author of the 'Mighty Dollar' [theater])—*Tramp through (sic) Europe—Col. Dick and Col. Jack. . . .*"[40] Other notebook references concerned the success of *Innocents Abroad*. Martí observed that this book which ultimately brought the publishers $75,000, was at first reluctantly considered for publication.[41] Another notation read (in English): "*Innocents Abroad* was black with handling before it was put into print."[42]

Martí the critic was at his best when he could honestly admire and praise a person. In Mark Twain he loved the homespun qualities which endeared the American humorist to the people. After he had heard one of Twain's lectures in New York, he told of the lecturer's popularity with his audience. He described his great head with its mane of white hair, his eyes which showed "experience, profoundness, and slyness," his long and eagle-like nose, his martial moustaches, and his hunched shoulders. With his way of giving detail that brings his characters to life, Martí described how Mark Twain would wink his eyes "as if to see better, or to prevent his thoughts from being guessed."[43]

Martí, however, did not seem overly enthused by Twain's humor, and the impression Twain, the lecturer, left on him does not appear to have been very favorable. But he was deeply moved and impressed by Mark Twain as the champion of social reform.[44] He was convinced that Mark Twain's sureness in writing came from his familiarity with many levels of life, and he was far in advance of many contemporary critics in seeing that the purpose of the "sharp Southern novelist" was to present all the contradictions and hypocrisies in contemporary American society. His style was well suited for this purpose, Martí noted, adding: "He draws with charcoal, but with swift and certain lines. He understands the power of adjectives and he piles them on a character in a way that the man described starts walking as if he were alive."[45]

The book of Mark Twain that Martí most admired was *A Connecticut Yankee in King Arthur's Court*, which he reviewed in January 1890 for *La Nación*, and which he described that same month in a letter to Gonzalo de Quesada as "a service to humanity, with light and characteristic language and a deep and meaningful message."[46] Martí correctly saw *A Connecticut Yankee* as an outcry against injustice, hypocrisy, and the abuses of power and wealth, and also saw the application of its message to his own day and age. He was enthusiastic, too, about the episode at the end of the novel which described the defeat of the 25,000 Knights. As he wrote to Gonzalo de Quesada: ". . . fifty-two young men (not men of years, preoccupied and corrupted), helped the Yankee to defeat twenty-five thousand fully armed Knights, who died taking knight-errantry with them."[47] Ivan Schulman notes that Martí's "interest in the fight of the few against the powerful many reveals the hand of the revolutionary faced with the overwhelming odds of the Spanish forces in Cuba."[48]

When most American criticism was content to compare Twain's book to Sir Thomas Malory's *Morte d'Arthur*, Martí recognized the relationship of the *Yankee* to *Don Quixote*.[49] He noted that *Quixote* was a "wise and painful portrait of a man's life" while the *Connecticut Yankee* with its honest indignation against oppression and poverty, is "a fight, cowboy style, with a lasso and gun." Still the *Yankee*, he assured Gonzalo de Quesada, could stand on its own feet and Twain owed not "a whit" to either Cervantes or Jules Verne. "It is a book of humor which calls forth tears."[50]

Martí did not regard Mark Twain as one of the major writers, but he did have high regard for his orginality and power of description. He credited Twain with having experienced life deeply and undergone suffering, two factors Martí believed were especially important to the development of a mature writer.[51] He had been put off at times by Twain's humor, regarding his jokes as "of the coarse frontier type." But all this faded when he read *A Connecticut Yankee*, and he was so taken with the work that at one point he said: "There are paragraphs in Mark Twain's book which make you want to set out for Hartford, to shake his hand."[52]

It is probable that the first North American author with whom Martí was acquainted was Henry Wadsworth Longfellow. Martí appears to have been familiar with Longfellow during his boyhood days in Cuba, for it was his belief that his teacher, Rafael María de Mendive, studied and read this American author, and the library in Mendive's school included a book by Longfellow with a dedication by the North American poet.[53] Later, in 1877, several years before he came to the United States, Martí referred indirectly to Longfellow. In writing of a magazine about Guatemala, which he planned to publish, Martí commented on the wealth of natural resources in the land, and continued: "Thus, when the first Christian prayer was raised heavenward from Plymouth, and when only the sorrowful laments of Hiawatha were to be heard in the North American forests, the extraordinary and fertile resources, which now sustain the people of the American union with miraculous development, were lying in neglect."

Longfellow, the author of "Hiawatha," was also one of the first North American authors to be mentioned in Martí's writing about the United States itself. It was published in *La Opinión Nacional* on March 22, 1882, and the part on Longfellow began with a reference to the death of President James B. Garfield. Martí went on to say that now another happy and famous man was near the doors of death. He wrote: "A cancer gnaws at the face of Longfellow, who four days ago completed his seventy-fifth year."[54]

Martí published two "literary portraits" of Longfellow. The overall message of the two articles was that Longfellow was a gentle, kind, good poet who wrote verses notable for their ability to enchant. Since Martí believed that the ability to delight the reader was an important function of poetry, he considered this quality in Longfellow as justifying his being ranked as a great writer. But not to be ranked in the same category as Emerson and Whitman. Martí noted that Longfellow lacked the suffering necessary to produce the purest lyricism. This made Longfellow chiefly a writer of pleasantries while Martí believed that literature should be much more than this. It must and should be at the service of humankind.[55]

Notes

1. José Martí, *Obras Completas*, Trópico edition, vol. XXV, ed. Gonzalo de Quesada y Miranda (La Habana, 1936–1949), p. 69. Hereinafter referred to as Trópico edition.

2. Martí, who was casting about for work in New York, was introduced to members of the staff of *The Hour* by a fellow Cuban, Guillermo Collazo. Like Martí, Collazo lodged at the home of Carmita Mantilla.

3. For the entire article, *see below* "The Metropolitan Museum of Art."

4. For the article on Goya, *see below* pp. 106–12.

5. Gonzalo de Quesada y Miranda, *Facetas de Martí*, (La Habana, 1922), p. 57; Félix Lizaso, *Martí Critico de Art*, (La Habana, 1953), pp. 7–9.

6. For the complete text of the articles in *Revista Universal*, *see below* pp. 35–73.

7. *Trajectory and Actuality of Martí*, Center of Studies on Martí, (La Habana, 1961), p. 38.

8. *See below* "A New Exhibition of Impressionist Paintings," pp. 118–24.

9. Trópico edition, vol. XL, p. 153.

10. José Martí, *Obras Completas*, vol. XII, (Havana, 1949, Editorial Nacional de Cuba), pp. 151–53. Hereinafter referred to as Editorial Nacional de Cuba.

11. José Antonio Portuondo, *José Martí, critica literarios* (Washington, D.C., 1953), p. 2. The essay on Bronson Alcott appears in *On Education: Articles on Educational Theory and Pedagogy, and Writings for Children from The Age of Gold by José Martí*, trans. Elinor Randall, Ed. with an introduction and notes, by Philip S. Foner (New York, 1979), pp. 47–53. Several of the United States authors were treated by Martí in relation to events of their time. Whittier and Lowell were mentioned in connection with the centennial celebrations common to the America of the 1880s. Harriet Beecher Stowe was lauded chiefly for her contribution to the antislavery movement in *Uncle Tom's Cabin*, and Helen Hunt Jackson was hailed for her concern over the injustice done to the American Indians. Martí's remarks on William Dean Howells came mainly in connection with his courageous stand during the Haymarket Affair in which he pleaded for clemency for the Chicago anarchists.

12. Andrés Iduarte, *Martí, Escritor* (Mexico City, 1945), p. 163.

13. Esther Elise Shuler, "José Martí: su crítica de algunos autores norteamericanos," *Archivo José Martí*, vol. XVI (Habana, 1950), p. 175. Shuler points out that in matters of style, Emerson and Martí were often alike, so that in some respects, Martí's tribute to Emerson sounds like Emerson himself. (Ibid., pp. 176–77.) In short, Martí often saw with Emerson's eyes.

14. Félix Lizaso, "Emerson visto por Martí," *Humanismo*, (Havana, 1954), vol. III, no. 23, p. 37.

15. José Martí, *Obras Completas*, Editorial Nacional de Cuba, vol. XXII (Havana, 1964–1966), p. 323.

16. Many of Martí's notebooks contain references to Emerson, and while they are brief, they are revealing. Thus he wrote in one place: "From Emerson—celestial sentences." Martí also included a number of direct quotations in English from Emerson in his notes, including: "The distinction and end of a soundly constituted man is his labor." (*Obras Completas*, vol. XXI, p. 39, 391.)

17. As late as 1950 it was believed that Martí had translated only one Emerson poem—the one found in *The Age of Gold* ("cado uno a su oficio" "To Each His Own"). However, additional translations of Emerson's poems by Martí have been discovered since then and are included in *Obras Completas*. All told, Martí undertook to translate at least five of Emerson's poems.

18. Lizaso, op. cit., p. 39.

19. Ivan Schulman, *Símbolo y color en la obra de José Martí*, 2nd ed., (Madrid, 1970), pp. 88–89, 109, 134, 150–51, 160–62. Esther Elise Shuler, Félix Lizaso, and Manuel Pedro González are among other writers who have noticed similarities between Emerson and Martí. González emphasizes that "Both epitomized and symbolized the finest human values of their respective peoples." (Manuel Pedro González, *José Martí: Epic Chronicler of the United States in the Eighties* [Chapel Hill, North Carolina, 1953], pp. 15–16.)

20. In a June 1887 article for *El Partido Liberal*, Martí contrasted Charles Dudley Warner's narrow-minded approach to Mexico and the Mexican people with Emerson's universality. In his account of a trip to Mexico, Warner was unable to sympathize with the country and its people. Martí attributed this to Warner's desire to judge everything by North American standards. Emerson, on the other hand, saw the human spirit evident in all peoples. (*Obras Completas*, vol. VII, pp. 54–55.)

21. Joseph Ratner, editor, *John Dewey, Characters and Events: Popular Essays in Social and Political Philosophy*, vol. I, (New York, 1929), pp. 75–76.

22. *Obras Completas*, vol. XXII, pp. 141–42.

23. *See* José Martí, *On Education*, ed. Philip S. Foner.

24. *Obras Completas*, vol. XXI, p. 232; vol. XXIII, pp. 17, 39.

25. *Obras Completas*, vol. XXI, p. 381; ed. Edward Waldo Emerson, The Complete Works of Ralph Waldo Emerson, (Boston, 1903–04), vols. XI, p. 442; vol. VIII, p. 37.

26. *See below*, pp. 149–67

27. Ethel Ríos, "José Martí: A Study of the Biographical Essays," unpublished M.A. thesis, Columbia University, 1947, p. 33.

28. Rubén Darío, *Los Raios*, Madrid, 1918, p. 238. Maurice Mendelson, the leading Soviet authority on Walt Whitman, observes: "The Cuban revolutionary José Martí was the first Latin American to respond to the poet's verse as a call for freedom." (*Life and Work of Walt Whitman: A Soviet View* [Moscow, 1976], p. 311.)

29. *See below* pp. 168–85 for the essay.

30. Most modern Whitman scholars, insist, however, that the earliest, best, and most memorable love poetry of Walt Whitman was written to a male lover. (*See*, for example, Gay Wilson Allen, *The Solitary Singer* [New York, 1962], and Ivan Marki, *The Trial of the Poet: An Interpretation of the First Edition of "Leaves of Grass"* (New York, 1976). In his study, *The Homosexual Tradition in American Poetry* (Austin, Texas, 1979), Robert K. Marten argues that Walt Whitman was the first to provide a voice for the homosexual in America.

31. *See below* p. 183.

32. Maurice Mendelson, praises Martí for having "faithfully conveyed the mood of the work," and adds: "But the poem contains more than just funeral tones. It does not make one think of death alone. Even on this occasion, the poem remains faithful to his life-affirming view of the world, to his love for people and his awareness that the people will live for ever." (Mendelson op. cit., p. 238.)

33. Some critics have argued that Martí's comparison is somewhat strained since the two poems are radically unlike in subject matter. Poe's is in no sense an elegy as is Whitman's. (Anne Owen Fountain, "José Martí and North American Authors," unpublished Ph.D. thesis, Columbia University, 1973, p. 85–86.)

34. Trópico edition, vol. XV, p. 196.

35. For a critical view of Whitman's position on slavery and black

Americans which asserts that "Whitman was a product of his times who was not able to truly transcend the rampant anti-black sentiment of his American society," *see* Ken Peeples, Jr., "The Paradox of the 'Good Gray Poet,' Walt Whitman on Slavery and the Black Man," *Phylon*, vol. XXXV, no. 1, pp. 22–32. However, Maurice Mendelson demonstrates the depth and profundity of Whitman's antislavery and abolitionist convictions, and argues that his antislavery sentiments were responsible for his being fired from a series of New York journals. (op. cit., pp. 132–39.) For a similar approach to this issue, *see* Joseph Ray Rubin, *The Historic Whitman* (University Park, Pa., 1973). Martí did not know that as editor of the *Brooklyn Eagle*, Whitman not only supported the war against Mexico in 1846, accused Horace Greeley, who opposed the war in the *New York Tribune* of "aiding and abetting the enemy in his 'open advocacy of the Mexican cause,'" but also wrote: "The more we reflect on the matter of annexation as involving a part of Mexico, or even the main bulk of that Republic, the more no doubts and obstacles resolve themselves away, the more plausible appears that at first glance most difficult consummation. . . ." (Allen, op. cit., pp. 82–84; Cleveland Rodgers and John Black, eds., *The Gathering of the Forces: Editorials, Essays, Literary and Dramatic Reviews and Other Material Written by Walt Whitman as Editor of the Brooklyn Daily Eagle in 1846 and 1847*, vol. I [New York and London, 1920], p. 130.)

36. *Obras Completas*, vol. XX, p. 132.

37. Portuondo, *op. cit.*, pp. 57–59. Portuondo notes a number of differences in approach to Whitman by Stedman and Martí. Thus while Martí appreciated Whitman's announcement of a new, just, and democratic era, Stedman complained of Whitman's emphasis on only the subordinate, the poor, and the humble classes. And while Martí wrote of Whitman's "vast and ardent love," the American critic displayed a distaste for Whitman's lack of restraint in speaking of sex and physical love.

38. For a summary of Walt Whitman's influence on Hispanic American poetry, *see* John E. Englekirk, "Notes on Whitman in Spanish America," *Hispanic Review*, vol. VI (1938), pp. 133–38. Englekirk comments on Martí's essay on Whitman, but confused Whitman's poem on Lincoln "When Lilacs Last in the Dooryard Bloom'd" with "O Captain! My Captain!" For a more recent study of the subject, *see* Fernando Alegría, *Walt Whitman in Hispano America*, (Mexico, 1954).

39. Ivan Schulman, "José Martí and Mark Twain: A Study of Literary Sponsorship," *Symposium*, vol. XV (Syracuse, 1961), p. 104.

40. *Obras Completas*, vol. XXI. p. 231.

41. Ibid., p. 397.

42. Ibid., p. 420.

43. José Martí, *Obras Completas*, editorial Lex, vol. I, (La Habana, 1946), p. 1577. Hereinafter referred to as editorial Lex.

44. For a study of this aspect of Mark Twain, *see* Philip S. Foner, *Mark Twain: Social Critic* (New York, 1968).

45. *See below* p. 191.

46. *Obras Completas*, vol. XX, p. 363.

47. Ibid. For a different analysis of the novel's ending, *see* Everett Carter, "The Meaning of *A Conecticut Yankee*," *American Literature*, vol. I, (November, 1978), pp. 437–40.

48. Schulman, "José Martí and Mark Twain," op. cit., p. 111.

49. Ibid., pp. 108–09.

50. *Obras Completas*, Vol. XX, p. 363.

51. Ríos, op. cit., p. 210.

52. *Obras Completas*, vol. XIII, p. 460; Iduarte, op. cit., p. 55.

53. *Obras Completas*, vol. VIII, p. 105. The reference itself is not dated, but Féliz Lizaso points out that on April 15, 1877, Martí announced that he would publish the *Guatemalan Review*, (*José Martí, Martyr of Cuban Independence*, trans. Esther E. Shuler [Albuquerque, New Mexico, 1953], p. 256.)

54. *Obras Completas*, vol. XIII, p. 225.

55. Ríos, op. cit., p. 141.

I
Art and Artists

Painting: Felipe Gutiérrez

In Mexico there is a prominent painter whose presence among us gladdens the few who know him, and pleases everyone who enjoys seeing the art of painting in strong and intelligent hands.

Felipe Gutiérrez paints with great brush strokes within great areas of shading. He does not dilute the light but disintegrates and contrasts it; he does not draw with lines but with experimental attacks of the brush. He does not use chiaroscuro but light and dark: a bold and luminous light and a dark filled with power and vigor. He opposes one to the other, does not reconcile them. His style is free and proper to a painter who has seen life in the canvases of Michelangelo,[1] Ribera,[2] and Tintoretto.[3] Gutiérrez paints rapidly, prolifically, and very well. He has something of the imposing coldness of Rosales. The Spanish artist painted with nerves and muscles rather than with colors. Gutiérrez goes hurriedly down that path.

1. Michelangelo di Lodorvico Buonarroti Sumoni (1475–1564), Italian painter, sculptor, architect, and poet, one of the greatest and most versatile artists of the Renaissance, who exerted enormous influence on the development of Western art.

2. Jusepe (José) de Rivera (1591–1652), Spanish painter and etcher, noted for his Baroque dramatic realism and his depiction of religious and mythological subjects.

3. Tintoretto (real name Jacopo Robusti) (1518–1594), one of the great painters of the Venetian school and one of the most important artists of the late Renaissance.

Sr. Sánchez Solés, the affable teacher, most faithful friend and wise deputy, is donating to the state of Puebla a collection of portraits of its governors: he has already given seven of them, and the latest is the work of this original painter Gutiérrez, highly esteemed in Italy, especially praised in New York, notable and renowned everywhere.

Gutiérrez has painted Sr. Juan Gómez, one-time governor of Puebla, former Minister of Law, and today chief justice of the state's Supreme Court.

It is bothersome to describe things in detail. Gómez is seated in an armchair that brings to mind Murillo's table and vase of flowers—not in the second stage of his life when he dipped his brushes in the colors of the sky, but in the first when he used the deep tones of an independent, austere and melancholy genius.

It is rumored that a bird once alighted upon the table before which Saint Anthony prayed. Although the Sevillians have always had that painting badly placed, this is understandable because of the hours of strong sunlight when Murillo's[4] table, with its ascetic reality, invites one to be seated beside it.

Gutiérrez' armchair has something of this quality; the dark shading of the arm upon the right leg is reflected in such a manner; that masterly hand holds a slightly opened book no less masterly than the hand itself, so naturally, that from this contrast of light springs an amazing truth. This part of the painting attracts the eyes: it is an essential incident.

Concerning the resemblance, it is said to be perfect. Gutiérrez drew it with his brush. From nearby, white speckles in the beard; from afar, a dark, decisive, frank and natural gray. One could desire more brilliance in the figure, but one does not wish to sacrifice to this quality the innovation of lighting and the vigor of modulation so dominant there.

There is too much ease in the garments, but it is not Gutiérrez' fault; it should be blamed upon this angelic city's tailors.

4. Bartolomé Esteban Murillo (1618–1682), the most popular Baroque religious artist of seventeenth century Spain.

They make them loose and comfortable: the painter copies what the tailors make.

In the painting's background a mere suggestion of a column, and a strange clarity, a clarity full of light that might, no matter how surprising, be properly called a shaded area. In short, a beautiful painting that reveals an original artist. He does not make lines, he makes brush strokes.

He is a painter in the grand manner; he would not please all tastes, but he probably surprises those who are fully accustomed to this. Gutiérrez' work somewhat satisfies the human aspiration to greatness. It is more handsome than beautiful. He will never paint a pretty picture, but when he so desires he will paint a great and amazing one.

The portrait of Gómez is a simple indication, painted hastily and carelessly, as it were; in Puebla he sketched the principal characteristics; here he finished this masterful portrait.

When Gutiérrez shows his paintings, his greatest worth consists in his displeasing a great many people.

On the other hand, he will have exceedingly sincere admirers, the most humble of whom will be

José Martí

Revista Universal (Mexico), August 24, 1875

A Visit to an Exhibition of Art

We are in San Carlos Academy. The courtyard has been tastefully furnished with white statues, a beautiful fountain, elegant patches of lawn, exquisite flowers, all embellished by a subdued light shed over the entryway along a spacious canvas that covers and protects it like a roof. This churchlike atrium is an invitation to art; live flowers prepare the eyes for the sensations of beautiful color; the women who go to visit the art galleries give us the preliminary kind of beauty which we need in order to fairly judge the canvases—and these we are going to pass over lightly, with the most fleeting glances, with only a first impression, since we do not claim to be critics or intend to have the last word.

We climb the steps and leave the sculpture galleries on the ground floor; we shall go through those thoroughly another time. Upstairs now, the view encompasses a series of elegant halls, all arranged with irreproachable good taste. At one side one's gaze extends the length of a corridor adorned with handsome decorative drawings; at the far end of the hall we see some rough sketches, and going a bit farther we can distinguish at the edges of those magnificent galleries something like a figure of Echave, filled with strength and vigor, a good mother of the emerging and original Mexican School of Painting. With more time we will make an analysis and comparison of the paintings, and come to the conclusion that there is a characteristic style here, all the more highly esteemed when revealed in an oppressive form of teaching and in the usual use of color—neither of which are in keeping with the freedoms and artistic flights of the spirit.

But this is to prejudge, and first we must see the exhibition in order to judge later.

The visit commences.

A student from the engravings department takes us to see the work of his fellow student Miguel Portillo who is exhibiting a good copy of Richard and a handsome portrait of that pallid and taciturn soul known in the country as Manuel Acuña.

We pass through the department of woodcut engraving, and here the work of Augustín Ocampo attracts our attention. Parra's *Galilean* is good.

We are made to remember that very beautiful things are usually seen in the die sinking prints, so we go to that hall and are pleased with our visit. This is certainly remarkable: Alberto Montiel works with utmost delicacy; these garments of *The Vestal* are natural and well defined; this *Belisario* is handsome; this *Pyrrhus* and this *Christopher Columbus* do honor to the artist.

José María Martínez is exhibiting many of his works nearby: another *Pyrrhus*, another *Vestal*, and a *Hernán Cortés*.[1] These are putting into the hands of his craft a reward which, for the number of his creations and for their merit, it evidently deserves.

Because of the figure in the print we draw back to take note of the Mining School facade, the work of Jesús Torres.

Here is a portrait of Sra. Josefa Ocampa de Mata; and who is the distinguished creator of this handsome subject? An artist who has made a fine copy of Archimedes and another of Minerva: a student who has had only one year of study in the discipline: Señorita Josefina Mata y Ocampo, one of Professor Navalón's better students.

Navalón on his part is exhibiting his designs for the Ristori medal and for the obverse and reverse sides of the Municipal Exposition prize medal. Good works: the artist's mastery and faultless execution are well-known.

1. Hernán Cortés (1485–1547), Spanish conquistador who conquered Mexico.

We shall pay no attention to the chalk drawings hall now, nor to the section where there are copies by persons not connected with the school, nor to the life drawings; we arrive at once in the hall of original paintings by artists who do not belong to the Academy.

Let us look at these by their order in the catalogue: this commissioned painting by Manuel Chavez is good; perhaps the ground is slightly spread out, but there is freshness and propriety in the execution of this pleasing subject.

Felipe Gutiérrez' portrait of D. Juan Gómez is here. The *Revista* has again commented upon the rare strength, magnificent style, and out-of-date determination that distinguish the work of this powerful painter who has been unwilling to exhibit in the competition his vibrant *Rebecca*, his superb heads, his studies of nudes, his many paintings of the customs of the people that were recently done with the expansive love that his country's affairs evoke in loyal spirits when they return to the land of their birth.

Here is a portrait of Sr. Matías Romero. It is the work of José Vargas, and is the best of all that he has sent to the competition this time.

Obregón is giving us numerous specimens of his talent with these difficult portraits, so correct and so similar, all belonging to the collection with which the respected and determined Felipe Sánchez Solés is honoring himself by honoring others. It has been Sr. Sánchez' wish that Puebla have a collection of the portraits of its governors; he has called together some State deputies, contributed considerable amounts of money, given profitable work to our well-known artists, and now all these portraits we are about to see are finished. The portrait of Governor Romero Vargas is a most exact likeness, although it could still receive some greater refinement in the whole. In Múgica y Osorio's there is not one detail that fails to reveal a conscientious artist. Another is of Gómez Pedraza, so remarkable for the facial expression, the flavor of the times, and the novel modulation and proportion with which the painter has executed the figure. There is a perfect portrait of Ignacio Mejía whose face is amazing and elicits praise from the least intelligent in the art of painting. In short, and as a worthy closing to this collection, the portrait of Sr. Rafael García, from whose shoulders hangs his characteristic cape, whose closed hands are astoundingly true to life, and whose facial features our remarkable Obregón robbed from Nature in an instant of artistic vigor. Obregón has long been honored by Mexican arts. And there is something else of his to praise: that full-length portrait of Romero Vargas, even if it does lack all the accuracy that Obregón might have easily obtained, is made remarkable for the facial expression and for the study in furniture of which he has made excellent use in this canvas.

Why do people move away from that small picture painted with pale colors? To enjoy the fine perspective which Augustín Ilizaliturri has achieved in it. His little canvas pictures one of the inner courtyards of Biscay College.

Here before us is *The Virgin* by Primitivo Miranda. Is it appropriate to make trifling judgments when talking about such a studious and experienced painter? Here is an irreproachable figure that is outstanding without the need of chiaroscuro for a warm yellow background, a color contrast difficult to achieve but which the celebrated artist's brush has overcome and beautified. That background, peopled with angelic figures wrapped in mists and clouds, so to speak, is completely original. Those angels aesthetically placed at the feet of an idealized figure of the Conception are exquisitely graceful. The drawing is excellent, the colors lively, vivid and natural. In short, this painting is the irreproachable work of a remarkable painter—pure in drawing, valiant in color, novel in composition, and demonstrating that the white hairs so nobly crowning the years that weigh upon the artist's brow do not exist in his brush.

And this miniature canvas which shows one sole figure of a musketeer, and immediately proclaims a fully experienced hand and the playful inspiration of a Meissonier?[2] It is obviously the work of Alejandro Casarín. It is a perfect musketeer who finds

2. Jean-Louis-Ernest Meissonier (1815–1891), French painter and illustrator of military and historical subjects, particularly of Napoleonic battles.

amusement in his loneliness by drinking to people's health all by himself, something rather unusual, but it can be excused because of the figure's grace and accuracy. Since Casarín is able to do better, however, he should do so. What has the young painter done with his Don Quixote in the mists? Can he have feared that the originality of his idea, and the difficulties he has had to overcome in its execution, might fail to be understood? Talents must trust their own power, for when the country creates a son, that son is duty bound to show all his progress, all his accomplishments, and all his hopes.

Petronilo Monroy is exhibiting two fine portraits; in that of Manuel Romero Rubio's wife the resemblance is perfect, the figure good, and the composition adequate and pleasing; we believe that there is too much color in Sra. Satur Lopéz de Alcalde's face. But a skilled hand is seen in both, and that portrait of Sra. de Alcalde departs from the commonplace because of its purity of line, perfection of drapery, true to life background, and beauty in general.

That other portrait of Juan José Baz, exhibited by Francisco Mendoza, is weak in color and the figure is sickly.

On the other hand, who painted these two portraits that boast of such a novel background, such softness of line, such a tranquil expression upon the old woman's wrinkled face, and so much docile languor in the southern face of the young woman? The artist's hand is skilled and bold. Let us look at the catalogue: both portraits are by a woman: she is the same young artist in the portraits, and the two subjects have Catalan names. The distinguished artist is Palmira Borrás de Coll. Observe these portraits: look at the furrows in the brow, the placid gaze, and the shadows from the old woman's chin. Look even more carefully at that background achieved with the use of green, that elegant and artistocratic head, those large, Arabian eyes widened with soft shadings upon the cheeks like those of the extremely handsome women of Italy and the lively beauties of Genoa and Marseilles, of the Mediterranean coasts, of Naples—because of being near the volcanoes—of Valencia, Málaga and Cádiz, because of a preferred love for the sun. Those two canvases justly attract the attention of the entire attendance at San Carlos.

A woman's name obliges us to a natural preference, and instead of blaming the landscape artist Coto for the false and disagreeable color and for the parallel bands of yellow with which he has damaged his poetic concept of the snow-capped Toluca mountains, let us enjoy those exquisite strawberries offered to us by the delicate hand of Srta. Elena Barreiro. She is exhibiting two paintings: one is this delightful picture of fruit; the other is a correct study copying a wax model, which elicits praise for the novelty of its idea, the successfully achieved shading, and the distinction and good lines of the drawing. This time justice does not need to grant its praises to gallantry; the teacher Pina introduces us to a remarkable female student.

Velasco: *Valley of Mexico*. Let us stop; let us stop and admire this most remarkable landscape, lovely as Nature herself, splendid as our sky, vigorous as our trees, pure as the placid waters of our majestic Lake Texcoco. Those clouds are the beautiful sky: they reach out, change form, are there in the distance and yet are here before us; this craggy ground is covered with plants native to our Valley; that blue water is ruffled by the passing clouds which it reflects; this man has placed himself at the heights of genius to obtain a good view of the entire proud expanse, the superb dynamism, the whole opalescent sky, all the atmospheric subtlety and wealth of mountains, and the magic quality of the light with which the virgin Mother America bared her breast in the center of the continent, an effort of aging creating in the sapless lands of the Caucasus and the weary regions of the Himalayas. The *Valley of Mexico* is a grandiose beauty: Velasco's handsome landscape is just as imposing.

Here the visitor's fantasy rests in admiration, and he leaves the pleasant work and the continuation of his visit until tomorrow.

Revista Universal (Mexico), December 28, 1875

A Visit to an Exhibition of Art (Continued)

Art is a form of Harmony. At times irregularity is artistic; but irregularity in painting must be logical in its fundamentals, as the whims of poetic fantasy must be consistent and grouped in unity. Monotony is a wild beast because it destroys everything, even the sanctity and customs of love. In painting, the parallel lines, symmetrical dots of color, uniform and alternating lines, geometrize the figure, vitiate the whole, and destroy the painting's grace and undulations with the harshness of straight lines. There is no beauty in rigidity: life is mobile, daring, abandoned, tender, active; the flesh has to be sensed and the nerves felt in an attitude of movement; if grief has been copied, tears must hang from the soft and silken eyelids; if fierceness has been imitated, angers must be collected upon the formidable furrowed brow. In painting, the simple is nonexistent: a first step is the beautiful, then the sublime. A painter must not be said to be accurate, but proud, innovative, spirited and grand. If Cordero has conceived of these truths, why has that which has become his own inspiration been reduced to affectation? Why in this painting of a family does he group those four heads in a parallel line—one of them so purely drawn, another so well lighted by a reflection of red, Cordero's favorite color; so rough the head of the young woman dressed in blue, and so lacking in expression that of the other young woman into whose white dress the painter has put so much care and conscientiousness? This group lacks perspective; those banana leaves lack realistic color; the placing of the figures lacks an objective. A painting must not eject from itself, because of its austerity, the beings who are alive in it; the space must be enlarged so they project from it; a roof of sky must be given to its landscape, and some relative extension to the number and size of the figures created upon the canvas. Let the details be faulty, but let there be harmony in the whole. A lack of proportion in that transparent white dress might be pardoned; one could pardon the rigidity of those hands that hold the flower-filled hat; one could demand of all the figures the elegance and accuracy indisputably possessed by the young woman in black, for she is remarkable for her placement, details, and completion. Finally, one might forget the total carelessness and haste with which that tree was drawn and completed; we could still overlook that inopportune and wretched water which unnecessarily adorns one edge of the canvas. But there is no excuse for that sky burning with a brilliance which the sun has never had. A painter who knew how to achieve those red reflections and use them to make a human face translucent by diluting a false light, is duty bound to reform his style and employ his forces and his original way of seeing things in the certain changes and multiple secrets of light. Anyone who has known how to embellish the false might well have accomplished and enlivened the true. The painter should make those figures more graceful and place them more naturally; group them so they do not present such monotonous symmetry; give them true color, accurate proportions, a ground adorned with flowers; give them some air and space, a truthful translucence and a horizontal perspective.

The hand that elegantly holds the little hat; the tamarind-colored dress that encloses a most realistic bosom; the scarf of perfectly fashioned lace; that other hand with which the young woman with the aristocratic profile supports a well painted cheek—would then add merit to this splendid whole. But even in these details, who copied these women without putting some soul into their eyes, and some grace and smiles upon their lips? Their lips are hard, their faces grim. This painting has been retouched and corrected; that is why it is harsh. Too much thought went into it; a painting should have nothing but inspiration and accidental color. In a word, much effort has been put into a work which could have been most beautiful; the artist has labored too much upon a painting which should have been, for its subject matter, an attractive and cheerful group upon a beautiful model landscape.

The artist painted large figures within a reduced space, persisted in the use of Dantesque color combinations, and gave more thought to a faithful imitation of his subjects' clothing than to the youthful mobility and lively expression in their faces. There is a mannered painter in this canvas, but there is a painter; proportion is lacking, but there is an idea; something beautiful was put into the details, but there is no splendor, reality, or appealing grace in the whole. Let the truth be stated, the spirit be tranquil, and the painter's name be respected, for he owes his shortcomings to a laudable although mistaken eagerness to create.

A sudden sadness envelops the visitor's troubled soul. An opaque spirit has drawn a feeble landscape. German Butze has used warm colors to make a faithful copy of the Chapultepec trees in whose shade dreams were born and grew in the candid soul that lifted their roots out of the oppressive surface of the ground. Vague as the branches of those trees were the dreams of that pure white soul: his is a true landscape when it so suddenly brings to mind the images of bitterness which oblivion will never be able to profane. Because it is profanation to shamefully forget the dead.

The painter of this landscape is Alemán, as his name should be: his beautiful tenuous composition is a fantasy of sadness about a subject filled with truth. There is something of Germania's clouds in this celestial blue; something of diaphanous serenity in the green of these leaves; something of the Danube mists in the veiled surface of these peaceful melancholy waters in the great forest. The painter gave to true form the vacillating hues of the spirit; he seems to have spread a subtle veil over the vigorous wealth of color with which the ardent American life has tinted the sky and clothed the branches of these witnesses of time which give an aspect of solemn old age to the paths of our most sacred forest.

Near the landscape Concepción Rosas is exhibiting a still life so perfectly executed that it would honor the hand of a master.

The painting is as valuable as it is small, because this time it is an Academy law that there is no work of a woman that does not deserve honorable mention—whether those strawberries that so constantly excite us in Srta. Barreiro's fine study; or that most gentle look that Sra. Palmira B. de Coll copied from her own eyes with her splendid brush and sensitive heart; or this simple but finished painting in which substance and true form was given to that which, in uninspired hands, might have been a passing occupation or a copy of little value. There is good lighting and a bold study of shading in this conscientious artist's painting.

The gaze rests pleasantly upon the three small landscapes exhibited by Ilizaliturri, one a finished painting and the other two slightly weak in color.

Primitivo Miranda has placed his good portrait of Morelos here. A stern figure, an adequate whole, a fine study of garments and truth in the objectives are qualities which fondly bring to mind the portrait of Hidalgo,[1] even more handsome than this one, which hangs like a venerable ghost in the studio of Guillermo Prieto, a good son of liberty and a favored companion of the Muses.

1. Miguel Hidalgo y Costilla (1753–1811), the "father of Mexican independence," was ordained a priest in 1789. In 1808 he joined a secret society in Dolores to oppose Spanish domination, and when he was threatened with arrest, instead of fleeing, on September 16, 1810, he rang the church bell in Dolores to call his parishioners to an announcement of revolution against the Spanish. Thousands of the poor, including Indians, flocked to Hidalgo's banner of the Virgin of Guadalupe. But eventually the movement was crushed, and Father Hidalgo himself was caught, defrocked, and shot. Father Hidalgo became the symbol of the Mexican Revolution, and September 16, the anniversary of the "Grito de Dolores" (Cry of Dolores), is celebrated as Mexico's Independence Day.

Vigor and daring have painted that portrait exhibited by Urruchi: it affirms a painter; it has challenged light and divested it of its vigor and contrasts. There is so much life in the face that it must resemble the person copied there; but although Urruchi's painting might lack this merit, it would always display a remarkable head and a background which could not have been achieved without a mastery of art and some audacity. Every line is a flourish and every shadow a reality; that painting is bold, novel and fine; lighting has been seen there in an original way.

We are finished with this hall, and courtesy has impelled us to complete our visit with another work by a woman, Srta. Francisca Campero. She is exhibiting upon a brightly colored canvas several copies which she groups under the heading of art, and which the catalogue lists as *The Quetzal*. A pure soul ought to see everything clearly; therefore there may be too much brightness, too much color in Srta. Campero's painting; but even so, there are some recommendable qualities in it; do we not perhaps have a desire to smell these blossoms? Do they not stand out realistically from their large flower vase so perfectly robbed from Nature? And that elegant pitcher beside it, does it not have a graceful shape and is there not a certain merit in its shadings and color?

There is no doubt that this examination exhibition is filled with promise; was there ever a woman's work that did not have some recommendable quality? Their mistakes are delightful, their creations tender; all produced by the feminine heart which, rather than the brain, is always sensitive and enthusiastic; woman's excellence consists in this higher sentiment.

And since our spirits these days are content due to constant association with works of inspiration and beauty, they shall again rest from their most agreeable task, meanwhile preparing their humble and impartial forces for a prompt return for further consideration.

Revista Universal (Mexico), December 31, 1875

A Visit to an Exhibition of Art (Concluded)

The spirit is always secretly disposed to talk of beautiful things. The spirit rejoices in all of its spiritual creations, and it is because the animating force is one, and there is a hidden brotherhood in all the ways of expressing being. Friendly feelings are more powerful than envy because there are more flowers in the world than snakes, and more blue clouds in the sky than the black ones that announce a hurricane. Let us return to San Carlos Academy, for it is a good place to forget daily trivialities: a place where so many youthful hopes, so many daring dreams, so much carefree trust of aspiring youth, are expressed in form and color. And youth sees the horizon clearly, for in the spirit's delirium one wishes to ignore the fact that since the fall of Lucifer the flying wings turned into nails that hold fast, into feet that take root, and into heavy clouds that suffocate the infinite germ of life which cannot fit into our molded and permanent austerity.

Color has more changes than words, just as in the gradations of expressions of beauty, sound has more variations than color. Since beauty conforms the spirit to all the indecipherable, the exquisite, the immeasurable and the vague, beauty is best expressed when one has more space for its expression, fewer obstacles in producing it, more means with which to reflect abstract necessity, mellow conception, the tempestuous or peaceful combinations of this presumption of the future, a religion of solitude and man's own home, all of which invoke capricious fantasy.

The soul enjoys music more than painting, and perhaps painting more than poetry. How sad it is for someone to stand before a lovely picture without feeling within himself the growth of a strange power, so to speak, and in his throat words of happiness and emotion piling one upon another without an exit! They are the laws of the eternal which escape to the legislators of the physical.

But let the wandering spirit return, return to the halls of San Carlos Academy.

Yesterday we said that Velasco had put the colors of genius into his landscape of the Valley. Why are Escudero y Espronceda's portraits placed beside this extremely handsome canvas? We should not wish to speak words of censure, and we withhold our judgment when something fails to merit our approval, for silence is eloquent enough and general opinion severe enough by itself. But Escudero has painted so many portraits, and so much has been said about him, and we were hoping to see such things done by his hand, that we were not very agreeably surprised at the exhibition by the large number of specimens which the renowned artist's strange manner of copying is giving us. It always happens that excessive praise diminishes that which it attempts to extol, and the impression that Escudero's numerous portraits have made upon us may be owed to inopportune exaggeration. Novelty in painting must never approach a complete falsity of coloring, inaccuracy in drawing, harshness in the subjects' clothing, lack of expression in their faces, and grace in the figures' placement. This painter should do much studying; he should see the actual colorings in Nature, should not damage his work by that vague shading in which he wraps his portraits, should set no limits upon achieving accuracy in the resemblances—because an artist who wishes to be something more than a portrait painter must accustom his brush to the riches, mobility, luminous strokes, and contrasts of color. The painter Escudero y Espronceda's inspiration must be given a different loftiness of thought, or what is misguided in him must be repressed; he should paint less in order to paint more. Perhaps the lack of accuracy in those works stems from the haste with which he paints them; perhaps a laudable desire to create has led him to depart too soon from the good rules of painting which do not oblige one to servitude but which undoubtedly deserve general observance and respect.

Amid Espronceda's portraits Cordero's *Virgin* is outstanding, for from the first instant it attracts our attention because of its original coloring. Rather than upon the main figure, our eyes fall upon the robust angel who fills the space by spreading roses at her feet. The artist's name and merit demand respect, but such a demand does not stop us from making general observations. There is quite enough strength in all the lines of this picture. A virgin makes clarity, nebulosity, and tenderness a necessity; there must be exquisite purity in the drawing, transparency in the drapery, an angelic expression upon the face, and one must sense the vagueness of an ideal concept in the figure's reality. Cordero's *Virgin* is the result of an inspiration more bold than tender; her face is not sufficiently delicate, her extremities are not perfect enough, the folds of her robe are too crude. The beautiful angel who attracts our first glances is more vigorous than celestial; we love and respect inspiration itself, and this figure has it, and this noble desire begins to appear in the two paintings shown by Cordero. The reddish manner in which he sees color is completely his own. But that angel with the sturdy arm, green robe, and illuminated by lighting that is more appropriate to hell than to the pure celestial spaces—is not as delicate in execution as the creation demands.

Lucifer could have been like that; Michael could have been like that when he subdued and abused the dragon; but the annunciating angel was never like that. In concepts all must be analogous: the Creator can be surrounded by manly angels, but a virgin, painted as the image of love in the midst of heaven, desires to have at her side, as a totality of purity, angels who possess something of the love, thoughts, and form of a woman. The shortcomings of this painting do not lie mainly in the harshness of the drapery, in the imperfect extremities, in the improper lighting, and in the heavy lines; it is a defect of essence; it lies in the fact that the execution fails to accomplish the creation: perhaps it lies in the creation itself. The woman of the heavens is not conceived celestially; the mysticism of a mystical painter did not create this concept; a painter who is too human could neither properly conceive nor execute a figure which was not in his own heart, and which certainly was not in the air he breathed, in the society in which he moved, in the needs which are completely alien to present day life. Why this violence of artistic aptitude? Why flee from the medium in which true inspiration is produced? When the earth was filled with oppression, the spirit flew more often to the heavenly images; today the freedoms are coming, and the Catholic virgins are going away. If religion is not in the soul, how can religious function be in the artist's brush? And although belief in dogma is produced by the overstimulation of a gentle character, or by the indelible habits of a Catholic education, the spirit does not pause in its uniform and analogous course because of the efforts of those who, out of respect or from the fullness of a loving nature, find some vague and grateful pleasure in remaining alone on the road.

All is moving and changing, and the paintings of virgins have passed. Make use of your imagination and creativity, for the fantastic exists in every age; but do not tie the imagination to dead ages, or oblige the brush to dip into the colors of the eleventh or fourteenth centuries. Today we populate our souls with phantoms: let us realize and produce them. When are the delicate qualities of love, the frowns of anger, and the constrictions of fear eradicated in the human face? And when is light extinguished in the soul, and when is there new expression in the eyes?

Strong painters should not look back upon schools which were great because they reflected a primitive age, for the age has passed and the greatness of those schools is more relative and historical than present and absolute. They should copy the light upon the Xinantecatl and the pain in Cuauhtemotzin's face; they should try to imagine how the victims who expire upon the sacrificial stone contract their arms and legs; they should wrest from fantasy the compassionate movements and bitter tears which Cortés's invincible love and the lamentations of his miserable brothers put upon Marina's face. There is greatness and originality in our history: let there be powerful and original life in our school of painting.

Since Cordero is so fond of the red tones of light, he should paint a picture of how one Indian wept bitterly on an afternoon—beside the young corn shoots trampled upon by the conqueror's war horse—over the blood-stained clothing of his brother, armed only with sticks and stones and who had perished while fighting an iron-clad horseman, aided by the thunder of God and yet favored by the powerful teeth of a mastiff!

Let us interrupt today's visit here: let us pause for a moment in this handsome courtyard in which the light has become artistic, and leave San Carlos Academy for tomorrow, saying that in these days of festivity there is no reason to envy the 1871 Exhibition of Paintings in Madrid where there still hangs one of Rosales' new canvasses, and it will not be long before we find some good Mexican painter like him.

Revista Universal (Mexico), December 29, 1875

Marat's Death

Painting, noble mistress of the spirit, put the colors of genius into Santiago Rebull's brushes. He conceived in his fantasy and accomplished upon his canvas such painting that he himself is establishing the pride of a school, the reputation of a name, and the illustrious life of a painter. Thus does one work, astonishing people; thus are wills conquered, admiration fixed in the mind, spirits made to dally. A sickly man has produced a vigorous canvas; see how bodily weakness completely fails to dim or perturb the creations of pain and of love.

Fierce pain and fierce love, and fear in those who appear in the shadows, and the energy invigorated by light—all this the creator of *Marat's Death*[1] gathered together and arranged in a totality that is rich in detail.

A beautiful homicide had to be painted—a homicide committed by the delicate hand of a woman. This subtlety added to the difficulty; it is quite right for blood to color the rough and work-worn skin of men, but who can restrain an involuntary shudder when seeing a woman's soft white hands stained with red, even if it be for some heroic crime? Two villains caused an appearance upon the scene of two heroines born at different times, but with a resemblance that proves the identity of the

1. Jean-Paul Marat (1743–1793), French politician, physician, and journalist, a leading exponent of the radical elements in the French Revolution. He was assassinated by Charlotte Corday.

human spirit. Judith's spike is Charlotte Corday's[2] dagger. Holophernes died because he was a unique tyrant; but in France, since the exaggeration of rebellion responds to the exaggeration of authority, Marat did not die by merely dying, for in the explosion the tyranny of many produced many tyrants. Every hatred was a despotism, and every French heart was an altar of hate, if hatred occasionally deserves veneration or altars. It is darkness that veils reason and obscures happiness. Vergniaud's[3] love might have saved France; the common people's hatred brought that country a reaction of misfortune which is not yet liberating its blood from the corrupt source of empire; by a law of history a pardon can be a mistake, but a vengeful act is always unhappiness. Conciliation is a nation's happiness.

But these are calm ideas, and when the country was a bonfire, a thought could not be reasonable. It was a blaze, and so it ought to be: it burned with the *Mountain*[4] and shed light with the *Fronde*.[5] The *Gironde*[6] was a blue sky and the *Mountain* a cloud pregnant with storms. It is true that the cloud was composed of centuries of infamy. Spiritual asceticism was to firmly unite a horror of the delicate with that of the crude: form exercises an invincible dominion in a great number of souls; and the soul of a woman who owed her extraordinary energy to chance, ought to

2. Charlotte Corday (1768–1793), the young Girondist who was the assassin of Jean-Paul Marat. Corday stabbed Marat in the heart while he was in a bath. Arrested on the spot, she was sentenced to death and executed.

3. Pierre-Victurnien Vergniaud (1753–1793), the most eloquent spokesman for the moderate Girondin faction during the French Revolution.

4. The Mountain referred to the Jacobins, the deputies of the left.

5. A series of civil wars in France between 1648 and 1653, during the minority of King Louis XIV.

6. Girondins were members of a political group in the French Revolution who were mostly well-educated, moderately rich professionals of republican leanings.

feel some tragic emotions, lofty repulsion, and majestic scorn toward those who embellished with life's young tendrils, and hastened with impulsive anger, the pure image of French liberty—impelled, betrayed and bewildered—which held out its arms in anguish to the sons of the noble South, without which it had never been able to see unbloodied the robe that other enraged sons tore apart in blind fury.

The eminent painter Rebull thought of that, and painted Charlotte Corday's figure with those thoughts and that horror in mind.

Not in vain did southern France preserve the Gallic dolmens: thus did it preserve the Revolution's priestesses who encouraged their parents to fight. Heroic Charlotte was to be compared with heroic Vetella. She dressed in white, had pure thoughts, was infused with greatness; if she had believed in the Catholic heaven, Charlotte would not have sat well upon the throne of Mary's affections. Mary is tenderness and Charlotte was energy and sublimity; a pure spirit, she had risen to an abstraction through the soliditude of a convent; she was ascetic in her conception of liberty; she read the vehement Reynal with love and the unhappy Rousseau with enthusiasm. The emigration of her brothers and sisters, the assassination of a man whom she may have loved, and above all the horror of an exquisite soul for the ferocious disorders of the popular movements, accumulated in her spirit, came together in an act of volition, and decreed her terrible heroic act.

Perhaps she did not walk upon the earth in her journey from Caén to Paris; she glimpsed the strange secrets and the heavens of martyrdom with pleasure. And we are now approaching Rebull's extraordinary painting.

Did the expression of pure liberty and the preacher of ferocious liberty fit into the same space? A loving soul excluded a heart devoured by the serpents of hatred and rancor, of envy and ferocity. Charlotte Corday had arrived in Paris; she failed to understand an environment poisoned by vipers.

There was Marat, the doctor who never healed a nobleman, the "whiskers" of the Republic, a pilgrim from Scotland, trader in a French market place, leader of the confined—perhaps wise, never mad, always cruel. He tried to be a monster and became one; he was crude and frightening, but logical; centuries of enslavement were to cast such a man out of his chains. He had the hypocrisy of virtue and even its concept, but never its worth; not in vain did his terrible name struggle upon the honorable lips of Loubet without finding an exit.

Conflicting, crowded and rudely paralyzed muscles constituted his outer form. As inner fire causes the earth's surface to suddenly rupture, so there must have been an inner volcano in Marat which had contracted and spread over itself the wrappings of that ill-fated man.

Since greatness is relative, the great painter conceived of the great instant: he united feminine beauty to energy and created Charlotte. Without a model—because Marat will not be reproduced until the history of European slavery ceases to be reproduced—Rebull arranged the muscles, gave artistic beauty to a bullish torso, bent the head backward at the moment of the supreme curse, and—huddled in the bath—the ruptured heart becoming compressed, the oaken log to one side, the poorly finished board upon the bathtub, papers scattered over the floor, and a few lines written upon an issue of *Friend of the People*—the painter executed a historic truth in this figure, caused astonishment with his harmony of detail, finished a perfect whole without unpleasant refinement, and at one end of his canvas reproduced the instant in which the agitator had just received Charlotte Corday's stab wound. We still do not look away from these marvels of the paintbrush; Marat has been stabbed; he has raised himself upon one arm whose contorted hand, that would have needed some definitive stroke from the master, clutches one end of the bathtub; he leans his head back and shows his chest muscles in all their vigor, his right hand covering the wound just received. The attitude is true; if the stabbing was administered in that spot, the contraction had to be as it was painted. And so too the agitator's figure, the naked body copying the tremendous nakedness of the soul; so too the rumpled hair which he was binding with a soiled handkerchief at the moment of his death. Marat's head might have desired somewhat greater historic fidelity, but the aesthetic concept did well in deviating from reality in this small detail. That surprising torso has obeyed every indication of the brush; it rises toward the shoulders, starting in a curve from the hips; the skin tones are faithful, their color in the bath, the bluish tint of the blood which has just undergone a sudden change. It is true that the artist cannot have had a model for Marat, but perhaps the muscles of his left shoulder and of the nearby thoracic region might have been indicated more clearly. That is the figure, created in all its savage vigor.

We are forgetting the perfection of all that surrounds him; let us see that other luminous figure taking a step forward and about to take another; she has not lost her feminine beauty in uniting the signs of a magnificent horror to her masculine majesty. Here one is inspired with total admiration: after dealing the blow Charlotte Corday could do no more. She performed her duty and was terrified. She sank her dagger and withdrew it; Marat's hand rose to his chest, the young woman moved a step back, knocking over a perfectly placed chair. Opening her right hand she drops the bloody dagger, and raising her left arm leans to one side as if to defend her body from invisible enemies, without taking her eyes from the wounded man or slowing her steps, for this has been the magic of genius, surprising Nature in the difficult moment of horror. A most beautiful head, faithful copy of that stern face! It has the knitting of her brows, the Grecian cast of her profile, the masculinity of her chin. Meissonier would try in vain to reproduce more beautifully the vigorous brush strokes of her coiffeur. The painter has conquered the laws of composition; any arm that cuts off the figure would harm the whole, but this arm does so and enhances it. The heroine has been given the kind of beauty she needed: a tragic beauty, the beauty of Medea with none of her disagreeable features. She is tall, broad-shouldered, small waisted. Her head rises most nobly from her neck. This woman is fearful, daunted, walking; she is leaving the painting as has the artist's genius left the petty shackles and annoying traditions of the school. Charlotte Corday's figure is so handsome that were the arms of the Louvre *Venus* returned to that statue, were the animated rigidity of terror given to the softness of its contours, and were it clothed with those irreproachable garments that enliven this creation of Rebull, the Louvre *Venus* would have been no other, no more correct, no more majestic, no more beautiful than the figure of the Mexican painter.

Let us now see all that surrounds those two culminating conceptions in the work. It is true that the dagger left Marat's breast all bathed in blood; but human blood is not so bright a red, nor must a few red spots distract the eyes from the principal figure which is beside them. The fallen chair is realistic; there is perfection in distance because in this painting there is total perfection. It is surprising to see the realistic quality of the papers which have fallen upon the floor in all directions; there is a handsome study of cracks and shadows in the log and its wooden support, well placed above the floor, for in *Marat's Death* all the laws of perspective have been observed. Perhaps the quill pen in Marat's hands should not be white, nor was it ever so white, nor does it seem possible that when a bird loses a feather it should fall where this one has fallen. Perhaps Rebull might have placed it in some other manner. But why must such a simple detail damage a concept in which there is sufficient historical truth, perfect arrangement, flawless execution, irreproachable animation, coloring, inspiration and perspective?

The shoes worn in those days could not be more realistic—those shoes of which it might be said, making efforts to employ exact language, that they are filled with emptiness, for so faithfully did the brush portray reality. And in the dark corner where one assumes there is a window, what a wealth of details, all adjusted to the character of the sullen man whom they surround! Hanging from the cracked stone are two pistols; upon a board shelf poorly fixed to the bare wall there is a flacon of medicine which tells us that Marat was ill. The brush has made strokes in the shadows of these walls as anger has made strokes upon that man's breast and bitten into it. Here is a spot of color, and it is a detail; there is a line, and it is a completion.

What a study of neck muscles in that Marat! In Charlotte Corday's attire, what haughty elegance, what natural folds!

If there were room for criticism in one's amazement, it might be said here, like a display of inopportune erudition, that at the moment when people entered the room, Charlotte was hiding behind an unseen curtain; but good taste is unwilling for aesthetic creation to be thus sacrificed to historic certainty. It might also be said that Charlotte wore white when she dealt the death blow to Marat; but this fidelity might have presented the artist with insuperable difficulties of color, such as how to free from harshness the contrast betwen the room's darkness and the figure's whiteness. A tenuous color, luminous as the heroine's heart, was required to outwardly enhance her inner character.

The artist may have been unaware of this, for greatness springs from the hidden without being elaborated in the brain; but it came to mind as he painted.

Even so, the brightness of the heroic image has somewhat compromised the reality of the light. Stepping back from the painting a bit, one finds Charlotte Corday's figure too luminous. To have received that much light, the room would have had to be lighter. But this exaggeration was necessary in order to emphasize the principal creation more pointedly. Reality is almost always monotonous, and a fine defect of fantasy, so to speak, is that which a distrustful critic probably has few scruples in pardoning.

Since we are obliged to focus our attention upon the most animated part of the canvas, we forget those perfectly French women appearing at the door to the room. Here lies the historic flaw: when people rushed in at the wounded man's cries, the heroine was hiding behind the curtain invisible here. How does that detail affect the animation of the whole? It is truly a good composition and adds one more incidental event to the painting.

This work seduces the eyes, captivates the will, and restrains the criticism upon one's lips. It is as terrible as the exploit which it embodies: more muscles in the arm and the monster is perfect. The painting is understood as a historical necessity; as a human entity it is abominated, as an artistic achievement it is admired. The artist has been able to do much: he has made Marat admirable. And Charlotte Corday is Victory, mother of military camps; she is Vetella, the Gallic priestess, and that is what the wife of the warrior Vercingetoux[7] ought to have been—a woman who cut off her husband's hand in order to appear before Caesar as a good traitor and deceitfully lure the barbaric Román hosts to their death.

Above all, we love that exquisite head with its exaggerated sweep of light and its most handsome coiffeur, and that hand which has dropped the dagger opening so beautifully, and that other hand which fright had not yet finished closing. We praise and are pleased with the bent and muscular torso in contrast to that other aerial and fiercely elegant feminine form. That which constricts his body is death; that which impels her is horror. In that extremely difficult foreshortening, Marat's unforeseen death is painted on the head with a single dot of color which that ever fortunate brush has been able to place upon the visible eye line. She leaves and he dies; she awakens interest and he terror; he deserves his death and she must save herself; he is as vigorous as the earth, she is as nebulous and light and tenuous and transparent as the sky. If the painting is faithful to the truth of the event, if the commentary is just, if by picturing the event the historical character of the personages and the judgment of future men are emerging, what more can one ask of an artist who gathered together upon a canvas all the barbarity of a political party, all the purity of a soul, the two exaggerations of spirit—the event and its consequences—the animation of truth and the future pages of history? That is greatness: comprehensive, perfect and combining parts to form a whole. That is the painting: it pleases the eyes, captivates the desires, is self-explanatory, and is felt and preserved in the soul.

This masterwork by one of its most illustrious painters is leaving Mexico: the land of superficial importance must now be

7. Vercingetoux (d. 463 B.C.), chieftain of the Gallic tribe, who led a major rebellion against Roman rule in Gaul. Defeated by Julius Caesar, he was forced to surrender and was executed.

important for the masses in talent and in art. A European museum would be honored by a painting such as this. It captivates everyone, and causes amazement in those who are seldom amazed. The painter of this work of art endures in his imposing figures, faithful use of color, and exquisite wealth of detail. There is truth in every line, and in all of them a rigid impression of genius in hostile or rancorous desires.

This is the painting: it attracts the will, arrests the gaze, puts joy and fascination into the soul, a desire to embrace into the arms, and instants of indelible happiness into the memory. Every beautiful work, every great work, redeems one moment of bitterness.

Revista Universal (Mexico), January 7, 1876

The Painter Carbó

Modest merit has an undoubted right to our attention; its own value creates an atmosphere, and its modesty enlarges and affirms it. So it is with José V. Carbó, an excellent draftsman, a most remarkable portrait artist, and a painter of a fine school who has just arrived in Mexico from Philadelphia in search of some Spanish American compatriots who will nourish his inspiration from more aesthetic springs.

Carbó studied in Italy with Pina; and Pina, who respects only those who deserve it and is not habitually indulgent, speaks of Carbó with affection and praise. The newly arrived painter is without doubt a perfect draftsman. A disciple of Mussini, he has learned from him a precise fidelity of line, a gentleness and truth in his modeling, and an authentic expression in his figures. We still do not recognize Carbó as a colorist; we know his portraits, his sketches of Mexican customs, his paintings whose rough outlines are appealing and whose execution remains in an unfinished state; but all that we have seen is good, beautiful and new. Whether it is the Hebraic physiognomy of Mr. D. David Fergusson, or the difficult brush strokes of a wrinkled face mistreated by the years, or the soft tones of a charming young face, these reveal precise strokes, strong shadings, a habit of portraiture, and such a mastery of art that with the first of his works one immediately places the newly arrived in the same category as our best portrait painter. And in addition to this we are amazed by the rapidity with which he works. He commences and finishes a portrait in a few hours, his haste detracting nothing from the merit of his work; this is a known fact, and no sooner was he established in Mexico than he had to enlarge his studio. His portraits of Fergusson and of a handsome young lady promptly made him famous.

Not from Mussini alone but from Overbeck[1] we remember observing the excellent quality of Carbó's drawing. Not in vain does he have diplomas from all the schools in Siena; not in vain does he keep his professors' letters in which they all refer to him as their *most beloved* disciple; not in vain was he several times given awards in New York and Philadelphia for his excellent cartoons.

Pencils and charcoal are putty in the hands of the newly arrived portrait artist, and such is his skill that, like his teacher, he draws correctly from memory. So did Overbeck, the famed Biblical painter noted for his pure lines.

In point of composition we do not know that Carbó has, nor do we believe that he attempts, those vast purposes and bold undertakings of his Sienese master. *The Expulsion of the Money Lenders from the Temple* is in Paris and admired by everyone. Like Paul Delaroche,[2] Mussini also painted in the idealistic and realistic style. A good follower of the classics, his likenesses are inspired by the superior paintings of the gentle and devout Fra Angelico,[3] a great Christian enamored of love and of heaven who imitates Giotto's gigantic inaccuracies when painting hands and feet. Mussini's trees are stiff and cold, his rocks rugged, his torsos energetic like those of a student who loved the scrupulously honest Vittoria Colonna[4] so intensely and so well.

1. Johann Friedrich Overbeck (1789–1869), German romantic painter devoted to depicting Christian religious subjects.

2. Paul Delaroche (1787–1859), French painter whose realistic historical subjects made him one of the most successful academic artists of mid-nineteenth century France.

3. Fra Angelico (real name Guido di Pietro) (1400–1455), Italian painter whose works embody a serene religious attitude and reflect a strong classical influence.

4. Vittoria Colonna (1492–1547), Italian poet.

The artist whom we are praising fails to reach this height nor has he been trained for it; but, a worthy and beloved student of his teacher, he has received from him the excellent qualities that have made Mussini one of the dominating forces in Italian drawing. Like that of the master in England and France, this highly esteemed quality of the disciple will inspire us with admiration.

Carbó idealizes in his concept, but adjusts it to Nature when giving it form. He copies but never dissembles; this, although it may be undesirable in oil painting, is the finest quality in Carbó's portraiture. Precision, smoothness, correctness and habit: these are all that a portrait artist needs, and the recently arrived painter has them all.

May Anáhuac be favorable to him; may the artist fare no worse in the land of art than he fared, for sterile art, in the land of Hamilton and Penn.

Revista Universal (Mexico), August 18, 1976

Sculpture: Francisco Dumaine

San Carlos Academy is in mourning; not for the death of a teacher, for every pupil who progresses is a budding teacher; these children of art later become strong and robust men.

Francisco Dumaine, sculptor of the notable statuary group *The Orphans*, an artist who sensed marble as good painters sense color, has left this earth. What better funeral wreath is there than the enumeration of his uncommon qualities?

Fame is usually as loquacious and capricious as it is aloof and unjust. Existence is always difficult, and lives destined for greater glory are more difficult still. Nothing is so simple and bitter, so distressing and hidebound, so exemplary and agreeable, as the life of an artist in which disappointment so often deceives the most cherished madness, in which zealous anxiety is always close to the difficult reward. His imagination realizes in hopefulness the mysteries created by his palette's colors, and there are more changes in the despondencies and exaltations of his spirit than in the combinations they can make with the picturesque elements of light.

And in their innermost agitations the souls of sculptors must be immense and wild and lofty. That daily battle with the stone's resistent inertia; that struggle of animated feeling rudely striking the inanimate material; that stony sloth confronted by human labor; that imposition of a beautiful soul into the indifferent rigors of a crude mass; that titanic fatigue for the sake of animating death, the most implacable of all inertia, must promote and inflame with passion all the forces of spirit, must fortify with energy the soul devoted to this perennial struggle, must endow with incredible strength the one who transports the fires of life and the blood's stimulating heat to the cold veined marble.

And what pleasure when victory comes! And what a victory this human triumph of creating a handsome child out of a hard and shapeless mass from the earth! How much spirit in that material! How much man in that stone! What tremendous perseverance, what mockery of death, and what loving fruitfulness and diligence in that apparently useless struggle!

This was undoubtedly the quiet life of the artist who has died, if in one unforgettable group a beloved name had not been justly written by his studio companions for days to come. It was written by those who shared their friendship, bitterness, and dreams with him; by those who know that Latin peoples are saved through art as Saxons through books, and in religion trust in beauty as an aid to all virtue, an invigorator of weak spirits, and a fruitful creator of greatness.

Perhaps without knowing it Dumaine belonged to the new sculpture, not to the useless albeit accurate adherence to the model—useless perhaps because of the very cold and conventional accuracy bequeathed to us by the Greek school; he might have imitated a Carpeaux *Bacchante* better than the Louvre *Venus*. If he had carved a Venus, he would have carved Canova's[1], as beautiful in sculpture as Corregio's[2] enchanting *Magdalen* in painting.

France has its own sculpture school, but what is wrong with this sculpture is that it is too French; it is fonder of confused form than of purity of expression; it copies a lily given to a mad love of the winds better than an erect lily with the shy freshness of modesty; in this school there is more sensuality than senti-

1. Antonio Canova (1757–1822), Italian sculptor and portrait artist. He was highly esteemed in his time.

2. Antonio Alegri, called "Corregio" (1489–1534), Italian painter of frescoes and canvases with mythological and allegorical subjects.

ment. And Dumaine was able to reflect solitude and bitterness in stone; his *Orphans* inspires love in the eyes of both soul and body; the accuracy of his portrayal is astounding, and the aching truth of his expression inspires sadness. Sacred Greece did not inspirit its statues with this fire; the nation of corporal affections could not very well imitate a spirit whose extension and sovereign origin it did not yet suspect. It was impossible for art to say its final words in the nation where Venus was a cult. Beauty may be loved, but Mary's beauty is loved Platonically: a nude woman is undoubtedly not woman's most beautiful form.

This laborious enlivening of the insensible is most difficult. This emerging school, this mellow sculpture, this spiritual statuary, have not yet found well-defined models, fixed lines, a definite path to follow for those who may be emancipated from the inexpressive although admirable ancient school. In painting, the days of Zurbaran's sullen saints and Ribera's somber ascetics are over. In statuary, the tepid copies of vigorous warriors and provocative Venuses have ended.

For his sensitivity, his studiousness, his originality, his conformation to the rules and his artistic talent, the unfortunate Dumaire well deserves the signs of the sincere grief with which his friends, his noble brothers and sisters, lament his death. He merits the posthumous praise which the enthusiastic lovers of national liberty render to his energetic talent, for national liberty encourages every belief of the modern spirit and every form of the new life.

Revista Universal (Mexico), July 16, 1876

Impulses of the Heart: A Play by Peón Contreras

There are some natures for whom evil and ugliness are impossible: namely Peón. He will be able to produce something less remarkable than his previous productions, but all he does will be sincere and characteristically beautiful.

The play of the night before last is a sensitive work of the mixed genre of *Struggles of Love and Honor;* it is not a copy of human characters, an impossible task for souls turned permanently toward heaven, but a presentation of a noble thought in corporeal form, more sung than explained, more sensed than proved. To be Molière[1] one must be aware of having been deceived by one's wife, and then forget it. Euripides[2] is above Aristophanes.[3]

Is it a defect not to be able to descend? In this case the disadvantage enhances the worth of the poetic spirit that has tended to become human: this is the only defect in the play of

1. Molière, stage name of Jean-Baptiste Poquelin (1622–1673), French dramatist and comic genius, who was to be acclaimed as one of the greatest of France's writers.

2. Euripedes (484 B.C.–406 B.C.), one of Athens' greatest tragic poets, author of some of the world's greatest tragedies. He left Athens in 408 B.C. for Macedonia, never to return.

3. Aristophanes (450 B.C.–388 B.C.), the greatest representative of ancient Greek comedy whose plays mainly satirized the social life, the fashionable philosophies and literature, and the aggressive foreign policy of Athens during the Pelopennesian War.

the night before last, a new dramatic comedy by a poet who feels drama in an excellent and exclusive manner. And there is some dramatic comedy in life, but it is not that of García Gutiérrez or López de Ayala or Larra Jr.; it is what the French seek in vain, a literature composed of exaggeration, intense violence, and phenomena; it is something the Spaniards will never approach, for they are too imaginative a people to become a real people; it is the unfamiliar in Germany, a nation of foggy rivers and foggy intellects; in language and essence it is a faithful expression of the contemptible and sublime vacillations, the monstrous and honorable thoughts, the redeemed miseries and fallen sublimities which, in turning around chaotically, expand the world. Men make mistakes, which is a human weakness, and they practice self-denial, which is intuitively divine. Plays are not limited to copying superficial defects, unprofitable copies, for they are always wrapped in exaggerated ridicule. They may copy the depths of the soul and the gravity of the mind in a beautiful form suitable for salons—French in culture, Athenian in incisiveness, and new in essence. The true comedy contains an inevitable amount of drama because the robust skeleton of grief is always waiting in the heart, at the door where smiles lurk. St. Augustine[4] did not utter his phrase for poetry; there is perpetual newness; poetry has many forms; a child of a phoenix and a Proteus, it brings to an end its diverse eras, and in the immensity of the analogous totality it develops by extending itself like every living thing, and each new soul brings soft and inaudible sounds of sorrows, revelations, and love to its harp.

The new is missing. In eroticism dignity and faith are missing. The theater lacks an exact copy, a natural presentation, a comforting preachment, and true realism. But they are bound to come.

However there are poetic entities, bards of the future, divine

4. St. Augustine (Augustine of Hippo, 354–430), early Christian father and author, the dominant personality of the Western church of his time, and generally recognized as the greatest thinker of Christian antiquity.

soothsayers of a vast blue religion. Had I not known that these poets move intentionally, I would say that they roam the earth mistakenly. If spirits had form, one would say that some had an earthy, others a cloudlike form. They live in an opaque light, enhance what they touch, embellish what they see, and exert a purifying influence wherever they talk. Like some future law, their messengers are not yet well understood. They are heard not merely attentively but ecstatically. Some works require examination, others contemplation. It is a susurrant language, a tenuous cadence, something of dawn and the distant warbling of birds.

And when talents of this kind invade the medium in which they live, the human medium becomes beautiful, and celestial talent becomes human. By doubling their faculties, they remain the same; but in their visible form they are better.

Herein lies the essential flaw of *Impulses of the Heart*. This work was not conceived for the pleasure of producing; it is useful to contemplate ugliness because it irritates goodness, and irritated goodness makes things very beautiful. Peón knows that wickedness is accidental, and that human kindness is essential. One is always born good; evil comes later. He conceived a plot in which a just man appeared evil and a lowly wicked man appeared good; and by some irresistible impulses of the soul he has made a woman lover blindly believe in the nobility of the just man whom she loves, and the repentant guilty one spontaneously restore the honor he sullied. A magnificent scene.

Perhaps at certain moments there is little attention paid to the details: a bird of the divine always has very restless wings. But the plot is natural, there is freshness and novelty in the play's resolution, there are some eminently dramatic lines which are going to remain fixed in memory and in the heart.

Among the emotions depicted by the poet there is one that is seldom used in the theater: intuitive faith; an intimate belief held by the fine young woman of the play in the loyalty of the man accused as a thief. And there is one noble act in addition to the constant ones engendered by this faith, the play's philosophical source: there is the revelation of the crime provoked in the guilty party by the generosity of the accused. And such is the power of good souls, and so has the poet Peón reflected them, that by amassing repugnant qualities upon the truly guilty one in his play, he embellishes him with repentence, illumines him with an absolute pardon, silences with heartfelt cries the sounds of animosity, and in the spectator's spirit itself there remains no memory of having seen a despicable live character upon the stage. The play's title is *Impulses of the Heart*, and it succeeds in making evil men beautiful, and in making the spectators convinced by this illumination of goodness. It is called *Impulses*, and it awakens them. Peón thus obtained that which was philosophically intended.

The somewhat melodramatic action flows easily and is justified; its rapid and brilliant structure, in which are blended the inaccuracies of a sketch done with masterly brush strokes, reveals the new and varied talent which so fortunately presents pure characters upon the stage, and clothes healthful lessons in morality with the gallantry of passion. It is not catechist morality, a usual rule of the spirit, but spirit itself that radiates loyalties and nobility.

With the structure somewhat sketchy, the details somewhat careless, the action dramatic and swift, the greatest merit in this new play lies in the vehement passion, the correct fluency, and the seductive charm of the language. That manner of speech carries one away. And the lyrical rapture is not inopportune in depicting real life; there is lyricism in every sentence, a delicate gentleness in every loving word.

One ends the five-line stanzas involuntarily, relishes the romance, is pleasantly satisfied with its spirited fits of energy. The ear is capitivated, and the spectator's body straightens up and then bends forward in order to be closer to the actor. That language plays, glides, runs as gently as a brook, swells like a river, spreads and becomes rough and angry as the sea.

It is a sensitive rather than an elegant language; in Peón's works language is truly a personage.

Those words love, and one expects to hear those lines weep.

What passions should be demanded of a work when it brings

to the stage those of a stirring and enthusiastic faith clothed with a woman's soul, a disagreement with a weak and sickly theater's usual dissemination of ugliness? Irrational passion is unworthy of men; we passionately love that which must always be rightly just.

What should be demanded of it in structure? A greater solidarity of detail, more humanity, since the poet is bent upon being human. And praise for his dramatic manner of weaving a plot, for the most beautiful second act, for the noble and exalted scene with which the play ends.

And what should be demanded of those earnest characters, that touching romance, that moaning language of the young girl in love? After the play is over the evening light fills the expanded soul with warm and tender relaxation.

One last sentence for the poet's honor: it was hard for him to be human.

Revista Universal (Mexico), October 12, 1876

The Metropolitan Museum

New York may be proud of its Metropolitan Museum of Art, of the precious ceramics collection and the highly interesting Japanese works to be found there. A well-arranged light adds to their real value of the objects accumulated. Old laces, ancient books, classic engravings, are placed side by side with the most remarkable products of Asiatic art. In the capacious halls everything looks clean and fresh; the mummies grin and the sarcophagi recall memories of ancient history, not of death. Classification and division have been as closely attended to, as if the director intended to prepare visitors for the study and not merely for the contemplation of the treasures.

As to the paintings, two collections, one of old masters, another of modern artists, attract the attention. A single glance is sufficient to ascertain that the former is not—unluckily—as valuable as the latter. The Flemish school[1] is profusely represented, but the great masters, if represented at all, are only so by commonplace works. But the exhibition of modern paintings makes honorable amends for the deplorable scarceness of old works of value.

1. The Flemish school represented the art of painting in the Low countries which produced two of the most historically and esthetically significant schools in the development of Western art. One was that of the fifteenth century in Flanders.

Such a painting as Mr. Chase's[2] *Poor Girl* reveals an uncommon strength, worthy of a master. Mr. Swain Gifford's[3] *Venice* stands comparison with the best bits of coloring. The *Broken Jug*, by Mr. Chase, is an important work, showing the obnoxious influence of the excessive love of novelty. Mr. Gifford's landscape is, perhaps, too warmly colored, yet the quietness of the sea, the elegance of the buildings, the reflection of the lights, give to the picture the appearance of a painting on steel. Mr. J. Brown's[4] *Violinist*, with his shabby clothes, his gray hair, and his blue eyes full of tears, is an affecting page of modern life. *Prisoners to the Front*, by Winslow Homer,[5] has all the ingenuousness of infancy and all the strength of primitive art. American art is in its cradle. It must be improved, but in an original direction; the old methods must be imported, but not the old ideas. Winslow Homer cannot be confounded with any other. His arrogant prisoner, his poor old man, his sympathetic officer, make up a striking scene—full of the gloom of war. His *Prisoners* could not be taken for a foreign work. He is an American painter and this is his first merit. Eastman Johnson's[6] *A Glass with the Squire* possesses the same quality, but not in such a high degree. The ridiculous figure of the squire has something of the caricature about it. The light is not taken from nature. The interior has been badly chosen. The art of painting does not

2. William Merritt Chase (1849–1916), American painter and indefatigable art teacher, important for his influence in establishing the fresh color and bravura technique of much early twentieth century American painters.

3. Swain Gifford is probably a reference to Sanford Robinson Gifford (1823–1880), American landscape painter who spent time painting in Italy.

4. John Appleton Brown (1844–1902), American landscape painter, especially noted for his painting of apple orchards.

5. Winslow Homer (1836–1910), American painter whose watercolors and oil paintings of marine subjects are among the most powerful and expressive examples of late nineteenth century American art.

6. Jonathan Eastman Johnson (1824–1906), American portrait and genre painter.

suffer the invasion of caricature. Satire can be usefully employed, as it has been by Kaulbach,[7] Goya[8] and Zamacois;[9] but satire is not useless mockery. Moran's[10] *Notre Dame* shows a fantastic talent. Nature is absent from the canvas. Memory guided the daring brush. The foggy spots of color, breaking forth from the dark night, are too straightly lined. The white stain behind the cathedral's towers has no natural significance. But imagination, boldness and the great difficulty of the subject speak in favor of the painter's ability. Arthur Quartley's *Morning Effect*[11] is a conventional work. It lacks inspiration. The tops of the waves are like darkish cottonbuds. The light effects have been, however, happily caught.

The welfare of our school of art calls for the following remarks: We have thought, but lack execution. The color employed in almost all our works is, with rare exceptions, shadowy and spotty. The faces are generally expressive, but the bodies are incorrectly drawn. The courage to paint American subjects is also highly needed. Bierstadt[12] and Whittredge[13] have opened this new path. Autumn leaves never had such a conscientious

7. Wilhelm von Kaulbach (1805–1874), German painter, illustrator, and muralist.

8. Francisco de G. y Lucientes Goya (1746–1828), was born near Saragossa and studied there until 1766 when he went to Madrid where he became deputy director of the Academy in 1785, and principal painter to the king in 1799. As a painter Goya had great influence on nineteenth century French painting, especially on Manet, and he has been called the last of the Old Masters and the first of the Moderns. For Martí's essay on Goya, *see* pp. 106–12.

9. Eduardo Zamacois y Zabala (1842–1871), Spanish painter of historical subjects.

10. Thomas Moran (1837–1926), American painter.

11. Arthur Quartley (1839–1886), American painter of seascapes.

12. Albert Bierstadt (1830–1902), German-born painter whose tremendous popularity was based on his panoramic landscapes, such as "The Rocky Mountains" in the Metropolitan Museum of Art.

13. Worthington Whittredge (1870–1910), American landscape painter of the romantic Hudson River school.

interpreter as Whittredge. Bierstadt is only rivaled by the Mexican Velasco.[14]

Amongst the European painters, the Germans are the most noteworthy in this collection. The "Crusaders" of Kaulback combines elegant fervor with grandeur of conception. His coloring is often too soft. Yet only Gustave Doré[15] could dispute the palm with him in invention and grouping. Knaus' *Holy Family*[16] is perhaps the finest painting in the Museum. The glass covering the picture spoils much of its beauty. The fine face of the young mother glows with rapturous love. The angels of Rubens[17] are not so slight and natural as those of Knaus. The virginity of his Madonna is perfectly human. Her purity is terrestrial. The cherubs surrounding her fly in the heavy atmosphere of earth. Two landscapes by Días[18] and one of Rousseau[19] are the best in the collection. There are two bright Madrazo's,[20] *A Courtyard*, by Rico,[21] and Alvarez's[22] remarkable *Our Forefathers' Diversions*. A royal fancy inspired the brilliant imagination of Alvarez; the Spring morning gave him his lively colors.

14. José María Velasco (1840–1912), Mexican painter famous for his "Valley of Oaxaca."

15. Gustave Doré (1832–1883), famous French book illustrator of the late nineteenth century.

16. Friedrich von Knaus (1724–1894), Austrian painter and craftsman.

17. Peter Paul Rubens (1577–1640), greatest exponent of Baroque painting.

18. Narcisse-Virgile Días de La Peña (1808–1876), French painter and lithographer of the group of landscape painters known as the Barbizon school.

19. Theodore Rousseau (1812–1867), French painter, leader of the collective known as the Barbizon school.

20. Martí is referring probably either to José Agudo y Madrago (1781–1859) or Federico de Madrago y Kuntz (1815–1894), both of whom were Spanish painters.

21. Martin Rico (1833–1908), Spanish painter.

22. Manuel Alvarez (1727–1797), Spanish sculptor and painter.

The group of ladies and priests is the only fault of this interesting canvas. The softness of light is surprising in the *Blue-dressed Young Lady*, by Madrazo. But his *Spanish Woman*, alone in a garden, notwithstanding the little bird flying around the upside-down parasol, is a violent caprice. *The Temptation of St. Antonio* by Leloir,[23] attracted great notice in Paris, and is worthy of it. Bourguereau's[24] *Music and Painting* has all the qualities and all the defects of its author. *Painting* is a very expressive figure. *Music* lacks expression. Rosa Bonheur[25] is represented by some pretty calves; the violet sky breaks too roughly on the green mountain in the background. Müller's[26] *The Call of the Victims of Terror* is a precious gem of expression, if not of purest drawing. The *Bodyguard of a Pacha*, by Pasini[27] might have been signed by Fortuny.[28] The *Call to Prayer*, by Gérôme,[29] gives a perfect idea of the quietness of this manner. The hour of prayer is a little indefinite. The city, emerging from the fog, is well treated. The general touch is exquisite. Jimenés Aranda,[30] Ruy Perez[31] and

23. Martí is referring either to Louis Leloir (1843–1884) or Maurice Leloir (1853–1940), both of whom were French painters.

24. Adolphe William Bouguereau (1825–1905), French painter and teacher.

25. Rosa Bonheur (1822–1899), French painter and sculptor famed for the remarkable accuracy and details of her portrayals of animals.

26. Friedrich Müller (1749–1825), German poet, dramatist, and painter.

27. Ludwig Passini (1832–1903), Austrian painter and engraver.

28. José María Bernardo Mariano Fortuny (1838–1874), Spanish painter whose historical and genre paintings won him a wide audience in the mid-nineteenth century. For Martí's discussion of Fortuny, *see* pp. 94–96.

29. Jean-León Gérôme (1824–1904), French painter, sculptor, and teacher, who often portrayed figures melodramatically and erotically.

30. José-Jiménes Aranda (1837–1903), Spanish painter and illustrator.

31. The reference is probably to Francisco Pérez Sierra (1627–1708), Spanish painter.

Villegas[32] uphold the honor of Spain. Aranda sees all nature as if it were slatecolored. A landscape by Church must not be forgotten. *The Monarch of the Plain*, by Sidney Cooper,[33] is a fine piece of animal painting. A smiling girl, by Meyer von Bremen, is full of relief and grace. A malicious cardinal, by Vibert; the original flowers of Roubbie;[34] the well-touched horses of Chehmouzki;[35] a head, by Nicol;[36] another head by Couture;[37] the works of Hunt;[38] *A Market*, by Tiffany;[39] a female beauty, by Gray;[40] the beautiful Arabs of Schreyer;[41] a charming Moor, by Tapiro;[42] Kaemmerer's[43] *Honeymoon*, and *Napoleon*, by Delaroche, are, with the foregoing, the works that at a first glance seem most worthy of the admiration of intelligent visitors.

The Hour (New York), 1880
[written in English]

32. Esteban Manuel de Villegas (1589–1669), Spanish lyric poet and artist.

33. Thomas Sidney Cooper (1833–1902), English painter noted for his depiction of cattle and sheep.

34. Probably José Robles Martínez (1684–1764), Spanish painter.

35. Probably Josef Chelmonski, Polish painter of the nineteenth century.

36. Père Nicol, French painter and glazier in Spain during the fifteenth century.

37. Thomas Couture (1815–1879), Academic painter best known for his portraits and historical pictures.

38. William Morris Hunt (1824–1879), American romantic painter or William Holman Hunt (1827–1910), British artist and prominent member of the Pre-Raphaelite Brotherhood.

39. Louis Comfort Tiffany (1848–1933), New York painter, craftsman, decorator, and designer.

40. Henry Peters Gray (1819–1877), American painter who was one of the most accomplished figure-painters of this country.

41. Gabriel Schreyer (1666–1730), German painter.

42. José Tapiro y Buro (1830–1913), Spanish painter of Oriental subjects.

43. Hans Julius Bernhard Kallmeyer, German painter of the late nineteenth century.

The Fifty-Fifth Exhibition in the National Academy of Design

As one enters these large halls, which, owing to the unfinished state of some of the works, resemble studios rather than galleries, there is something which attracts marked attention. Among so many incomplete pictures, so many landscapes which resemble chromos, so many figures painted with a few dashes of color and a few confused lines, amidst so much negligence and incorrectness, there are a certain freshness of primitive art, unmistakable originality, grandeur, boldness and love of freedom. The walls are replete with pretentious imitations. Landscapes, which are a painful sign of artistic poverty, abound. Portraits—another poor species of art—are also very numerous. Historical subjects, which reveal intellectual refinement and solid culture, are unfortunately in the minority. Fields too clean, very transparent rivers, banks too pretty, blotty skies, steamships and wharves, isolated figures and unsightly groups, are the most frequent subjects of the works now on exhibition. The coloring, in general, lacks animation. The outlines are vague and incorrect. General Grant's portrait, for instance, appears to have been painted during a foggy morning, and another, by Alden Weir,[1] looks like a ghost emerging from the darkness. In judging works of art, the spirit which animates them and the manner of

1. John Alden Weir (1852–1919), American painter, famous for his lyrical and intimate art.

expressing it must be considered. Unfortunately, we cannot as yet consider the general spirit of the American school of painting, because there is no school here. To copy nature, to imitate European masters, to give color to caricatures, is not to create a school. There are famous names among our artists: Winslow Homer, Eastman Johnson, even Arthur Quartley (when he paints carefully), Moran, Porter, Brown, Gifford. All these and others like them, at least choose American subjects and treat them, as a general rule, in an intelligent way. But this is not sufficient to give significance to the art of a country.

The art of painting has two principal guides—imagination and intelligence. From intelligence is born the classical, from imagination the romantic school. The romantic painters are the impressionists: the classic ones the academics. About an impressionist painting, nothing else can be said than "Here is talent." This praise should not satisfy true artists. If talent exists, it must produce great works. When we imitate, we often imitate what is bad. In painting, as in literature, Americans keep their jealous eyes on European glories. We grumble at them, but we remain slaves to them. While this servile admiration dominates us, we shall never be able to produce anything worthy of the New Continent.

Of these impressionists and classics—although the last are in lamentable minority—the Academy is composed. Two portraits well represent the two schools. *The Portrait of Miss H.* by Douglas, shows the free manner; *The Portrait of a Lady*, by Porter, the finished school. The brush in the hands of Douglas has been moved by an arrogant and rebellious spirit; in the hands of Porter, as if guided by a slave of the science of coloring. Draperies and fresh tints are predominant in Porter's work; vigor and reality are admirable in Douglas: but a craving for effect greatly mars the latter's picture. It is true that figure of the young lady dressed in black may be said to be in bold relief and to look at you with almost human eyes. But that yellow background, is it the studio of a painter (as stated in the catalogue), or is it a bale of hay, or an antique drapery, or the wall of a miserable garret?

In many of the pictures there is great incorrectness of drawing. Drawing can only be neglected by those artists who are perfect draughtsmen. One can become a good impressionist when he has been a long time an academic. But to paint lies, to dare to present a picture unworthy to be hung on the walls of a Long Island hovel, will never be the way to elevate the art of America. The picture *Neighbors* is a sample of this unpardonable negligence. There are only a quantity of stains, supposed to represent faces, painted with whitewash, without any expression; a yard is there represented with trees that would bring a blush to the cheeks of a beginner. Genius beautifies the monsters it creates. Without genius, the monsters alone are apparent.

Strictly Confidential, by F. Wood,[2] is a delightful and modest composition. It has American character and European refinement. *The Little Negroes*, by Winslow Homer; the various landscapes by Moran; the delicate works of Brown; a colored caricature, *Bulls and Bears;* a remarkable Bashi Bazouk; A May Day, by Thompson;[3] *The Turner's Shop*," by Hall;[4] *A Quiet Moment*, by Sartain,[5] are the best in the collection.

The Hour (New York), 1880
[written in English]

2. Francis Derwent Wood (1871–1926), English sculptor and painter.

3. Launt Thompson (1833–1894), American sculptor, famous for his portrait busts.

4. George Henry Hall (1825–1913), popular American painter.

5. William Sartain (1843–1924), American painter, or Samuel Sartain (1830–1906), American painter.

Fromentin

A man who acts frankly, thinks boldly, disdains the prejudice of others and obeys faithfully the commands of his conscience, is always sure to be honored and respected in the future, when the ghosts of servitors of vulgar prejudices are forsaken. Such a man was Eugène Fromentin,[1] a close observer of nature, a careful delineator of its movements, and an exquisite writer. He was conspicuous both as an artist and as a literary man.

Mérillat,[2] Descamps,[3] and Delacroix[4] painted Egyptian scenes, but that country never had such a faithful interpreter as Fromentin. He never painted badly, but he never did as well as when he transmitted to the canvas the splendid dawns, tempestuous forenoons and ruddy twilights of the land of the fellah. His soul, thirsty for vigorous impressions, hating all things vulgar and extravagant, loving the sun, space and liberty, revelled in that land of dreams and colors. Those far countries are the natural resorts of romantic minds. Fromentin felt himself to be a son of the Nile's divinities, and with filial passion and fidelity, honored their memory with the most conscientious and attractive reproduction of their splendors.

1. Eugène Fromentin (1820–1876), French painter and author, best known for his pictorial scenes of Algeria.

2. Louis Mérillat, French painter.

3. Jean Baptiste Descamps (1706–1791), French art historian and painter.

4. Eugène Ferdinand-Victor Delacroix (1798–1863), greatest French Romantic painter, famous for his use of color.

If one should try to mentally represent Madrazo, it would be in the shape of a charming boy, painting outdoors, smoking, with hat thrown back and palette covered with red and green colors. Munkacsy[5] would be thought of as a hard traveler, crossing a wide forest, looking around with large shadowy eyes. Fromentin appears to the imagination as a noble Arab, mounted on a superb horse, the white burnous reflecting the brilliant sun of Egypt, his deep eyes revealing the power of an inspired soul.

Fromentin, when alive, was not praised enough. He saw the truth and followed it; he never sought for a transitory success by flattering the caprices of the public; he looked for that legitimate success the rewards of which are found only in the solitude of the conscience and the truth of the work. Brilliancy appeals strongly to our feelings, yet, when the surprise is past, it is disdained; but true merit recovers its power, too late alas! for its possessors. The enthusiasm now evoked around the light of Fortuny, the masked women of Madrazo, the little musketeers of Meissonier, the soldiers of de Neuville[6] and the madness of color of these painters, will, under the influence of a critical examination, be considerably tempered; and then the artists who painted nature as they saw it, with a firm hand, will occupy the chief places now stolen from them by capricious and blind fashion. There is many a famous master, the whole of whose works cannot be compared in value to a single painting by Fromentin.

Genius has its counterfeits. Fromentin was not one of them. He harmonizes purity of lines with brightness of colors; the expression of his figures with the exact representation of the surrounding nature. He is as conscientious towards his backgrounds as toward the dark eyes of his charming heroines.

An astonishing blending of the beauties of other painters is his principal characteristic. He has the delicacy of Meissonier,

5. The original name of Michael Lieb born at Munkacs who lived from 1844 to 1900. He was an Hungarian historical and genre painter. For further discussion by Martí of his work, *see* pp. 125–34.

6. Alphonse-Marie de Neuville, nineteenth century French painter.

without his minuteness; the light of Mérillat, without his excesses; the softness of Gérôme, without his varnish; the excellences of his brethren in art, without their faults. He was an honest and refined man and painted accordingly. He had the noble haughtiness of the *ancien régime* and the dash of a really artistic nature, and his brush follows the arrogant movements of the mind which guides it.

Fromentin's mastery of light in his *Canges sur le Nil*, of movement and gest in *Sachki*, of the art of grouping figures in the *Village au bord du Nil*, and of miniature painting in the delightful *Bac sur le Nil*—are unequaled. *La chasse au héron* raised him to the pinnacle of art. His continuous success, his kindness to minor artists, his devotion to work and his seasonable change of subjects, maintained him in this high position. No one who ever called on him for good advice retired without it.

Arab Women, one of his best works, expresses in the most happy way the majestic and indolent beauty of the daughters of the East. In *A Marching Tribe* the caravan seems to be actually breathing the air of the desert. *A Muleteer's Inn* made a sensation. *The Country of Thirst* is his masterpiece. The darkness of the sky, the gloomy clouds, the whirling sand and the parched air give a frightful expression to those unhappy souls, whose violent contortions and desperate looks reveal the terrible anguish of thirst. The foreshortening is admirable. Even the burnous folds are full of spirit. When life grew troublesome for Fromentin, his powerful brush became sorrowful, and the striking colors were replaced in his palette by dark tints. As he painted with his soul, his painting followed his feelings. His pictures of Venice, not painted in the conventional, loud, bright manner of Ziem, were considered mournful and unreal. Critics judged them wrongly. Fromentin was too sincere a man to represent Venice in a more poetical way than she deserves. The city of canals is not always the city of colors. The proximity of death disturbed the impressionable soul of the painter; a dusky tint covered his works in his late years. This state of mind influenced the character of his painting; but the *Great Canal* and the *Mole* do full justice to his stay in this famous city.

Rhamadan and *A Fire* were two of the last paintings projected by Fromentin. The entire canvas of *Rhamadan* was never on the easel; the conception was buried with the author. Only isolated sketches, considered today as inestimable treasures, show the strength, originality and extent of the intended work. The sons of Nature are adorning their mother in a lovely country. A golden light illuminates the figures. The wild soldier, the poor fellah, the tired woman, throwing themselves on the sandy ground, sing and pray. *A Fire*—another grand conception—never got out of its embryo.

Fromentin had the instincts of an adventurer, restrained by the habits of a born cavalier. He had the boldness of genius, without its turbulence and disorder. Ardent as an innovator, he was precise as an academician. He improved the rules of art without breaking them. He opened a new path to the art of painting without forgetting the old ones. As a creator, he was a spiritualist; as a worker, he was a faithful copyist of Nature. His imagination was always bridled by his supreme idea of the aesthetics of art. His respect for the truth, his wise employment of colors, the arrogant movements of his brush, his original views and fantastic travels, and a literary refinement embellishing and purifying his poetical impressions, are his great characteristics. The admirable painter of the great Orient was the elegant writer of *Mustapha*, *Bridah*, and *Sahel*.

The Hour (New York), April 10, 1880
[written in English]

The Runkle Collection

Amongst the many rich collections of pictures to be found in New York, none is more fastidiously chosen than that of Mr. Runkle. A glance at its treasures suffices to prove Mr. Runkle a connoisseur in art and an amateur of the poetic branch of painting illustrated in landscapes. Rousseau, with all the mysterious repose which distinguishes him, Corot,[1] prolific of dreamy sylvan scenes peopled with nymphs, Daubigny,[2] who depicts nature under colors as sombre as those of Dupré[3] are vigorous and solid, Millet, who succeeds in giving stability to his own vagaries and Díaz, at whose magical touch a peculiar blue light emanates from dense shadow—all these illustrious masters of landscape art are represented in M. Runkle's collection. Díaz, who has reproduced the nude women of the Italian school, the blue draperies and the smile of nature in his moments of tender revery, is the painter of two little pictures which recall his works on exhibition at the Metropolitan Museum. They bear the imprint of his favorite effects of light, of which the most

1. Jean-Baptiste-Camille Corot (1796–1875), French painter, noted primarily for his landscapes, who inspired and to some extent anticipated the landscape paintings of the Impressionists.

2. Charles-François Daubigny (1811–1878), French painter noted for his naturalistic painting of landscapes and his use of color which greatly influenced the Impressionist painters.

3. Jules Dupré (1811–1889), French artist who was one of the leaders of the Barbizon school of Romantic landscape painters.

notable is a bit of blue sky, pure and limpid, in the midst of a dark canvas, whereof the thick forest and the water which reflects the dense foliage of the overhanging trees only serve to throw it into more vivid relief. Another autumnal sketch, filled with the subdued light of an October day, and a third picture, representing a woman recumbent on the grass, her back turned, and, with a wave of her hand, dismissing a charming Cupid, who steals from the trees in the vicinity, are full of interest and artistic merit. The effect of light in the latter work, as it passes through a clearing in the opaque foliage and falls on the figure of the woman and of the little Cupid underneath, is really remarkable.

Between Millet's[4] two pictures it is difficult to make a choice. One depicts a female figure, pure in drawing and harmonious in color, and sketched with a bold, free hand, uniting at the same time the ease of Díaz with the mysterious suggestiveness of Corot; the other, whose inexhaustible beauties permit close inspection, is based on an effect of moonlight. A woman advances alone from a dark background, her back turned to the moon, which illumines the horizon with steady and sustained light. Detaille contributes a *genre* picture, *Les Incroyables*, to this collection, which is wanting in the easy grace and vigorous realism of his later works, but in which he gives, nevertheless, a faithful copy of the fantastic idlers of Barras' day.

Mr. Runkle possesses one picture signed with the name of the great Gérôme. The painter of Moorish women was in London during the siege of Paris, and whilst there executed this charming work, minute in the treatment of figures and misty in perspective. The picture represents the house of the English painter Turner,[5] to whom three street musicians, veritable and picturesque Italians, offer their salutations. The accurate contour of their forms is well defined by the early morning light,

4. Jean-François Millet (1642–1679), French painter famous for his landscapes.

5. J. M. W. Turner (1775–1851), British Romantic painter, famous for his landscapes.

which illumines at the same time the ribbons and flowers of their hats. The little Italian, his cheeks distended as he plays his pipe, abandons himself with youthful delight to the pleasures of his art, his aged companion is evidently less charmed with the treadmill of professional labor. Jacquet[6] contributes an interesting picture, which might be called *Rêverie*, but is, in fact, *Autumn*. Similar to the charming female figures in the work entitled *Rêverie*, the subject of his sketch dreams under the trees, which cast their autumn leaves at her feet. One hand rests on a book, the other, neatly gloved, hangs listlessly at her side. An indescribable air of dreamy melancholy pervades the features of this lovely woman, quite in keeping with the subject of the piece.

One of the most charming elements of this collection, however, is a little picture by Boldini.[7] In color it suggests Madrazo, in light Pasini. A young woman, whose exquisite, dainty head peeps from a hammock and out of a cloud of white drapery, ornamented with pink ribbons, is gracefully swaying to and fro under the trees. A fairy foot protrudes from the folds of her dress, and from the variegated masses of bright color one would say that a butterfly had shaken over the canvas its wings of many hues, but these caprices of color only intensify the grace and harmony of the drawing.

The Hour (New York), 1880
[written in English]

6. Jacquet d'Arras, French tapestry weaver in fifteenth century Italy.

7. Giovanni Boldini (1842–1931), fashionable Italian portrait painter, noted for his elegant likenesses of leaders of European society and leaders in the arts.

A Statue and a Sculptor

In the turmoil of Parisian life, where events distinct and varied follow each other in rapid succession, a young sculptor named Suchet[1] received at the last Salon his medal of honor, at the same moment when a grateful public paid homage at Ville d'Avray to the commemorative bust of the dead painter Corot. A certain analogy is thus suggested between the youthful débutant on the threshold of a brilliant career and the old artist dying in the fullness of years and plenitude of distinction. Around this bust is twined a branch whereon is perched a bird with folded wings—touching souvenir connected with the burial of Corot. As the friends of the great artist and man of genius stood by his grave, ready to scatter over his remains the first handful of earth which separates eternally the living from the dead, the vibrant note of a bird from a neighboring bough thrilled their souls with a sense of undefined joy and superstitious dread. This parting song seemed a fitting tribute to the French painter, who was first to convey in his works that vague sense of harmony, echo, perhaps, of past things, or forerunner of things to come, such as leave in one's heart the song of birds. Corot enveloped his figures, as did Díaz, in a warm, luminous shadow; his oaks, viewed too closely, are but blots on the canvas, but, seen from afar, as they should be, are bathed in the indolent glow of a

1. Joseph François Suchet (1824–1896), French painter of marine life.

great forest, where the winds, laden with perfume, kiss lightly and reverently the leaves of the sturdy tree. In all that the great and prolific painter touches, one sees the evidence of a nature true, dreamy, and impassioned. He invests his trees with life. They are filled with spirits lacking form, wandering amongst the leaves, invisible, like those dwarfs of the Danube, who, the better to see without being seen, carried for their protection the blue rose.

The Hour (New York), 1880
[written in English]

A Remarkable Mexican Painting

There has been on exhibition in New York a picture which has more than ordinary attractions. Its composition, its size, the minuteness of its details, the number of figures which it contains, and the historical events which it depicts, make it a subject of special interest. The picture is about twelve feet by six and contains between two and three thousand figures. In one place they are crossing a lagoon; in another, defending a fortress; here crowing a king and there killing him; first worshipping his horse and then carrying the same horse's head on the point of a spear. Here they crown a conqueror with roses; there they fight against him. There are some strikingly original points in this work. But, although the figures are most lifelike and are the production of a practiced and bold hand, yet they are hard and carelessly drawn. The figure of the horse, for instance, is very roughly finished.

Judging from the style of composition and the colors used, the picture is probably two hundred years old. There is no doubt that about that time there existed in Mexico a school of painting which was discouraged by the admirers of the Spanish masters, with whose works the churches and museums in Mexico are filled. History and mythology were subjects then prohibited by law. Only religious pictures were allowed to be painted, and it was with such pictures that Villalpande covered the walls of the convents and churches with paintings which still astonish all those who see them. Evidently, this picture must have been painted to order for some rich person or corporation—perhaps for one of Cortés' train, or more probably still for the hall of the *ayuntamiento*,[1] or for the Viceroy. No private person could have paid for a composition which must have taken the painter some years to complete. The painting is on wood and, to prevent its being stolen, one of the owners of this picture had it cut into ten pieces.

To one familiar with the history of the conquest of Mexico, one look at this painting will suffice to demonstrate the grandeur of the land of Montezuma.[2] The general tone of the picture is sombre, but bright spots relieve it. Every scene in the occupation of the Mexican capital by Cortés seems to be compressed in it, from his imposing entry, to the *noche triste*, when the inhabitants so fiercely revenged themselves upon him for his temerity. From these lifelike representations the reality of those terrible days can be imagined. The battles, processions, vessels, castles, volcanoes, and the blue lagoons of that period are seen in this great picture. Were it only for the truthfulness with which it represents the costumes of the inhabitants, the weapons of the Spaniards, the pomp of the emperors and the singular contrast between the two peoples facing each other—the Spaniard accoutred in steel, the native half naked—the picture would be well worth seeing. This artist's deviation from the beaten path, his transition from slavish ideas to a free scope of the study of nature, his absolute disdain of imitation of masters or conventional colors and his contempt for the opinion of a prejudiced school, all tend to make this great painting well worth studying.

The Hour (New York), 1880
[written in English]

1. An *ayuntamiento* was a town hall, city hall or city or borough council.

2. Montezuma (1466–1520), last Aztec emperor of Mexico who confronted Hernán Cortés.

Fortuny

Mariano Fortuny[1] was the most daring colorist and the most romantic and clearsighted genius among modern painters. Fancy, boldness, and fervor are striking in his works; but powerful thoughts and transcendental ideas never disturb his hand. He was a revolutionist; he gave new color to the brush, new rules to perspective, and new softness to brilliant hues; but this great departure from the beaten paths of art, however much admired it may have been, did not result, as it should, in giving a fixed and decided standard to modern art. Fortuny painted more and better than any other artist of his time, but he could have done more than he did. It is, perhaps, the fault of the epoch, not of himself; but a true genius opens new paths for the expression of beauty. Energetic thought, like light shining through the darkness, illuminates the spirit of the times and endows the future with a worthy and durable reproduction of the present. Fortuny is worthy of admiration; he was the creator of a school of painting and treated with admirable dexterity many special subjects; but the American artists must not imitate him. If we are obliged to imitate, instead of asserting our own originality, let us wait for some one who can represent the majestic side of the character of our age.

It would be a vain effort of memory to recall all Fortuny's works. No artist can be ignorant of his fecundity, his poor

1. For other reference to Fortuny, *see* p. 78.

cradle, hard infancy, and brilliant youth. The owners of his pictures are now made famous by the possession of them. If we judge the author by his *La Vicaria*, *Academicians Examining a Model*, and *A Tribunal in the Alhambra*, the most fervent praise becomes inadequate. If we look at the richness of his draperies, the magnificence of his foldings, the leaves of his colossal roses, the grace, variety, and life of his figures; if we pay attention to the scrupulous exactness of his nude figures, the picturesque dress and mien of his Arabs, his gaily attired academicians, his fragrant, sumptuous gardens—nobody excels Fortuny. His light blinds us. All is surprising and marvellous in him. His palette had secrets that no imitator, even though he be Pasini, could discover. He reminds us frequently of the ancient masters. His *Spanish Lady*, now in Mr. Stebbin's collection, shows the vaporous clearness of the face and mysterious darkness of the shadows commonly used by Rembrandt.[2] He even improves on the old painter. Never could Rembrandt have given such passionate expression to his figures. The ardent passion of Andalusian women glow in her countenance, to which the tender shadows are a fitting relief.

Little has been said about the sketch of *The Battle of Wad-Ras*, an unfortunately unfinished picture, dedicated by the grateful artist to the Deputies of Barcelona, who sent him to Rome. It is in the Museum of Madrid. Never was a brush so powerful, never did a fantastic mind conceive so many varied groups of dying horses, wounded Moors and white burnous floating in the air. There is elegance in the horrors he paints. A band of blue is a distant mountain, red spots are bloody brooks, small black points are soldiers crossing the river, and a saffron line is the sunset. A battle is really there, and a truly African battle. Lively colors are mingled with astonishing skill, and a soft covering color, as if produced by the bright splendor of all the others, sweetens with a delicate tenuity the strong glare of red, green, white, blue, and yellow.

2. Rembrandt (1606–1669), most creative and influential Dutch artist of the seventeenth century.

Don Federico Madrazo, Fortuny's father-in-law is fond of showing a delightful little genius, with butterfly wings—a masterpiece of color. The atmosphere, supporting and surrounding the charming child, is sky-blue, and everything is floating in air. One of the wings is pierced in the middle. The hole is perfect and has the color of the canvas. There is no doubt about it, and one feels sorry at the damage. He raises unconsciously his hand in the direction of the slender wing, and a frank laugh behind testifies the father's enjoyment of the triumph of his son. The hole is painted.

Fortuny masters all difficulties; he transmits in the picture the real and strong impressions received by him; he indicates a horizon with a single line; he painted without drawing, but he had drawn much before painting. He did not mark the outline with a careful brush, the most pure outline being in his eye. It seems as if he had assisted at the conception and birth of light. He knew the difference between the blush of a pure cheek and the tender tint of a delicate flower. Warm light, extraordinary perceptions, exquisite drawing, an absolute mastery of all the means of the art, gave the Catalan painter the most remarkable individuality among European artists. But his graceful ladies, his nude soldiers, his gardens, figures and ornaments of the Renaissance, were only one side of his portentous genius. He died when he was beginning. He invented a wonderful manner, and was anxiously looking for a subject worthy of him. But he did not live long enough: he died famous only as a great painter of light.

The Hour (New York), March 20, 1880
[written in English]

Edouard Detaille

He is but thirty, and has already painted his thirtieth picture. Celerity, vigor and truth in art—and sometimes in spite of art—these are his characteristics as a painter. To judge the man we need take but one trait. When his country was in danger, and other artists were mourning her misfortunes in safety, Detaille,[1] already famous, flung aside his brush to shoulder a musket and sacrificed his nascent renown to his country. One of the first pictures which drew public attention to Detaille was *A Rest During the Manoeuvres at the Camp of St. Maur*. He was but twenty years old when the *Rest* was exhibited. Three years later he himself was resting at St. Maur from more arduous manoeuvres. He had already been highly spoken of for his *Cuirassiers Shoeing Their Horses*. His first picture, like all first efforts, was a weak and cold piece of work. It was more of his master's picture than his own.

Detaille was Meissonier's pupil. It was with him that he improved his drawing; with him, too, he traveled in the South of France. But his best teacher was the South itself. It was thence that he drew his warmth of tone, his youthful ease and his boldness of movement. The most striking feature in Detaille's works is not correct drawing—for this is too often neglected; nor carefully chosen color—for this he cares little about; not the mannerism of overcareful finish—for this he hates; but it is the

1. Edouard Detaille (1848–1912), French painter best known for his accurate portrayals of battles and military life.

perfect solidarity of the painter and his work. It makes you feel that all you see upon the canvas lives and throbs in the artist's heart. His age and his tastes are shown in his works. You see that he is young, brave and heedless; that he is a first-class soldier. He does not draw his inspirations from his master, for the pupil disdains that which enchants the teacher. Detaille considers a thing as finished which Meissonier would think scarcely begun. It is his highest merit that he worked under a master like Meissonier and valiantly escaped his influence. Detaille's conceptions are quiet and complete. He paints with surprising rapidity. He is carried away by his ideas. There is no trace of a slow or tardy hand in his canvases. He has the fiery spirit of Gros, the bold grouping of Horace Vernet[2] and the proud independence of Géricault.[3] Detaille thus enjoys the benefit of a worthy parentage. Is he a good son? Yes, but he is rebellious. He admires his ancestors, but when he is at work forgets them. He does not stop to ask how any of them would have done what he has to do, but does it in his own way. He is too prolific to be minute. His genius disdains his talent, and he has all the recklessness of youth. Knowing that he can overcome dangers, he does not think of the risk, and, instead of going round an abyss, leaps over it. But the incorrectness of rapid work does not affect in him the charm of a frank and free nature. You see on his canvases none of the artificial gloss of varnish, which takes so much from the real strength of painting. His soldiers are really firing; they smoke, also, real cigars; his dead are indeed dead, and his horses are real horses, though sometimes he neglects them, as in a watercolor belonging to Mr. Stebbins, and sometimes makes them somewhat chimerical, as in the *Engagement Between French Dragoons and Russian Cuirassiers.*

A glance at Detaille's face is enough to open the heart to him. He will remain always young, even if he lives to be an old man.

2. Claude-Joseph Vernet (1714–1789), French landscape and marine painter, famous for his fifteen paintings, "Ports of France."

3. Théodore Géricault (1791–1824), French painter famous for his animal and sporting paintings.

There is a savour of the bivouac as well as of the *Café Anglais* about him. When the god of battles does not disturb his spirit with the rush of his bloodstained wings, he paints charming types with a careful and caressing hand. *The Interior of a Coffee-house*, *Reading the Papers*, *Exquisites in Luxembourg*, are among them. The faults of some of his military pictures must be excused on the ground that he neglects color and drawing only when engrossed by the fervid inspiration of war. Repose and conventionality have no room in such cases. If his subject be peaceful, Detaille elaborates his figures, studies their drapery and arranges the effects of light with loving attention. If Mars guides the brush, he goes where the fiery god leads him. This is the reason of his shortcomings; in him the artist does not control the man. Nearly all of his military pictures are celebrated. Every one knows that most touching one, *Les Vainqueurs*, wherein the suffering of the conquered French is told almost with grandeur. The Prussians, calm and haughty, are leaving Paris; they ride away smoking, and beyond, in the snow, lies the capital silent and suffering. It is a sad picture. The *Infantry Regiment on the Boulevard* has been much praised for the variety of the groups, the animation of the faces and the sober strength of the ensemble. *Saluting the Wounded* is one of Detaille's finest works. The figure of the general is admirable, though his back is turned; but the group is so powerfully rendered that one can almost see his face. The position of the horses is very happy. A *Reconnoitering Party* is full of life. A soldier is reporting what he has seen; the enemy is near; he signifies the direction by a clever turn of the thumb; he is worn out and has just halted. The officers, while listening to him, hastily mount their horses. All is action and life—the soldier who speaks, the listening officers and the poor horse exhausted with fatigue.

There is no room left here to speak at length of his other great pictures: the *Charge of the Ninth Cuirassiers*, the *Dragoons of the First Empire*, the *Scene in the Franco-Russian War*, *In Retreat*, the *Defense of Champigny*. Modern painting can show few pictures as true, as animated, as natural as the last-mentioned canvas. It is replete with life, with not one detail out of place. The picture is full of figures; some are only waiting—but what animated waiting it is! Those on the wall opposite seize on everything that can fortify their barricade. Looking at this canvas, one can count every heart's beat and hear the words on every lip. It is a pity that, yielding to modern prejudice, the picture has been kept within so small a size. In our days lightness and littleness are too much sought after, and everything suffers from it. Detaille is a patriot and an artist in the truest sense of the words. Nature has endowed him with golden wings. His genius is a beautiful and eager child, caressed by ever-smiling fairies and nursed at France's breast.

The Hour (New York), February 28, 1880
[written in English]

The French Water-Colorists

The last exhibition of the French Water Color Society (their second one) was a success and no cloud obscured the brilliancy of a veritable festival. The French water-colorists have created a school of their own—light, flexible and ethereal. Fortuny himself, with all the attractive power which belongs to genius, could not control these fresh and original talents. The two great opposing schools of genius and talent here, as everywhere, contend for the mastery. In the water-color exhibition of this year two artists, Jacquemart[1] and Français,[2] carry on the strife. Français is the more conscientious. Jacquemart the more spirited. To Jacquemart nature is a lovely girl of twenty; to Français she is a reasonable pretty woman; but beauty is at its best when it does not stop to reason. Jacquemart's peculiarities are worthy of study. He does not touch and retouch his outlines caressingly, he does not study deeply, he disdains the false effects produced by violently contrasted extremes, and from this very truth and frankness arises, as with Detaille, a certain haste and carelessness which, though not merits in themselves, bring out other virtues. Jacquemart does not love, like Meissonier, to paint a horse hair by hair or a tree leaf by leaf. Though he has not yet reached the heights of art he is well on the way, observing with accurate eye all that he encounters. When he

1. Hesden de Jacquemart (1384–1409), French-Flemish painter and miniaturist.

2. François Louis Français (1814–1897), French painter.

looks at brilliant Genoa, at pretty Marseilles, at the sunny road of San Carlo or the green valley of Gorbio, he does not distinguish each object around him. He sees a mingling of colors, shades fading vaguely into one another, all the beauties of nature melting into a wave of harmony. One line suffices to place a mountain ten leagues away from another; we comprehend the space between and see the summits, though there is before us only a little water, mixed with some bluish-black and some dark green colors. We take refreshing walks in these superb landscapes. Jacquemart secures all these effects by a method at once simple, broad and transparent, Français paints like an academician; his skill is remarkable, but his coloring, thoughtful, studied and carefully prepared, inspires no enthusiasm. They say, "He is a good painter"; but they do not say, as they do of Jacquemart's work: "This is nature." Heilbuth's has been called the great picture of this exhibition; it is entitled *Les Fouilles*. There is an English-looking old man, who surrounded by ruins, pretty curiosity seekers and exaggerated tourists, points out the site of vanished monuments. It is a new subject. These stylishly dressed people are a bit of life in a forgotten cemetery. One would think the sun itself—very well painted, by the bye—a stranger among that yellow rubbish. The melancholy of history is in the picture. But it is a good representation of tourist life. Heilbuth does not idealize his women, for the very good reason that they do not need it. There are painters, Meissonier at their head, who never paint women. Others, like Henner,[3] paint women only. Heilbut makes faithful copies of them. When he chances to come across a lovely young girl he makes her lovely, but heaven help us when his model is not handsome.

There are two charming pictures in the exhibition by Detaille, much less harsh than his previous works in this style. In some of his water colors, as in some of his paintings, the figures look as if they had been cut out with a pair of scissors and

3. Jean-Jacques Henner (1829-1905), French painter, best known for his pictures of nymphs and heads of young women and girls.

grouped on the shining paper without any softening shadows. This time the earnest artist has succeeded better. He has an impressionable retina and never forgets what he sees. He saw London, its gray sky, its wide streets, its cold coloring, and he seized on the poetic side without adopting its monotony. Though true to his subject, he has gallicized England and dressed her out to appear Parisian. In his *Retour de l'Exercise*, one of Detaille's most remarkable works, we see some pretty and very English-looking girls on horseback, a lovely mother running with her child to see the soldiers go by—those lifelike soldiers of Detaille—and a wretched-looking man, whose back is toward us. Architecture is a quicksand for artists—the best are often wrecked on it. Detaille has escaped its dangers in his *Interior of the Tower of London*. It is, as usual, a military subject, but these walls, with their color of old stones, so hard to render, how well they are done! As to the figures, to make them live and move is one of the gifts of Detaille's genius.

Louis Leloir is, as usual, the painter of voluminous and bizarre costumes, well and strongly drawn. We have his captains in huge feathered hats, his Flamands in yellow boots and his pompous men with martial moustaches. Rubens[4] gave the full force of his genius to the draperies of his colossal figures; and it is in the style of Rubens, though without his grand inspirations, that Leloir dresses his mousquetaires. His mind always works in harmony with his fancy, and from this rare union comes the much talked-of picture, *L'Assiégé*, which is neither more nor less than the temptations of poor St. Anthony. A hermit at his window, emaciated and solitary, throws restless glances from side to side as beautiful visions appear before him.

Louis Leloir is not the only fan painter of the season; there are also Jourdain,[5] happy observer of the rustic beauties of Boujival, Villerville, Maurice Leloir, brother of Louis, and Lambert,

4. Peter Paul Rubens (1577–1640), considered greatest exponent of Baroque painting, painting in Antwerp, Brussels, Paris, and Madrid.

5. Francis Jourdain (1847–1950), French architect and craftsman.

the painter of cats. His *Congress of Cats* surpasses all his other works in the exhibition. This fan recalls the *Voices of the Night*, a good picture, which is still to be seen at our Academy of Design—a picture which, in spite of the Flemish gray tint of the whole, is of some merit. Lambert has studied cats frolicking, cats quarrelling, cats fighting and cats making love; and he has no rival in this odd specialty.

Mlle. Lemaire's flowers are also worthy of praise; they are not unlike those lovely ones by Roubbie which enrich our Metropolitan Museum. One sees the caressing breeze lifting the rosy leaves and the drop of dew is round as a pear on the calyx. Mlle. Lemaire is said not to be so happy in her figure painting.

The *Sombrero* and the *Torera* are two pretty bits by Worms, who has heated his imagination in the sun of Seville and Granada. Vibert has dared and conquered the great difficulties of red and manages its different shades with unsurpassed dexterity. Some of his Cardinals look as if painted in blood, but this is in the dreaming hours of his fertile talent, luckily, however, he is almost always awake. There was once a French painter of rare merit, who lived under all the rulers of the first third of his century and was loyal to each one in succession. Isabey[6] was celebrated for his miniatures and for his great talent as an ornamental painter, also for his style of dressing and adorning the women whom he painted. Today we have another Isabey; he is full of fantasy, like those other water-colorists: Lamy, Barou[7] and de Beaumont.[8] Jacquet, a fine artist, first appeared in a study à la Watteau.[9] It is true to the flowery age of Boucher[10] and Lebrun,[11] but it is as yet impossible to judge

6. Jean-Baptiste Isabey (1767–1855), French painter of miniatures.

7. Michel Baron (1653–1729), French water-colorist.

8. Claudio-Francesco de Beaumont (1694–1766), Italian painter.

9. Jean-Antoine Watteau (1684–1721), French painter of "scenes of gallantry."

10. François Boucher (1703–1770), French painter, engraver, and designer, whose works are regarded as a perfect expression of the French Rococo period.

11. Charles Le Brun (1619–1690), French painter who performed many commissions for the French government.

of the force and vigor of his coloring, or of the originality of his talent.

To conclude, Gustave Doré sends a perfect gem, a caprice which only connoisseurs will enjoy. It is a pity to fly too high, for at such an elevation one can only be seen by the far-sighted. Doré's work is an *Illustration de Molière*, a panel, covered with boldly painted, vividly colored birds. From its brilliant color and the bright harshness of its contrast, it might be taken for the work of that much admired Russian, Vereshchagin.[12]

The Hour (New York), June 12, 1880
[written in English]

12. For Martí's discussion of Vereshchagin, *see* pp. 135–47.

Goya[1]

Never did a woman's black eyes, or blushing cheeks, or Moorish eyebrows, or small, sharp red mouth, or languid indolence, or whatever of beauty and delight exists in the sinful thoughts of Andalusian love, with nothing attempting to reveal it outwardly or deface it—never did these find richer expression than in *La Maja*. She is not thinking of a man; she is dreaming. Was Goya, conqueror of every difficulty, perhaps trying to endow Venus with clothes to give her an Andalusian hue, a human luster, a feminine, palpable and true existence? Here you have it.

Therefore what rivalry in these legs so daringly outstretched, lying side by side, one against the other, separated and joined at the same time by an opportune fold of yielding gauze! But with Goya these legs—delicately languishing and appropriately tapered because thus they are more beautiful and natural at the young and passionate age of this Venus—the position of these legs is reminiscent of the handsomest of Titian's reclining Venuses.[2]

1. Martí's notes on Goya were found in one of his memorandum books from the year 1879, and were therefore edited while he was in Madrid during his second deportation to Spain. For other mention of Goya, *see* p. 76.

2. Titian (full name Tiziano Vecellio) (1488–1490), painter of the Venetian school whose mastery of handling color and the technique of oil painting made him one of the greatest artists of the Renaissance.

One cannot deny a human existence to this Maja, a crude and fortunate violation of every convention. Were she to rise from her cushions and come to kiss us, it would seem a very natural event and our good fortune, not some Germanic dream or fantasy illusion. But she is not looking at anyone!

Her eyes are an infinitude of distracted love. One never tires of seeking oneself in them. Herein lies the painter's subtlety: vuluptuousness without eroticism.

Goya made a deep study by the scaffolds, among the executioners of Corpus Christi and Holy Week. He enjoys painting holes for eyes, thick reddish dots for mouths, ferocious amusements for faces. Where there is scarcely any color one sees a surprising effect of coloration because of the fortunate arrangement of those colors he does use. As if to pile up the difficulties, he generally employs the lively ones. He prefers and loves the dark tones: grays, murky hues, browns, blacks, smokey shades, broken by dabs of green, yellow and red—bold, unexpected, and brilliant. Nobody demands of Goya the outlines which in *La Maja* show that he knows how to frame within them a superbly graceful figure. Just as on a night of restless sleep one's brain is filled with infamous dancing specters, in this manner he pours them upon the canvas, whether in *The Burial of la Sardina* where the ugly approaches the beautiful, and the dancers seem to be a great lesson and a great intuition, not noble, live human beings but disinterred, painted corpses; or in *The Insane Asylum* where almost one single tone threatens to absorb, by the darkness of the walls, the rosy-toned yellowish-gray men. In that strange canvas of naked figures one prays, another groans; this fellow—a happy figure!—takes hold of a foot, his other hand holds up a flute; he decorates his head with a deck of cards. Another pretends to be a bishop, wears a tin mitre and dispenses blessings; this fellow tears out his hair with one hand and clutches a lance with the other; that one, angrily pointing to the door, displays a three-cornered hat with a turned-up brim; his face has been painted so bright a red that he resembles an Iroquois Indian with a headress of tall feathers. A coarse-featured woman with white hair kisses his hand, her erect head wrapped in a shawl; she has taken that man for a Franciscan. To puff up these creatures with pride, some poor devil blows upon their bellies. Are not these naked bodies perhaps all the miseries taken out into the market place? Worries, vanities, human vices? How else would they have been permitted to him? He gathers them all into one tremendous definitive judgment. Religion, monarchy, army, worship of body—all of them appear here exposed without clothing, so that these naked bodies are a good symbol of meditation and shame. This canvas is a page of history and a great page of poetry. Rather than form, the audacity of having scorned it is the surprising thing here. Genius embellishes the improprieties it incurs, especially when incurred voluntarily and for a greater magnificence of purpose. Genius embellishes the monsters it creates!

This *Corrida de Toros in a Town*, in such a round and spacious bullring, preserves no more of the fantastic than basic color. To you, the prim, here is a powerful and useful triumph of expression over a vague triumph of color. It looks like a canvas of splotches, but it is a finished painting. A young bull with sharply pointed horns and certainly a too sharply pointed snout comes down upon the picador who turns on him; turning his back to us and goading the bull, he is the best figure in this panel. There at the barrier, a great number of people. Behind the bull, a little wag who is a good runner. Beside the picador, the barrier man. Behind them, two of the matador group. Over yonder, another picador. On this row of seats, some white dots which are undoubtedly elegant young lasses in white mantillas, lace mantillas. "Force yourself to guess what I have attempted to do," says Goya. Imbued with the importance of his idea, he passes angrily over what he may be judging, and for him it is an unnecessary frenzy of color. Here he seems to let one see how he worked, failing to cover with paint the outlines which he hastily, and with a firm bold hand, sketched for the drawing. Two heavy black lines, between them a yellow strip, and here is a leg. When he wishes, what an opportune blending of colors or shades of the same color, which make of this canvas, at first glance rather lackluster, a magical effect of lights! That is how he paints the picador's jacket.

Here also is the celebrated life-sized *Tyrant* María Fernández: the famous actress María del Rosario. Fleeing from all contrary conformity as if to counterbalance the bad, Goya falls into his own conformity. He opposes his disdain for form with his love of it. And this occurs in painting as well as in politics. Exaggeration in one extreme gave rise to exaggeration in another. Goya's almost absolute lack of expression brings about his almost unique solicitude for spirit, for the source idea in the painting. His worship of color, with a marked irreverence for subject matter, made him scorn color as the mannerists used it, and made him be concerned especially with the subject. But due to that rare gift of his unquestioned genius, his secret lies in the profound love of form, which he preserved even in the midst of his intentional forgetfulness, his intentional deformities. Let those over-elegant, profusely embroidered white silk clogs with trimmed heels and sharply pointed, upturned toes that cover the inimitable feet of the *Tyrant* tell whether or not this is true. For with a marvelous although hasty and perhaps unintentional study of nature, that privileged eye penetrated everything. He might have been a great miniaturist, that artist who was a great revolutionary painter. The *Tyrant*, resting the weight of her robust body upon her right foot, has the left supporting it a bit to the side. Notice this invincible cult of elegance in the entire figure: the etherial material of the light-colored gown, the pale carmine sash, obviously satin, whose golden flecks, overcoming all the difficulties of the overlaid color, closely touch those never highly celebrated clogs. This face is not the indolent Arab face of *La Maja*. This face also burns, but in so doing its gaze also threatens. She challenges with her entire body. It will be given to love, but only to love. And it will dismiss without appeal when it tires. Her heavy brows, heavy to the space between them and arching widely outward, denote great energy. Out of those eyes—a regal impression—just as rapidly flow amorous effluvia, maddening glances, the sweetest of promises, torrents of torrid kisses, as if robbing the face of gentleness; and with that strange coarseness that angers women, those eyes flash and sparkle as if she were annoyed with anyone who might look at her and copy her. These women of Goya have all the handsome qualities of his nudes with none of their monotony. A misty brilliance surrounds *La Maja.* The *Tyrant* stands out boldly from an ashen blue background, with merely the slightest of a diffused blue atmosphere in the general background enveloping that splendid figure. And yet since she comes forward at quite a distance from balustrade and fountain behind which some trees, gardens, water, and a lawn can still be discerned, that white, gold-embroidered gauze gown strikes the eye; on one side following the slope of her body, rising and dallying a bit toward the waist, and on the other falling in masterly folds. Breaking the difficult line from neck to elbow, since the right arm is supported by a hand resting upon her hip, is that briefest of sleeves that barely covers the gold—the sleeve also embroidered in gold, like the gown from which springs the décolletage; although not precisely chaste, it is yet inoffensive and not too revealing here. Because although encircling it an exquisite breast is disclosed, a wide carmine sash girdles the waist and crosses over the left shoulder, breaking the monotony of the standing lady's straight, white-skirted gown, as was the style in those days. I seem to be rewarded by her loving glances for the long moments I spend in studying her. And I seem to believe she is alive and loves me. What abandonment and what audacity there is in passion! The left hand, emerging from the sleeve that covers almost the entire arm, is dangling and could be more elegant and less heavily shaded. The flesh has its radiance, for it still shines among those somber colors. The gently turned throat is as human and handsome as the "Tyrant's." The neck, unblemished; the hair, curly, fallen over the forehead and drawn upward over the coiffed head like an unruly cap, and caught high to the left with a small shell comb. I do not know how to bid her goodby.

When *La Maja* sees me pass by she seems to smile, although a bit jealously, quite sure that the *Tyrant* has not surpassed her. What a bosom has *La Maja*, more nude for being half clothed with a bodice of neutral trim, open and gathered at the sides and made of the immaculate fabric that shelters those most gracious goblets of love! *Ma guarda e passa.* For this painting belongs to the San Fernando Academy.

Goya's self portrait, although painted upon his own panel, looks as if it were by Van Dyke. But with more humanity, even in the flesh; with all the play of shade and all the arched sweep of eyelid; with all those sinuosities of the human face—tight-lipped mouth, deep dimples, prominent eyes with a startled look in them. Here upon the candid brow a lively yet gentle stroke of light out of which float those tiny close-growing hairs. The rest of the face a strong rose tone, skillfully unbroken but blended into shading, and on this other side, here at the neck, a dark chest and shading. As if some light were taken from here, some shade from there, and he made that face like the human spirit. This canvas seems to have been painted by another artist. By means of the exquisite beauty and extremely delicate use of color in this panel, he tried to show—not through lack of skill but systematically and through conviction—that he was scornful.

Inquisition paintings. They ooze blood: red from the living, purple from the dead. There a virgin, blind and faceless—oh admirable painter, oh presumptuous boldness, oh sublime imperfection!—is present at the scourging, carried upon a litter. Naked bodies fend off the lash with their gestures, by bending over, by flailing their arms; white linen, to rob the body of shame, hands bloodstained from their waists. That man's arms are bound to a plank behind his back. These men's faces are covered, the rest have theirs uncovered. Wrapped heads. By those hollows beneath the linen one can divine their terrified eyes, their clamoring mouths. A procession, onlookers, a night that frames the painting and gives it an appropriate atmosphere. Banners, trumpets, a cross, lanterns. Form? The naked figures are admirable. Powerful leg muscles. All the various positions of suffering mankind avoiding the lash; one feels the weight and pain of the last blow upon all of those bodies bending over to escape the next. Felicitious new flesh tones; not for that reason greater care than with the rest of the canvas carelessly painted at will, for thus are the confused forms lost in the dark of night. Great backs, strong arms.

What an excellent painting is this other! A convict on the scaffold, his head covered with the conical hood and fallen upon his bleeding chest, is dying. Behind, upon an ignominious tribunal, some round-cheeked, cretin-cheeked friars—this one with black blotches for eyes, suggesting a sinister look; those, revealing brutal indifference; these, aged Dominicans with mended skulls hung with white: poorly concealed rejoicing. Two judges before the scaffold, the one with all the terrors of hell upon his ample forehead, the other white-haired with prominent cheekbones, bony jaws, bushy eyebrows, forehead lit with a sinister light as if convinced that he has done well; he holds out his hand, by some admirable whim painted red. Each of Goya's apparent errors in drawing and color, each monstrosity, each deformed body, each exaggerated hue, each deviant line, is a harsh and dreadful censure. Here is a great philosopher—this painter—a great vindicator, a great demolisher of all the infamous and terrible. I know of no more perfect work in human satire.

Goya's two portraits of the Duchess of Alba are famous. In one reclining upon a *lit de repos*, the duchess wears Spanish attire and rests upon an elbow in a half-lying position. The venerable art critic Paul de St. Victor owns this painting.

Nude in the other, her high separated breasts point outward. Baudelaire said of the painting: "*Les seins sont frappés de strabisme et divergent*."[3] Ah, Baudelaire! He wrote poetry as if he were carving white marble with a sure hand.

3. "Her breasts are wall-eyed and point outward."

Ancient American Man and His Primitive Arts

Hunting and fishing, dodging the ocelot and the puma and the colossal pachyderm by means of his flint; hiding away from the mountainous trunk that sheltered the attack of a tusk, primitive man in the Quaternary period roamed the forests of America. Perhaps he spent his wandering and hazardous life in loving and self-defense, until the Quaternary animals disappeared and nomadic man became sedentary. It was inappropriate that he used the same flint points to kill the stag as to carve its resistant horns; he fashioned axes, harpoons, knives, and tools out of antlers, bone, and stone. Man feels the desire for ornaments and immortality when he is barely aware that he thinks; art is the form of the one, history of the other. The desire to create invades him as soon as he is free of the wild animals, and in such a way that he loves truly, or preferentially, only what he creates. In later and more complex ages, art can be the product of an ardent love for beauty, but in former times it was nothing but the expansion of a human longing to create and conquer. Man feels jealous of the creator, and delights in giving to stone a semblance of life and animation. A stone carved by his hand appears to him like a defeated god at his feet. Satisfied, he contemplates his work of art as if he had set foot in the clouds. Man's vital yearnings must give some proof of his power and leave some record of himself.

The troglodites of the Vesère caves in France[1] used sharp

1. The Paleolithic art of the Old Stone Age was discovered in the Vesère caves in France near Geneva as early as 1833.

pieces of flint or quartz to carve their images of the tremendous mammoth, the astute seal, the revered crocodile, and the friendly horse upon elephant tusks and gold teeth, upon the shoulder blades of reindeer and the shin bones of stags. Those brutal profiles run and bite and charge. When the artist wanted to make something in relief, he made his cuts deeper and wider. Truth has always been man's burning passion. Truth in works of art is the dignity of his talent.

When the Vesère troglodyte was covering the empty spaces of his animal scenes with drawings of fish, and the man of Laugerie Basse was representing on a stag horn a vibrant hunting scene in which a happy youth with unkempt hair, expressive face, and naked body—followed by full-breasted, high-hipped women—shoots his arrow at an enraged and terrified stag, the sedentary American was already impressing grape leaves or cane stalks upon the soft clay of his vessels, or marking imperfect lines with the point of a shell upon his objects of clay, often inlaid with colored shells and dried in the sun.

These first relics of American man have been found in guano beds covered by a deep layer of earth and dense overgrowth, although never among metal objects or animals of the Quaternary period. And since these poor specimens of an ingenuous art are covered by earth as deep, and underbrush as tangled, as the layers that now permit us to see only short stretches of the palaces with carved and painted walls that belonged to the fierce and glorious men of the Mayapán empire, it is impossible to assume that the American of those times had little artistic instinct. As our eyes can clearly see, we must admit that there were refined and historic peoples of great wealth as well as primitive and savage peoples living in the same age. Now this very day when locomotives rush through the air, and a rock that is objectionable to man can be broken into invisible atoms like drops of tequila tossed high out of a glass, are there are not some barbaric tribes still carving quartz, digging up boulders, worshiping idols, inscribing pictographs, making statues of priests of the sun, this very day? The human spirit has not been developed along rigid areas or zones, or as a mere walking emanation of a state of the earth, or as a flower of geology, let them say what they will. Men being born in the forests now, in the midst of this advanced geological condition, are still fighting animals, living by hunting and fishing, hanging strings of pebbles around their necks, carving stone, horn and antler, going naked with unkempt hair, like the hunters of Laugerie Basse, like the elegant warriors on Iberian monuments, like the inglorious savages of the African capes, like all men in their primitive stages. Man's spirit—the spirit of each individual—contains all the ages of Nature.

Rocks existed before the knotted cords of the Peruvians, and the porcelain necklaces of the Araucanians, and the painted parchments of Mexico; and the solemn forests were the first records of the events, fears, glories, and beliefs of the Indian peoples. For painting or carving their symbols they always chose the most beautiful and imposing places, the priestly places of Nature. They reduced everything to action and symbol. Although expressive in themselves, as soon as the land suffered an earthquake, or the lakes overflowed, or the people moved to a new location, or the nation was invaded, they looked for a smooth-surfaced rock and carved, inscribed or painted the event on granite and with sienna. They had no use for stone that was crumbly or perishable. Among the arts of primitive peoples who show degrees of inaccuracy similar to that found in American art, nothing can compare to it in quantity, eloquence, boldness, originality, and ornamentation. These Americans stood at the dawn of sculpture, but at the high noon of architecture. In early times when they had to carve stone, they limited themselves to line alone; but once their hand ran free with drawing and the use of color, they worked in relief, overlaid, chased, embroidered, and decorated everything. And when they built houses, it hurt their eyes to have a single area of paving or roofing that did not display a curled plume, a warrior's crest, a bearded old man, a moon, sun, serpent, crocodile, macaw, jaguar, a flower with huge and stylized leaves, or a torch, carved on the surface of the stone or on the head of a timber. And their monumental stone walls are of a richer and more exalted workmanship than the subtlest work of an expert weaver of textiles. It was a noble and impatient breed of men, like one who begins to read a book at the end. They by-passed the small and were already on their way to the large. Love for adornment was always a gift of the sons of America, and they excelled because of it; so too is it responsible for making the fickle character, the premature politics and the ornate literature of the American nations somewhat offensive.

The shapeless dolmens of Gual do not approach the beauty of Tetzcontzingo, Copán and Quiriguá, or the profuse wealth of carvings at Uxmal and Mitla; nor do the harsh drawings in which the Norwegians tell of their voyages; nor do these vague, indecisive, and timid lines used by the enlightened peoples of southern Italy to paint the man of primitive times. What is the intelligence of American man if not a chalice open to the sun by a special dispensation of Nature? Some peoples search, like the Germanic; others build, like the Saxon; others understand, like the French; still others excel in the use of color, like the Italian; none but the man of America, however, can to so great an extent be dressed with natural clothes, as it were, by the certain concept of a facile, brilliant and marvelous pageantry. Only peoples in their infancy—for not all of them take shape in the same way, and a few centuries are not enough to form a people—only those in a state of emergence were susceptible to the attack of the valiant conquistador who, with the subtle cunning of an old opportunist, could discharge his ponderous weapons among them—a historic misfortune and a natural crime. The slender stalk was forced to remain erect so that the entire and full-fledged work of Nature might then be seen in all its beauty. The conquistadors stole a page from the universe! Those native Americans were the ones who called the Milky Way the "highway of souls"; the ones for whom the universe was filled with the Great Spirit whose breast contained all light, with the rainbow crowned as if by a plumed crest, encircled as if with colossal pheasants, the proud comets parading the spirits of the stars between the drowsing sun and the motionless mountain. Those were the people who could not, like the

Hebrews, imagine a woman made out of a bone and man out of mud, but who conceived of both as born at one and the same time from the seed of the palm tree!

La América (New York), April 1884

A New Exhibition of Impressionist Painters

We will go where all New York is going: to the exhibition of the impressionists which opened again by public demand. Visitors were drawn to it out of the curiosity inspired by such boldness and extravagance, or perhaps they were conquered by the brilliance and daring of these new painters. It is difficult to make one's way though the crowded galleries; there they are, all of them: naturalists and impressionists, fathers and sons, Manet[1] with his severity, Renoir[2] with his Japanese overtones, Pissarro[3] with his mistiness, Monet[4] with his exuberance, and Degas[5] with his gloom and shadows.

None of them has yet been victorious. The light defeats them, for it is a powerful conqueror. They seize it by its

1. Edouard Manet (1832–1883), French painter and printmaker who was an important forerunner of the Impressionists.

2. Pierre-Auguste Renoir (1841–1919), among the most popular of the painters originally associated with the French impressionist movement.

3. Camille Pissarro (183?–1930), French impressionist artist.

4. Claude Monet (1840–1926), French artist who was the initiator of the impressionist style of painting.

5. Edgar Degas (1834–1917), French painter and sculptor, considered to be one of the masters of modern art.

intangible wings, forsake it brutally, clasp it in their arms, ask favors of it; but the wicked coquette slips away from their assaults and entreaties, and all that remains upon their impressionist canvases from that magnificent battle are those flaming ridges of burning color which resemble living blood poured out of their wounds by the broken light; anyone who tries to scale heaven is worthy of it.

These are the strong, the masculine painters. Weary of Academy ideals that are cold as a copy, they want to drive Nature, quivering like a naked slave, into their canvases. Only those who have engaged in hand to hand combat with truth, in order to reduce it to a phrase or a line of poetry, can know how great is the honor of being conquered by it!

Elegance alone is not enough for virile spirits. Every man carries within him the duty of adding, of taming, of revealing. Guilty is the life spent in the comfortable repetition of truths already disclosed. The young artists find the world a painting of silk, and with their grandiose pride of a student they want an artisan of sun and soil. Satan sat down before his easel, and in his magnificent illusion of vengeance wants to spread over the canvas, held fast like a criminal upon the rack, the blue sky out of which he was hurled.

The world's art is being emptied upon New York in the odor of wealth. The rich to boast of luxury, the cities to encourage culture, the taverns to attract the curious, all these buy the finest and boldest work of the European artists for large sums of money. Whoever knows nothing about the paintings in New York knows nothing about modern art. Here is the Mecca of every great painter. Here are the two Napoleons of Meissonier: the Olympic youth of Fribourg and the hardened man of the retreat from Moscow. Here is Fortuny's *The Beach at Portici*, the unfinished painting where light itself seems brisk and winged, seems to have been an accomodating model; this happy painting looks like a basketful of sunshine! Was this not where Morgan's colossal sale took place?

But that entire collection of masterworks, even if so opulent and varied, failed to leave in one's spirit that creative restlessness and delightful fascination left there by the sudden appearance of the strong and the true, as shown by the impressionists. Rivers of green, plains of red, hills of yellow; seen *en masse*, that is what the crazy canvases of these new painters resemble.

They look like clouds dressed in their Sunday best: some all blue, others all violet; there are cream-colored seas, purple men, a green family. Some of the canvases enthrall one immediately. Others, at first glance, give one the desire to destroy them with a good hard punch; at second glance, to respectfully salute so courageous a painter; at third, to tenderly caress the artist who struggled in vain to empty upon his canvas those far distances and intangible subtleties with which his intense colors softened the misty light.

The impressionists come from the naturalist painters; who is unaware of this? They come from Courbet,[6] the bold spirit who understood no other authority than the direct authority of Nature, in both art and politics. They come from Manet, who refused to have anything to do with porcelain women or powdered and painted men. They come from Corot[7] who, with the mysteries and vibrations of a lyre, put into his painting veiled voices that filled the air.

And all of these come from Velásquez and Goya, those two Spanish giants. Velásquez[8] created anew the forgotten men; Goya, who as a boy drew with all the gentleness of Raphael,[9] descended wrapped in his swarthy cape into the entrails of the human being, and with their colors described his voyage upon his return. Velásquez was the naturalist, Goya the impressionist. With a few red and grayish blotches Goya painted his *Insane Asylum* and *Court of the Inquisition* both of which send

6. Gustave Courbet (1819–1877), French painter who was the leader of the "realists" in nineteenth century French painting.

7. Jean-Baptiste-Camille Corot (1796–1875), French painter famous for his landscapes.

8. Diego Velásquez (1599–1660), Spanish painter of the seventeenth century.

9. Raffaello Sanzio Raphael (1483–1520), Italian painter and architect.

deathly chills down one's back. Like a bloody and eternal portrait of mankind, there they are—the great skeleton of vanity and evil. Through the round eyes of those hooded men one can see the stairs descending into hell. He was acquainted with the court, with love and war, and he painted death naturalistically.

Arriving at art in an age without altars, the impressionists had no faith in the invisible, and suffered no pain from having lost that faith. They enter life in the advanced countries where men are free. For even though a column of aromatic smoke rises from their breasts among the roses of their orgies, so to speak, a virile and enriching love for mankind replaces a pious love for the mystical painters, and this because of the nature of those who are beginning to feel equal. It is a known fact that the dust of the earth, the bones of men, and the light of the stars are all made from the same substance. What painters yearn for, having no enduring beliefs for which to fight, is to put things upon canvas with the same splendor and luster they exhibit in life. They want to paint upon the flat canvas with the same three dimensional quality that Nature uses in her creations deep in space. They want to obtain with tricks of the brush what Nature obtains with the reality of distance. They want to reproduce objects clothed in the floating and irridescent garments with which the fleeting light illuminates and clothes them. They want to copy things not as they are in themselves, because of the way they are made and seen in the mind's eye, but as they are seen when a momentary caress of light gives them capricious effects. Due to an insatiable soul-felt thirst they strive for the new and impossible. They want to paint the way the sun paints, and so they deviate.

But the human spirit is never futile, even when it has no desire or intention to be transcendental. The human spirit is essentially transcendental. All rebellion of form carries with it a rebellion of essence. And that same angelic force with which life's loyal sons, who carry within them the elfin spirit of light, are trying to leave created by the hand of man a nature as splendid and bright as that which is constantly being fashioned by the elements set to boiling by the Creator—that same angelic force, through an irresistible fondness for the true, through a natural union of art's fallen angels with the fallen angels of existence, is leading them to paint with fraternal tenderness and with brutal and sovereign anger, the wretchedness in which the meek and lowly live. Those are the starving ballet dancers! Those are the sensuous gluttons! Those are the drunken laborers! Those are the dried up peasant mothers! Those are the perverted sons of the wretched! Those are the women of pleasure! And they are impudent, bloated, hateful, and brutal!

These unfinished and sincere pages of color do not give forth the subtle but venomous perfume which so pleasantly scents so many fine books and elegant paintings where sensual villainy and crimes of the spirit are entrusted with the temptations of talent. Rather, from those brutalized young lasses, those coarse mothers of fishermen, those bony choristers, those humpbacked peasants, those saintly little old women, there rises a spirit of ardent and compassionate humanity which, with the healthy energy of a farm hand, casts aside false pleasures and obtains a place in the . . . .

How can we leave these exhibition halls that are so defaced by the many figures with no drawing to them, by the many violent landscapes, by all this Japanese perspective, without once more paying tribute to that canvas of Manet whose crude style of painting opened the way for those outdoor passions, without pausing before Lerolle's *The Organ* with its superhuman organist, before the splendid paintings of Renoir and those profound and gloomy canvases of Degas. How can we leave before looking once more at that astounding *Study* by Roll,[10] bringing to mind the Pasiphaë legend[11] from which comes poetry as fragrant and ripe as fruits in season?

The Renoirs shine like glasses of Burgundy in the sun; they

10. Alfred Phillippe Roll (1846–1919), French painter and sculptor.

11. A legend in Greek mythology, the fabulous monster of Crete, half man and half bull, the offspring of Pasiphaë, wife of Minos, and a snow-white bull.

are bright, flashing canvases, full of thought and challenge. There is a Seurat rising in rebellion: the short stretch of shoreline, green and without shade under a noonday sun, the river like cotton. A bather is a violet blotch, a dog a yellow one; blues, reds and yellows are mixed with no regard for art or amount. Monet's canvases are orgies, Pissarro's mists. Montemard's are blinding with all their light. The Huguet[12] portrayals of the Arabian Sea inspire a friendly feeling for the artist. The Caillebotes are wonderfully courageous: some little girls in white dresses in a garden, with all the fire of the sun; a dazzling and implacable snowfall; three yellowish men, naked to the waist, sweeping a floor, and beside one of them a glass and bottle.

How to count these canvases if there are more than two hundred? Some are exasperating, some astounding, others, such as Renoir's *Young Girl in the Theatre Box*, arouse one's love like a living woman. This mountain appears to be falling, that river seems to be rushing over us. Is it not true that Manet painted a study, in light reflected from a conservatory, of three full-length figures upon a balcony, all green?

But out of all those aberrations and flights of color, out of that conventional use of the transitory effects of Nature as if they were permanent, out of that absence of graduated shadings that swallow up the perspective, out of those blue trees and red fields and green rivers and lilac mountains, what strikes the eyes—as sad upon leaving the place as when one has been ill—is the powerful figure of Renoir's oarsman in the courageous painting *Rowers on the Seine*. Some coarse young girls are bargaining about their favors at one end of an improvised table under an awning, or removing the seeds from some purple grapes on a tablecloth heaped with the remains of lunch, the whole painted in tones of jewel-like brilliance.

The vigorous rower, standing behind them, his masculine face shaded by the wide brim of a straw hat banded with blue, raises his athletic torso above the whole—hair combed high,

12. Jaimes Huguet (1415–1492), Spanish painter.

arms bare, body cast into prominence by a short flannel shirt—in the burning sun.

La Nación (Buenos Aires), August 17, 1886

The Munkacsy Christ

Today we will follow all of New York to see the painting of Christ by the Hungarian artist Munkacsy.[1] Painters, poets, journalists, clergy, politicians are shouting "Eljem, eljem!" meaning "Hurrah!" wherever Munkacsy appears in his current visit to New York. They cheer his name as if to enhance the fame and fortune of his canvas. Yesterday the city's distinguished men gave him a banquet and upon the wall, above his head with its heavy shock of hair, "Istem-Hozott" or "God brought you to us" was spelled out in letters of flowers. The luxurious manner with which he was treated while traveling is reminiscent of the way Rubens lived—a man who wanted everything dripping with gold and silver, and who even enjoyed seeing the pomp and splendor of jewels upon feminine flesh itself. In Washington he was celebrated with great feasts, brocade tablecoths, halls hung with red damask, the wealth of kings. But his sublime Christ, in the modest tabernacle where it is on view, is receiving even more honor than the artist. By some secret magic of the paint brush, the white linen robe gives forth a great light which dominates and intensifies everything around it, restfully drawing together all the varied movement of the whole, and investing with captivating majesty a solitary body from which the linen cloth hangs in graceful folds.

Ah, one has to fight to fully understand those who have fought! To fully understand Jesus it is necessary to have come

1. For an earlier mention of Munkacsy, *see* p. 84.

into the world in a darkened manger with a pure and devout spirit, and to go through life touched by the scarcity of love, the flowering of cupidity, and the victory of hate. One must have sawed wood and kneaded bread amid the silence and transgressions of men. This Michael Munkacsy, now married to a rich widow who lends the charm of a palace to her house in Paris, was in his early years the "poor little Miska" from Munkacsy Village. He was born in a fortress in the days when the Russians were laying waste to Hungary, and when the entire lovely country of forests and vineyards looked like a cupful of colors shattered by a horse's hoof.

Those souls never saw the sun. People were starving to death. Munkacsy's mother died of hunger. His father died in prison. The robbers born in wartime killed all who remained in the house and left no one alive but him, close to the body of his aunt. The child did not even know how to laugh. A poor uncle put him to work as a carpenter's apprentice. He worked a twelve hour day for a peso a week. Some school children, grieved to see that sad but eager face, taught him to read and write, and he caressed those letters with his eyes.

Not knowing why, he began painting the chests in the carpentry shop with heroic scenes of Hungarians and Serbians wearing their shaggy helmets, close-fitting boots and curved daggers. Finally his uncle began to prosper, and sent him away to regain his strength. The place seemed like heaven to Miska, for there he saw a portrait painter who managed his colors so well that they brought to life at will all those heroes that the boy had painted upon the carpentry shop chests. Miska pleaded with the portrait painter so fervently that he succeeded in staying with him to learn to paint. He was such an apt pupil that within a few months he gave drawing lessons, and painted the family of a tailor so much to "Sr. Cloth Cutter's" liking that the man paid him for his work with an overcoat.

In those days he was already an avid reader, and the heroic types and periods in history assumed the task of invading his soul with light—a soul that death, war, and the orphanage had clothed like a darkened funeral parlor. But the Hungarians, with their stubborn black eyes, are worshipers of Nature, of naked passions, of an open home and a free and joyous countryside. Their music is epitomized by Liszt,[2] their poetry by Petofi,[3] their orators by Kossuth.[4] They drink new wine from wineskins, and love with a consuming ardor. When playing their spirited music they have the storm-tossed mane of a charger, the voice of a flower, and the call of a dove. This is the land of those colorful Gypsies and their gay and picturesque caravans, their lovemaking with the scent of early fruits, their curly headed vagabonds who fall in love with queens.

Life flowers and overflows there, comes out of cannons, and rules and preserves its regal aspect even in vice and effeminacy; all those vagabonds resemble princes whimsically disguised as beggars. Foreign ideas troubled Munkacsy as if they were bridles. His love of Nature was racial and inborn, and he preferred life to books. He found it absolutely necessary to create, and had that thirst for truth, unknown to the learned, that makes men great. Men are like the stars, for some of them give out their inner light and others shine with the light they reflect. How could Munkacsy paint his gloomy memories, but with the sorrows of his soul, the very colors that have given him no joy? One can see what he carried in his inner self; man places himself above Nature and alters her light and harmony at will. This is how poor Miska trained his impatient hand; and since he came from those who have their own intrinsic law and color, from which the artist in him overflowed, he always searched in his subject for the picturesque. But it was from his soul, which too seldom saw the sunlight, that he extracted the lugubrious

2. Franz Liszt (1811–1866), one of the great composers of Romantic music and the greatest pianist of his time.

3. Sandor Petofi, killed December 31, 1823, Hungarian lyric poet and national hero, whose songs during the Hungarian revolution of 1848 inspired the entire Hungarian population.

4. Louis Kossuth (1802–1894), symbol of Hungarian revolutionary nationalism who inspired Hungary's struggle for independence from Austria in the 1840s.

tones so well fortified by his own superiority, from which only love and the kind of glory that attracts enlightenment were later to be separated. In that black bed of pitch, however, shone the eyes of a Gypsy.

And did that courageous, direct, self-possessed man have to amuse himself by clothing mummies, by fondling masks, by grouping academies? Not at all. Life is full of enchantment and the picturesque. When he felt his strength mature and given praise in exhibition halls and competitions, that which occurred to him to paint, with much uproar from the usually placid Knaus, was a living sign, a famous canvas entitled *The Last Day of the Condemned Man*. The man under sentence is praying face down upon a table whose white tablecloth sets off a crucifix standing between a pair of candles. His poor moaning wife leans against the dreary wall; their little daughter stands between them; at the door to the cell a soldier holds back the crowds. The painter put into that work all his poor man's pity, the color of his solitary soul, his new man's courage.

He was awarded the Paris prize; his art and his very existence have grown with legendary beauty and swiftness. Every one of Munkacsy's canvases is an attack. He is a well-known artist in the outside world, but in his own home his wife's affection gives him the courage to earn that fame. She praises his creations, returns to his hands the palette laid aside by his sense of sterility or despair; she alights upon his shoulder like a hummingbird, to whisper into his ear in such a way that he fails to realize that her voice is not his own, that arm too high, that eye not attentive enough, that slightly brutal foot a slur upon her Miska. She drives away the last vestiges of his sadness. She softens his daring groupings, brings greens and blues to his studio. Not the umber; that she cannot make disappear completely, for when a soul is baptized by darkness some salt is left upon the brow, like a diamond rose, and there is pleasure in darkness. White does not attract him either, for this takes the painter out of himself with epic boldness.

Every day, the force of ideas nourished the creativity of this spirit that evolved the pulsating beings of his canvas principally from inside himself, with little aid from books, and because of his admiration for intellectual power he began to feel a deep affection for the blind and wasted Milton as being representative of the finest model of the strength and beauty of ideas. And then, to further emphasize his indigence and depression, he rose higher to a love for Christ before whose triumphant light he grouped the most fearsome and active powers on earth: egoism and envy. He has intentionally accumulated apparently insurmountable difficulties, and has been eager to make the human mind triumph by means of its own splendor. He has succeeded in investing an ugly figure with supreme beauty, and in dominating with a figure in repose all the ferocity and brilliance of the passions animatedly contending for that figure.

That is his Christ. This is his strange concept of Christ. He does not see him as charity, as charming resignation, as immaculate and absolute forgiveness not at all applicable to human nature. The pleasure of controlling one's anger is applicable indeed, but man's nature would be less lovely and efficacious if it were able to stifle its indignation in the presence of infamy, which is the purest source of strength.

He sees Jesus as the most perfect incarnation of the invincible power of the idea. The idea consecrates, inflames, attenuates, exalts, purifies; it gives a stature that is invisible but can be felt; it cleanses the spirit of dross the way fire consumes the underbrush; it spreads a clear and secure beauty which reaches the soul and is felt in it. Munkacsy's Jesus is the power of the pure idea.

There he is in a loose-fitting robe, thin and bony. His wrists are bound, his neck stretched out, his tight lips partly open as if to make way for the final bitterness. One feels that evil hands have just been placed upon him; that the human pack of hounds surrounding him has begun to sniff at him as if he were a wild animal; that he has been harassed, beaten, spat upon, dragged by force, has had his robe torn to shreds, and has been reduced to the lowest and most despicable condition. And that instant of extreme humiliation is precisely the one which the artist chooses to make him emerge with a majesty that dominates the powers of the law before him, and the brutality pursuing him, without the aid of a single gesture or a visible muscle, thus making Christ emerge with the dignity of his garments, the height of his stature, the exclusive use of white pigments, and the mystical aureola of painters!

And there is no more assistance from the head, from the noble downcast eyes in their hollow eye sockets, from the sunken cheeks, the tight-lipped mouth revealing a human courage still, the calm and admirable forehead above the temples sparsely covered with hair like a canopy over the brows.

The secret of that figure's singular power are the eyes! Anguish and aspiration are clearly seen in them, as are resurrection and life eternal! The winds can strip trees bare, men can topple thrones, fire from the earth can decapitate mountains; but even without the violent and sickly stimulus of fantasy, one can feel that his glance, by means of its natural power, will continue to shed its fire.

All things will bow before those eyes which focus all the love, affirmation, splendor, and pride that the spirit can hold. Jesus is near the four wide steps leading to Pilate's[5] council chamber, and Pilate appears to be prostrate before him. Pilate's tunic is also white, but Jesus' robe, through no visible trick of the brush, shines with a light quite unlike that of the cowardly judge.

Wrath runs rampant beside him, insolence is bold, the law is being debated, loud are the demands for Jesus' death. But those courageous and inquiring eyes, those frenetic and impudent faces, those talking and shouting mouths, those angry upraised arms, instead of deflecting the strength and light of his fulgurant figure, focus upon it and put it into sharp relief by contrasting his sublime energy with the base passions surrounding him.

The scene is set in the vast and austere praetorium. Through the entrance in the background, which has just admitted the

5. Pontius Pilate (d. A.D. 36), procurator of Judea who condemned Jesus Christ to be crucified.

multitude, one can see a patch of glorious sky shining like the wings of Muzo's[6] blue butterflies.

At the left of the canvas the excited crowd pushes toward the figure of Jesus. The painter refused to place him in the center, to have that one extra difficulty to overcome. A magnificent soldier raises his lance to drive away a peasant, and the man shouts and waves his arms: an imposing figure! There is that bestial type among all peoples—beardless, with a large mouth, flattened nose, wide cheekbones, small gelatinous eyes, low forehead! He overflows with that insane hatred of despicable natures for the souls who dazzle and shame them with their splendor. And without any artful effort or violence in contrast, the painting most forcibly projects its two-fold moral and physical opposition: the virtuous man who loves and dies, and the bestial man who hates and kills.

At the right is the Roman Pilate, his white toga bordered with the red of the patricians; one can guess by the softness of the folds that it is made of wool. The modeling of Pilate's figure is astounding; in a recess of the council chamber he seems to be alive. His eyes bespeak his troublesome thoughts, his fear of the populace, his respect for the accused, his hesitation in lifting one hand from his knee as if wondering what is going to become of Jesus.

Caiaphas the fanatic can be compared with the finest creation in art. His head turned toward the pretor, he gestures imperiously to the crowd that demands Jesus' death; that white-bearded head rebukes and compels; from those lips come cruel and impassioned words.

Two doctors seated to the left in the council chamber look at Jesus as if they had never been able to fully understand him.

Beside Caiaphas an old man has his eyes fixed upon Pilate whose head is bowed. A wealthy Sadducee, white-turbaned and white-bearded, gives Jesus his total attention; richly clothed and self-satisfied, he is seated upon a bench, his right arm bent,

6. A village in central Colombia.

his left resting upon his thigh; he is the detested rich man of every age! Wealth has made him swell with a brutal pride; humanity is his footstool; he is worshiped for his purse and its bulging contents. Between him and Caiaphas some priests argue about this legal case, one with a stern expression in his eyes, one with the assurance of a petty lawyer. Another, leaning against the wall as he stands upon a bench, calmly surveys the turbulent scene. Behind the Sadducee and close to Jesus, a marvelously realistic peasant leans over the railing in a violent posture to see the prisoner face to face. Above the peasant's head and beside the column of the arch that wisely divides the scene, a young mother with babe in arms fixes her devout eyes upon Jesus—eyes and figure so reminiscent of Italian madonnas. There in the background, to break the row of heads, stands a bearded Bedouin holding out his brutal arm to Jesus.

It is impossible to see this gigantic canvas without having one's mind, already weary of so much inferior, patchwork, and fallacious art, assaulted by the memory of that era of fixed ideals in which painters treated their churches and palaces in the grand manner.

That light from the captive Christ, which draws the eye to him as the inevitable end of one's perusal of the canvas; that sturdy and spacious arch which instead of robbing the Christ of effect heightens and completes it; that forceful, new and lively group of men; that knowledge of how to make the most exquisite colors stand out from the somber background without the use of artifice—colors as warm and rich and mellow as those of the old Venetian school; that sure and harmonious concept in which none of the less important figures lose power and relief when subjugated to the central and principal one; those eloquent facial expressions that tell of their owner's consuming passion; that masterful boldness of detail, contempt for artifice, contrasts and direct light; that truth, grace, and movement, and the patch of sky which from a distance inflames and perfects them—all these things indicate that the poor Miska of Munkacsy Village, who now lives in Paris like the king of painters, was one of those magnificent spirits, so rare in this age of pressure and crisis, who can intimately embrace a human idea, reduce it to its component parts, and reproduce it with the energy and intensity required of works that are worthy of the approbation of the ages.

Not in vain has this painting been shown triumphantly throughout Europe. Not in vain did Paris give the admirable Valtner the medal of honor for his brilliant etching of *Christ Before Pilate*. Not in vain, in this century whose chaotic and preparatory greatness could not be reduced to symbols, does this canvas of Munkacsy move and excite both the critics and the people at large, even if some of its figures are indeed violent, and if some of its composition may appear to have been added to the main idea as an afterthought, for decorative effect, and even if the artist's faith in the religion he commemorates has been lost.

True genius never rushes to the admiration of men who need to be great in spite of themselves. But can it be merely a faculty for composing in the grand manner, a strength and brilliance in the use of color, a harmonious grace in arranging the figures, an impact of the work as a whole—can it be all this, in these days of rebellious beliefs and new subject matter, that assures such wide popularity to the familiar matter of a religion gone down to defeat?

This painting contains something besides the pleasure produced by harmonious composition and the liking induced by an artist who impetuously addresses and splendidly completes a courageous work of art. It is the man in the painting who delights and arrests one's judgment. It is the triumph and resurrection of Christ, but as he lives his life and because of his human strength. It is the vision of our own strength in the pride and splendor of virtue. It is the victorious new idea aware that its light can free the soul without any extravagant and supernatural communion with creation; it is ardent love and disdain for self that took the Nazarene to his martyrdom. It is Jesus without a halo, the man subdued, the living Christ, the human, rational, and courageous Christ.

It is the courage with which the Hungarian Munkacsy—his

artist's intuition foreseeing what his study corroborated, understood and accomplished (for his passions and motives were always one), and ridding himself of legends and weakly portrayed figures—it is the courage with which he studied in his own soul the mystery of our divine nature, and with the brush and a free spirit stated that the divine resides in the human! But one's fondness for the pleasing error is so forceful, and the soul so certain of a more beautiful figure beyond this life, that the new Christ does not appear to be completely beautiful.

La Nación, (Buenos Aires), January 28, 1887
Dated New York, December 2, 1886

Exhibition of Paintings by the Russian Vereshchagin[1]

Soft music could be heard from outside, as if inviting comparison. It reached the doorway from the whispering within like sounds from a church. Artists, rich men, sweethearts, Quakers, idlers, craftsmen, all have gone—and even twice—to the art exhibition of the Russian painter Vereshchagin. Paris has praised him for his use of color; the Austrians have maligned him for his Mary, mother of Jesus. By means of his intensity, exuberance, and epic candor, he reflects his native land.

This Russian will bring about some changes. He is a patriarchal child, a stone with blood, ingenuous, sublime. He has wings of blood and claws of stone. He knows how to love and to kill. He is a fortress with swarms of bees in the merlons and snakes in the moats, but he keeps a dove inside. Beneath his dress coat he wears a suit of armor. When he eats, it is a banquet; when he drinks, an entire bucketful; when he dances, a whirlwind; when he rides a horse, an avalanche. His enjoyment amounts to frenzy; when giving orders, he is a satrap; when serving others, a dog; when loving, a dagger and a rug. Animalistic creation shines from his Russian eyes with matutinal clarity, as if Nature had just finished carving man into a wolf or a lion, and woman into a she-fox or a gazelle. The light in his

1. Vasily Vasilyevich Vereshchagin (1842–1904), Russian painter noted for his war canvases as well as for "The Crucifixion."

Russian eyes comes from eyes that have something of the fire of the Orient; they are gentle as a quail, changeable as a cat, troubled as a hyena. He is a man of passion and color, of growling and cooing, sincerity and strength. He moves heavily in his French cape, like a bearded Hercules in the clothes of a child. White-gloved, he sits at table where a bear is panting.

Artists, rich men, sweethearts, Quakers, idlers, craftsmen, clergymen—all have gone to see Vereshchagin's exhibition for the second time. And they say that those somber, resplendent, crude, livid, yellow canvases, painted with milk, painted with blood, stand out huge and radiant from among the mild and discreet tapestries through whose deep folds the querulously trilling notes of music fade away, like birds that seek asylum. Like a curtain drawn aside, a curtain of the silent hue of dusk, revealing the Caucasian caverns with their crevices of dazzling snow! "An exhibition," says one viewer, "of a Cossack horse with a silken bridle."

The crowd gives way at the door. A group of rich old ladies rushes to a tapestry. The ladies feel it, smell it and say that it is better than their own, which until they saw this one was the best. Others buy a portrait of the artist—high, shiny forehead, eagle eyes, nose like a beak of a bird of prey, powerful jawbones, a whole community of whiskers. Others enter to see the curiosities first: the room where two Mujiks with blouse and boots serve tea from a brass samovar, tea with sugar and lemon wedges, the cups in the shape of a skull, the silverware like lace from far away Cashmir; the wool from Tibet where the priests in their clownish caps give off a stench, and the saints wear masks and make flutes out of shin bones like the lovesick Indians from Peru, the base open like the flower of a Jerusalem cedar, and where the sheep have silken fleece; a corner of the marble screen from the mausoleum of Tamerlane the Terrible; a pointed hat of a dervish; the fountain where the Bokharan heroes presented the heads of the defeated Russians to the Emir of Samarkand. And ivories and laces and crosses and cloth of gold and priests' vestments and caparisons.

The entrance tapestry, with its blue and grayish boughs, is raised, and there is the city of Jaipur,[2] sumptuous Jaipur in all its noonday splendor. Flowers at its feet, the burning sky above, multitudes at the windows, rose-colored palaces, a retinue of elephants bearing the prince of the land and his conquerors in the gold and ivory *howdah*. This is the popular painting, the canvas painted in full sunlight, with neither tricks of shading nor of varnish! These are the firm and honest tones of Nature, upheld with epic courage by the hand of a conqueror upon a canvas stretching from wall to wall, and it makes us bow before it and blink! The colors are fresh, the unexaggerated colors of truth, the unadorned colors of objects in the open air, not those of the academies, honeyed and rhetorical! That power of expression, those light shades superimposed without being spoiled or running together, cause such astonishment. So amazing are those dark tones softened and clarified, as it were, by the splendid whole, as if scalded by the vast amount of light and the haze of sunshine above the mass of heads, that it takes some time to find a defect in this canvas and perhaps in all of Vereshchagin's cold and processional art. For the hand to paint well, the soul must burn. Fire must not be taken out of one's heart and replaced with a book. Thought directs, selects, and counsels; but art, superb and destructive, comes from the untamed regions of feeling. It is great to seize the light, but only to inflame that of the soul.

There in the gold and ivory *howdah* they go in peace, incredible as it seems! The Rajah of Jaipur, with his useless beard, and the Prince of Wales, with helmet and red tabard coat; but they ride in the *howdah*, confused and insignificant, never guessing that this triumph is India's funeral cortege.

And so went the procession, as a matter or course; but art must give the meaning of things, not just their appearance. When it gives their appearance, as here, even if here that appearance is painted with sunshine, it fails. There goes the pompous retinue, with princes for heroes, and gold embroidery,

2. A city in India.

and silver-chased war clubs. First go the standard bearers with their four-colored banners, and the buglers with their long-tubed bugles. The elephant is entirely covered with jewels: the wealth of precious stones weighs down his trappings on both sides. The harness crownpiece is embossed with amethyst and sapphire roses; labyrinths of pearls and strings of larger pearls adorn the ears. Beneath the crownpiece the yoke is decorated with pictures in red and green velvet, the tusks are ringed with gold, and the trunk is painted red to the halfway mark. Five elephants can be seen, the foremost animal appearing to leave the canvas. Beside each of them go red-clad macebearers and those in white, carrying feather fans, and horses with all their trappings, colored bridles and feathered forelocks. The green feathered saddles are studded with gems, the blankets are of silver, the horses' chests and flanks are adorned with blue plumage. The horsemen ride wearing corselets and gauntlets, with bucklers at their sides, lances in the lance buckets, broad-swords in their belts, and floral-patterned helmets upon their heads. Their legs are encased in greaves and thigh guards, their stirrups made by a jeweler's hand, with emeralds and fine silverwork. They move along in the sun. The dust glitters.

And that painting was going to be the last of a tragedy in color, for like all truly powerful minds, Vereshchagin in his maturity tends toward the vast and the symbolic. An execution stirs up, releases, stops the blood in his veins; and he paints various ways of killing, the Roman crucifixion, the Hindustani bombardment, the Russian scaffold, as he sees them or as they would be if he did see them. He is present at the Plevna campaign and will make numerous sketches of it, from the first snow-covered trench to the greenish-black hospital where the Turk expires biting the dust.

He goes to Palestine in search of color, and will paint upon canvases resembling caskets of jewels everything from the tombs of Hebron, where the populace throws stones at him to prevent him from profaning Abraham's rest, to the troglodyte hermits who live by carving crosses, among the toads and snakes in the caves of the meandering Jordan, like the tatters and lice of a conquered religion. He copies a famous building, defying dangers and obstacles, defying lone miles of traveling to copy mausoleums, palaces, and rival mosques.

With wire rather than brush he paints a fleshy background in full sunlight, a rabbi with spectacles and skull cap, a typical rabbi; and he climbs over ravines and brambly ground looking for types of interest to Russians and who figure in the Russian's surroundings—the mustachioed Magyar, the large-nosed Syrian, the togaed Armenian, the Circassian with pointed fez, the man from Mingrelia with his air of authority, the Kurd of sheeplike profile, the lean Turk, the handsome but sad Bulgarian, the buskined Wallachian, the magnificent Moldavian. Alas, it is art in chapters, but not in song.

For what is self-evident in this painter, as in all those of his race, is that universal sin of contemporary art, which seems more obvious in Russia because of the contrast between his energetic childhood and his culture brought from ancient peoples. It is an excess—ever present in man—of the faculty of expression over that of creation, an excess of the power of distributing color over that of conceiving subjects worthy of it. It is an excess of the craftsman's skill over the artist's rapture and ability to capsulize. It is too much attention paid to painting the exterior aspect—which demands no more than an eye for observation, judgment in selection, and cleverness in arranging colors, to reproducing (upon that other canvas in which the exterior aspect is used truthfully and in ways that elicit that intimate caress) a mixture of the submission and pride with which man in the presence of beauty, whether animated or inert, is recognized and esteemed as a living and fraternal part of the rest of the universe.

And in Russia this restlessness of contemporary man becomes worse, because from the barbarous and conquering types who have merged with the herculean Slav, there arises at the same time this strength of hand and character, this need for extension inherited from their feudal and combative ancestors—wild as the mountain peaks, melancholy as the steppes—and this terrible fear by which they are rotted by an alien civilization before condensing into a civilization of their own. The prince as well as the mujik, the *Kaías* as well as the *Isvotchik*, the palace that drinks champagne as well as the farmhouse that drinks vodka—all can feel their beards fall over their hopeless breasts because their hearts are living without freedom.

They believe in nothing because they do not believe in themselves, but the *knut* with its pointed hooks is forever held over the back of the working man—a walking rock—and of the *barina* who owns and despises him: they both suffer from the weight of life without the decency of being able to exert their free will, a misfortune greater than the weight of outraged love, greater than the loneliness of a poet's soul. Divested of the joy of universal freedom, they suffer from the pain of slavery, comparable only to the pain of eunuchs. And with the frenzy of irremediable mutilation, and the impetus of their equestrian race, they pour over those they consider most unhappy, with rage and cruelty, the compassion they feel for themselves.

And where is there art without sincerity? Or what honest man will use his strength—whether it consists of fantasy or reason, beauty or belligerency—in mere ripples, embellishments, or imaginings when he is faced with temples that resemble mountains, prisons from which there is no return, palaces which are whole towns of palaces, walls built upon the shoulders of a hundred races at once, the hecatombe from which, when corruption comes to light, will emerge the splendor that stuns the world; when he is faced with Herzen's[3] "pyramid of evil"?

Justice first, art later! The man who in times without honor amuses himself with the niceties of the imagination and the delicacies of the mind, is a female! When one fails to enjoy freedom, art's only excuse and sole right to exist is to place itself at freedom's service. To the bonfire with everything, even art, to feed the flames!

3. Alexander Ivanovich Herzen (1812–1870), Russian journalist and political thinker who originated the theory of a unique Russian path to socialism, peasant populism.

And from what does the artist live but from his country's feelings? Let him use himself, by the very things that invade and move him, in the conquest of righteousness! And since the direct defense of justice, the dramatic commentary, the eloquent composition, are forbidden to the Russian because of his own terror as much as by law, the only means, the only courage, the only protest, the only and indirect defense, the wingless and voiceless prayer of the despairing Russian, is his painting—ugly if need be, foul-smelling if need be—of the misery he contemplates, of the heart-rending truth! "I hope," says Vereshchagin with the lines of Pushkin,[4] "I hope that men love me, for my art serves truth and I plead for the downtrodden!" Later, to rest and regain his strength, he will paint, free and great for the first time, the majesty of Nature.

In Russia, alas for the man who is outspoken in his pleas for the downtrodden! And the painting, it does not go from house to house like the true-to-life manuscripts of Tolstoy who needs a live model; the Russian painting, which can be more daring, perhaps with the sanction of the anguished monarch, is meant to implore men's grace by means of the horror it inspires for the hundreds frozen to death, for the peasants cut down in a mass slaughter by a sweep of the cutlass, for the thousands in Plevna bleeding to death in the rain puddles.

With that national character of objective contemplation, with that habit of observation and copying, how can this painter reflect—with drama elevated to priesthood by French saintliness and Spanish energy—the action of combat, the rage of the cavalry, the face-to-face encounter in the trenches? If he paints a battle scene, he will veil it in heavy smoke, perhaps to say that all is smoke, as when his tzar—from the hill upon which, seated in his campaign chair and surrounded by his generals with their lavender sashes around their waists—sees in the distance, through the smoke rising behind them, that Russia is fleeing from the Turk, and that Allah is cutting the tails off the Cossack colts. Or he will paint the scene before the battle, with the

4. For further discussion of Pushkin, *see* pp. 284–93.

soldiers stretched out in the wheat field, finger upon the trigger and over their shoulders blankets yellowish as the sky, and standing to one side the commanding officers in their caps bound with red braid. Or after there is nothing left of the hostile Turks in Shipka but heaps of corpses piled in the snow throughout the silent hamlet, he will take a walk to Skobelev, followed by the flag, to escape upon a white horse facing the troops who frantically toss their caps into the air at the foot of the mountain that shines like silk. Or after the fight he will paint, with newly shed blood, the wounded lying upon their stomachs, or crouching, or twisted, or dying. The gray-caped sentry's face is torn to pieces. A general, dress coat over his shoulders and head bowed as if about to receive the Host of death, stands beside a man who has just expired, his face with the look of mud. Another corpse, arms spread and legs contracted, smiles out of a greenish face. Here a soldier carefully lifts his splinted leg as if it were a friend. There a soldier clutches his hanging arm. Another compresses his lips as he vainly tries to stand up from amid haversacks, canteens, and broken guns. Among the dead and wounded still others are smoking.

As if to lend some animation to the cold painting, an officer speaks in passing to a woman in charge of food and drink. A wounded soldier vainly asks to enter the crowded tent. One man turns away his eyeless face. The ridge of mountains is yellow, the sky fleecy. And the heart fails to be moved by that painting of an idea composed as if to instruct, because the visible calm of the artist, the wooden quality of the bodies, the mute feeling in that canvas where the agony of dying and the dignity of death are missing, contrast sharply with a theme that demands glances that tear, bodies that crumble upon giving up the spirit, crisp and broken lines, violent and fleeting foreshortening, and an apparent confusion of technique which enhances and contributes to the subject at hand.

But where solitary death holds sway and man has ceased to suffer, Vereshchagin finds the ever-missing sublimity, perhaps because upon canvas he scorns the men he knows, and it is there that one wants somewhat more than the groupings and colors of figures: one wants the solemn course of the Danube, scattered here and there, as the only color in the wondrous snowfall, with Turkish corpses abandoned by the victorious army along its line of march, with the only sentries the telegraph poles, so eloquent in such solitude, and the only friends the birds as they peck at the capes or alight upon the boots of the dead. Or those other days, full of majesty and tenderness, days in which the two last friends, standing in a pasture covered with whitish corpses, beneath a sky growing overcast and rainy in the East—the commanding officer in battle dress and the priest in his sepulchral chasuble—are burying, with a grief that penetrates one's bones, and softly intoning a prayer to the rhythm of the incensory, the squadron cut down by the Turk with a single assault. Faint sounds of music, grieving and despairing, come from among the tapestries as if given to us with gentle hands. The crowds want light and contentment. The crowds are going to see the holy pictures.

These are sunlight full of color, moss-covered courtyards, peeling walls, black wells and doorways, and phosphorescent seas upon whose shores the fair-haired and white-robed Jesus lingers, or converses with John, or curses the wicked cities, or weeps disconsolately. What is religion but history? Jesus walks beside us, and dies in anguish because he finds no one to help him in his good works! John preaches beside us, in his camel hair shirt and with his terrifying words. Good men salute him from a distance, and shopkeepers laugh at him from among their loaves and amphoras! Vereshchagin understands them as men, and as men he paints them, or as figures of landscapes in which he considers the blue of the water more divine than the anguish of the "Lamb of God," or the fierceness of the apostle, or the meekness of those locust and wild honey breakfasts upon the banks of the Jordan in the shade of the tamarinds.

And perhaps if it had not been painted as a sketch, it would be one of the most notable canvases of our times, for its frank concept, for the skill with which the artist uses natural contrast with Jesus' surroundings to make his divinity clearly felt—that sketch of Vereshchagin in which he paints Joseph's family in an humble courtyard with the father and his apprentice grouped to one side, and Mary appeasing the newborn's hunger at her breast, another son at her feet, and a boy dissolved in tears, his arm over his eyes, while two more of about age ten lie upon their stomachs discussing things of no more moment than little balls and spinning tops. Above Mary's head the family wash is drying, a rooster close behind, the hens feeding at the foot of a stone stairway, and upon the lower steps, so that he seems to be higher than all the rest, Jesus is reading.

The canvases, all of them small, are painted with shades of amethyst, flowers like blood, violet shadows, thick stone walls like flayed flesh, and rusty greens. As if he were taking a man's pulse on an open vein, Vereshchagin reproduced in full color that dead sea with its trees of ashen fruit. He copied that hill half-covered with blossoms, where Moses died before the promised land; that Valley of Jericho which yesterday was a garden but today is a vale of spiders, scorpions and snakes; that grave of Samuel where he summoned the Philistines to battle; that well where Gideon tried his soldiers, and abandoned for their laziness the ones who stopped to drink. There, upon canvases that could be worn as medallions in rings, is Jacob's well where Jesus talked of days gone by with the woman of Samaria; Beisán the strong that never opened up to Israel; famous Capernaum, today all weeds and ruins, where Jesus lived in his own house and healed so many people; thankless Bethsaida where he multiplied the loaves and fishes and gave sight to the blind; the fields of flammable pitch where Sodom and Gomorrah perished in the fury of the flames; the plain from which one can see Mt. Tabor surmounted by the castle where the assumption of Jesus is said to have taken place; and the Mount of Temptation in whose grotto, once lavishly covered with frescoes, now live the good monks who give alms to the birds and the Bedouins out of their meager store of beans and olives, onions and garlic, and a little black bread.

And in a canvas where the rachitic figures of Calvary, painted in a panoramic style, are in front of a wall of red and moss-covered stone blocks, stand the people of Galilee in their festive attire, gazing at the crosses. A horse shows its rump. An Arab watches from his donkey, his staff lying across the animal's back. In the background some wealthy Moors come riding richly caparisoned horses. The canvas offends against that feigned simplicity like a snare. Off to one side, not upon the stony ground like a mother seeing her son upon the cross, but standing and covering her face with her hands, is Mary. A robust girl in a white robe implores her with beautiful sorrow. Another woman's sorrow is evident in the frown that sets her apart from the rest. An English-looking Jew is having his purse snatched by a pickpocket with a long blond beard and a striped shirt.

And there the curious pause, not to see an admirably painted canvas with a red stone door and a flower covered lawn at the entrance where, beside a pair of handsome brutes—one white and the other black—some Arabian grooms are waiting, in hooded capes and fine silk shirts; not to deservedly acclaim the portraits of a dishevelled, sun-bronzed Butanese with honey-colored eyes and emeralds in his earlobes, and his thick-lipped wife carrying their son upon her back.

No, what the curious come to see, considering art in terms of mere size, is a brightly colored newspaper engraving that represents, with nothing more powerful than the live body of a soldier, an execution by cannon fire in Hindustan where the guilty Hindu, tied to a post at the cannon's mouth, is being shot to pieces. It is neither art nor does it inspire the desired horror, for it lacks in realistic force that intense quality which, in the beautiful as well as the ugly, constitutes the artistic skill of another canvas where throngs of people, as in a white bull ring encrusted with color, crowd together at the height of a snowfall that sprinkles the caftans and fur cloaks with snowflakes, to see two culprits, like two worms, hanging from a scaffold.

But what a way Vereshchagin has, in these miserable canvases, of emphasizing white upon white by using masses of color! What a way of painting the famous window built by the great Mogul Akbar in honor of his holy counselor Selim-Shirti, so that one can actually see that translucent marble! And how he painted those copper-faced guards of the shrine huddled at the well in their togas and turbans as white as the lattice screens, talking together in the fiery sunlight of high noon!

Then there is the milk white Taj Mahal mirroring its delicate cupolas, that seem to have been carved with a needle, in the reflecting pool bordered with cypresses and autumnal boughs, a pool to whose lullaby, beneath the foliage of airy marble, sleeps that favorite who loved the Shah Jehan. And now we see the Mosque of the Pearl beckoning us to enter through its noble series of arches carved out of ivory rather than pearl, with its rows of reverent Mohammedans standing shoulder to shoulder with bowed heads, calling forth the unseen creator. Now the vestibule with its double-mouthed cistern and babouches at the door. Cool as morning is the vestibule of that mosque where the green- or yellow-clad Ottoman entreats Allah's protection from the wailing Jewish tradesmen. Next, with its green and gilded domes; its *orujinaia* palace filled with treasures; the magnificent Tower of Ivan presiding over the vast marvel; the Gate of the Savior through which no one passes bareheaded; the Pantheon of the tzars, bristling with spires; its mass of superimposed storeys like the palace at Babylon; its protective bastions and its Moscow below—the colossal Kremlin, the rose-colored Kremlin.

And now as we leave with the crowds, of what consequence is that tiger by a palm tree watching a vulture hastening to satisfy its hunger upon a cadaver disputed between them? Or that veil-like canvas of a dawn in Cashmir? Or that lone palm tree, black sentry of the Delhi ruins, reflected in Yellow Lake at sundown?

The music does some good now as it comes from among the tapestries, sending its fluent and hymnal notes like necklaces of little diamonds. Never upon so vast a canvas did man create the luminous sky with more power and truth. But why paint it? Is there anyone who has not seen the sky? Below where the black vulture, sole inhabitant of all that purity, soars with outspread wings in search of the unburied soldier, earth-covered boulders like giant *bucarés* lift their flowers of snow upon the mountain peaks. Drowsy clouds awaken in the sun, and like the mists of morning wander gently as if moved with pleasant langour by invisible maidens. Furrowed by shadow, the snow-covered peaks rise high. The airy cloud floats, releases its haze, soars and vanishes, leaving the calm blue sky triumphant.

Thus does light crown the faithful artists who are saddened by the lack of a pleasant ideal in these changing times; for in spite of schools and grammars, they set up their easels out in the sun and find in Nature, comforting as the light of dawn, the peace and the epic poem that seem to be lost to the soul. Vereshchagin paints his portraits as if with a dagger; he paints the Samaritan sea as if with diluted sapphires, almost making one desire to die in it. He reproduces what he sees as if he had looked beneath its shell, to better possess it. His marble glows and his Indian air radiates light. A vigorous son of a frightened and disfigured nation, he knows how to make use of man in his canvases only when, far from his dismal country, he finds him agile and gracious; when he paints man it is to serve him. He neither composes nor consolidates nor creates; his spirit seems not to have been opened to great art, the art that is able to extract the soul of things, or produce harmonious feelings by means of detail, or flood one's entrails with delights—except in those vast and solitary canvases with mountains, oh Russia, like your sorrows, and with valleys, oh Russia, as frozen as your hopes.

La Nación (Buenos Aires), March 3, 1889
Dated New York, January 13, 1889

II
Literature and Literary Figures

Emerson[1]

There are times when the pen trembles, like a priest tempted by sin who feels he is unworthy to perform his ministry. The agitated spirit soars, seeking wings to carry it upward, not a quill to taper and shape it as would an engraving tool. Writing is painful and humiliating, like hitching a condor to a wagon. When a great man disappears from the earth he leaves a trail of purest splendor, a desire for peace and an abhorrence of noise. The world is like a temple profaned by the commerce of cities, the tumult of life, and the bustle of men. One feels like shedding one's feet and sprouting wings. One lives as if in starlight, as if resting in a meadow of white blossoms. Pale, cool fire fills the silent immensity of space. Everything converges toward a summit, and we are atop it. The earth at our feet is wrapped in shadows like some distant world of long ago. And those rumbling wagons, those hawking shopkeepers, those tall chimneys that spew out their whistling blasts, that clashing, strutting,

1. Ralph Waldo Emerson (1803–1882), American transcendentalist essayist, poet, and philosopher. Emerson left the Unitarian pulpit because he felt he needed a new approach to God and man. His oration on "The American Scholar" called for a fresh, individual approach, and his "Divinity School Address," delivered at Harvard and critical of conventional interpretations of Christianity, barred him from the University for many years. Emerson helped edit *The Dial* with Margaret Fuller. For other references to Emerson, *see* pp. 18–25, 146–67.

arguing in the lives of men, seem to us in our chaste and comfortable retreat like the sounds of a barbaric army invading our mountaintop, tramping its slopes and angrily tearing the great shadow behind which rises, like a tremendous battlefield, the great, tumultous, shining city where warriors of stone carry red lances and wear golden breastplates and helmets. Emerson is dead, and sweet tears fill the eyes. We are not sorrowful; only envious. Our hearts are brimming with tenderness, not grief. Death is a victory, and when a man has lived a good life, his hearse is his triumphal chariot. Our tears are of pleasure, not grief, because the wounds that life inflicted on the hands and feet of the deceased are now covered with rose petals. The death of a just man is a celebration in which all the world stops to see the heavens opening. Men's faces are radiant with hope, they carry sheaves of palms for carpeting the earth, and with their swords held high they make an archway under which passes the body of the victorious warrior, covered with golden straw and boughs. He who gave everything of himself, and did good to others, goes to his rest. He who labored badly in this life goes to labor again. And the young warriors, after jealously seeing the passing of the noble conqueror, whose still warm body radiates all the greatness of peace, return to the tasks of the living, so they themselves may deserve a carpet of palms and an archway of swords!

Who was this man who died? Well, the whole world knows. When he was alive, he shook from his shoulders all those cloaks and from his eyes all those bandages with which the past has encumbered men, and lived face to face with Nature, as if the entire world were his home, the sun his own sun, and he a patriarch. Here was a man to whom Nature opened and revealed herself, and held out her many arms as if to enfold within them the whole body of her son. He was one of those to whom is given the greatest knowledge, the greatest calm, the greatest joy. All of Nature trembled before him like a new bride. He lived a happy life because he put his desires outside the world. His entire life was the dawn of a wedding night. What raptures filled his soul! What visions swam before his eyes! What tablets of the Law were his books! His poetry, what flights of angels! As a boy he was slender and timid, giving the impression of a fledgling eagle or a sapling pine. And then he became serene, kindly, and radiant, and young and old alike would pause to see him pass. His step had the firmness of a man who knows where he must go; his tall, frail body was like those trees whose tops sway in the pure breezes. He had the lean face of a man made to be withdrawn yet eager to come out of himself. His forehead was like a mountainside, his nose like the beak of birds whose haunts are near the summits, his captivating eyes were calm and filled with love, as if he had seen the unseen. The mere sight of him made one want to kiss his brow. The great English philosopher Carlyle, who rejected the world with Satanic strength and brilliance, referred to a visit from Emerson as a "heavenly vision." Whitman, who had found a new poetry in Nature, thought "blessed" the time he spent with him.[2] The reputable critic Stedman[3] saw "a pure light burning in the town of the Concord seer." Alcott, the noble old man with a young outlook,[4] the thinker and singer, considered it "a misfortune not to have known him."[5] People would go to see him as if he were a living monument or a supreme being. There are some men of mountainous stature who level the land before and after them.

2. In his poem, "By Emerson's Grave," Walt Whitman (1819–1892) wrote: "How shall I henceforth dwell on the blessed hours when, not long since, I saw that benign face. . . ."

3. Edmund Clarence Stedman (1833–1908), American author and critic. In citing this phrase from Stedman, Martí may have been referring to his statement: "Of Emerson I have said elsewhere that his prose was poetry, and his poetry light and air." (E. C. Stedman, *The Nature and Elements of Poetry* [Boston, 1892], p. 58.)

4. For Martí's essay on Bronson Alcott, *see* pp. 47–53 in *On Education*, volume 3 of the collected writings of José Martí, ed. Philip S. Foner (New York, 1979).

5. Martí is referring to Alcott's line in his dedicatory poem which reads: "Misfortune to have lived not knowing thee!" (See Bronson Alcott, *Ralph Waldo Emerson, An Estimate of His Character and Genius* [Boston, 1882].)

He was not familiar but he was kind, for his was the imperial family all of whose members were to be emperors. He was as fond of his friends as if they were lovers; friendship for him had something of the solemnity of a forest twilight. Love is greater than friendship in that it produces children. Friendship is greater than love in that it creates no desires, nor the fatigue of having satisfied them, nor the pain of abandoning the temple of gratified desires for that of new ones. He lived in an aura of enchantment. His voice sounded as if coming from a messenger of the future speaking from out of luminous clouds. It seemed as if the men gathered to hear him were bound together by an impalpable strand of moonlight. Wise men would go to hear him and come away regaled and reprimanded. The young walk long miles to see him, and he would receive the trembling pilgrims with a smile, have them sit around his sturdy mahogany table covered with books, and, standing like a servant, serve them his fine old sherry. Some of those who read but fail to understand him accuse him of showing little kindness, because, made for perpetual communion with greatness, he thought little of personal matters, regarding them as unimportant things of chance and unworthy of telling. The woeful lamentations of these little poets! Men must be told what is worthy of a man and able to exalt him! It is ants' work to go about telling one's petty sorrows in lackluster rhymes! Grief should be modest.

His mind was priestly, his kindliness angelic, his rages holy. When he saw men enslaved and thought about them, his words seemed to be the Tablets of the Law shattering again on the slope of some new biblical mountain. His anger was indeed Mosaic. Emerson shook off the trivialities of commonplace minds the way a lion swishes its tail to rid itself of horseflies. Argument for him was time robbed from discovering truth. Since he said what he saw, it irritated him when anyone questioned what he said. It was not the anger of vanity, but of sincerity. How could he be blamed if others lacked the enlightenment of his eyes? Will the caterpillar not deny that the eagle flies? He looked down upon sophistry, and since for him the extraordinary was the commonplace, he was amazed by the need of having to demonstrate the extraordinary. When he was not understood, he shrugged; Nature had spoken to him, and he was a priest of Nature. Revelations were not affectation with him; he did not build worlds of the mind; he put neither will nor mental effort into his poetry or prose. All his prose is poetry, and one echoes the other. He saw behind him the creative spirit that spoke to Nature through him. He saw himself as a transparent eye that could see everything, reflect everything, and was eye alone. What he wrote seemed to be fragments of shattered light falling upon him, bathing his soul, intoxicating him with light, and bouncing off him again. What was he to think of those vain little minds going about on the stilts of convention? Or those unworthy men who have eyes but refuse to see? Or those idlers or flocks of sheep who would rather use the eyes of others than their own? Or those figures of clay who walk over the land molded by tailors and shoemakers and hatters, adorned by jewelers, and endowed with senses and speech but nothing else? Or those pompous phrasemakers who are unaware that every thought is mental anguish, and a flame kindled with the oil of life itself, and a mountaintop?

Never did a man live freer from the pressures of men or of their times. The future did not make him tremble, nor was he blinded in passing through. His inner light brought him safely over those ruins we call life. He knew no bounds or shackles, nor was he a man merely of his own nations; he belonged to mankind. He saw the world, found it incompatible with himself, felt the pain of answering questions men never ask, and became introspective. He was kind to men and faithful to himself. He was trained to teach a creed, but he handed over his clerical robes to the believers when he felt that Nature had thrown her noble cloak upon his shoulders. He obeyed no system, because to do so seemed like an act of blindness and servility; nor did he create one, for this he considered an act of a weak and base and envious mind. He buried himself in Nature and emerged from her radiant, thus feeling like a man and therefore like God. He recounted what he saw, and when he could not see, said nothing. He made known what he perceived, revering what he could not perceive. He looked upon the universe with his own eyes, and spoke its special language. He was a creator in spite of himself. He knew divine joy, and lived in delightful and heavenly communion. He knew the ineffable sweetness of ecstasy. His mind, his tongue, and his conscience were never for hire. He radiated light as if from a star, and embodied the full dignity of humanity.

That is how he spent his life: seeing and revealing the invisible. He lived in a sanctified city, for there, weary of slavery, men decided to be free. Kneeling on the ground of Emerson's native Concord, they fired the first shot, from which iron this country was forged, at the English redcoats.[6] He lived in Concord, which is like Tusculum,[7] a town inhabited by thinkers, recluses, and poets. His house was spacious and solemn like himself, surrounded by tall pines, as if symbolic of their owner, and shady chestnut trees. The books in this sage's room looked more like guests than books; all wore an everyday appearance and had yellowed pages and well-worn bindings. He read everything, a preying eagle. The house was gabled, like the dwelling of one who lives in constant upward flight, and plumes of smoke streamed from the high and pointed roof like that mist of ideas that sometimes seems to drift out of a great and pensive mind. There he read Montaigne,[8] who saw things for himself and spoke true words; Swedenborg,[9] the mystic with the oceanic mind; Plotinus,[10] who searched for God and came close to

6. It was at Concord at North Bridge, on April 19, 1775, that the Americans counterattacked with effect after being repulsed the same day on Lexington Green. In Emerson's famous words, the "embattled farmers . . . fired the shot heard round the world."

7. Tusculum was an ancient city, now in ruins, in Latium, Italy, southeast of Rome; the Roman writer Cicero had a villa there.

8. Michael Eyquem Montaigne (1688–1772), famous French author of books and essays.

9. Emanuel Swedenborg (1688–1772), Swedish scientist and theologian whose followers founded a religion, the Church of New Jerusalem, in his name. The Church claimed direct mystical communication between the world and the spiritual realm and affirmed Christ as the true God.

10. Plotinus (205?–270 A.D.), Egyptian-born Roman neo-Platonist philosopher.

finding him; the Hindus, who came humbly and trembling to the evanescence of their own souls; and Plato,[11] who saw into the divine mind fearlessly and with unparalleled results. Or he would shut his books and his corporal eyes, and give himself the supreme pleasure of seeing with the soul. Or when an idea, seeking its precise expression, struggled on the lips like an animal caught in the brambles and fighting to be free, then flaming with anger, he would pace the floor, restless and excited, like someone moved by an alien will. Or he would sit down wearily and smile sweetly, like a man who sees something solemn and gratefully caresses his own spirit for having found it. Oh, how rewarding to think well, and what kingly joy in understanding life's purposes! One smiles at the appearance of a truth, as if at the sight of an extraordinarily beautiful young girl, and trembles too, as at a mysterious betrothal. Life, usually so awesome, becomes ineffable. Ordinary pleasures are instinctive with rogues. Loving and thinking impart to life the most delicate pleasures, for what clouds in the sky are lovelier than those that cluster and drift upward in the soul of a father looking at his child? For why should a man envy saintly womanhood because she suffers or gives birth, since a thought, with its birth pangs and subsequent rejoicing, is also a child? It is a noble and intoxicating moment when one knows the truth. The sensation is not one of ascending but of repose. One feels a filial tenderness and a father's confusion. Joy makes the eyes sparkle with fire, infuses the soul with tranquility, and imparts to the mind a caress of soft wings. It is as if the brain were peopled with stars: an inner firmament, vast and silent, illumining the tranquil mind on a solemn night! A magnificent world from which one turns and gently leads by the hand all man's handiwork, as if with pity for the insignificant, and the plea that it not disturb the sacred bliss. Books that seemed like mountains a short while ago now appear to be withered grapes, and men seem like

11. Plato's ideas had a great influence on transcendentalists like Emerson. Platonism, the philosophy of Plato, emphasized the ideal forms as an absolute and eternal reality of which the phenomena of the world are an imperfect and transitory reflection.

invalids to whom one brings a cure. And trees, mountains, the enormous sky, and the mighty sea seem like our brothers or friends. Man feels as if he were a creator of Nature. Reading stimulates, fires, enlivens, and is like a gust of fresh air that blows away the ashes from the embers, baring the fire to the air. One reads great books, and if capable of greatness a man is better able to be great. The noble lion awakens, and vigorously shakes from his mane the golden flakes of thought.

Emerson was a subtle observer who saw the delicate air become wise and melodious words on men's lips, and he wrote as an observer and not as a ponderer. Everything he writes is a maxim. His pen is not a paintbrush that dilutes, but a chisel that carves and trims. He leaves a pure phrase the way a good sculptor leaves a pure line. He likens a superfluous word to a wrinkle on the form, and with a stroke of his chisel the wrinkle vanishes and the phrase is smooth and clean. He detests the superfluous. When he says something, he says it all. At times he appears to jump from one subject to another, and at first glance the relationship between two connected ideas is not always plain to see, but what to others is a leap, to him is a natural step. He strides from mountaintop to mountaintop like a giant, disdaining the trails and footpaths where the pack-burdened pedestrians plod far below, and to whose eyes this towering giant looks small. He does not write in clauses, but in catalogues. His books are summaries, not demonstrations. His thoughts seem isolated, but the fact is he sees many things at once, and wants to say them all at once and just as he sees them, like a page read by lightning or in such a beautiful light that one knows it must disappear. He leaves the deciphering to others; he cannot lose time; he merely sets forth. His style is not baroque; it is clear. He purifies, cleanses, examines, distills it, and reduces it to essentials. His style is not a green hillock covered with sweet-smelling flowering plants; it is a basalt mountain. Instead of serving language, he makes it serve him. Language is the work of man, and man must not be its slave. Some of us do not fully understand him, but a mountain cannot be measured in inches. They say he is obscure, but when have great minds escaped this accusation? It is less humiliating to say we do not understand what we read than to confess our inability to do so. Emerson does not argue; he establishes. He prefers the teachings of Nature to those of man. He feels that a tree knows more than a book, that a star teaches more than a university, that a farm is a gospel, and that a farmboy is closer to universal truth than an antiquarian. For him there are no candles like the stars, no altars like the mountains, no preachers like the deep and tremulous night. When he sees the bright and joyful morning cast off its veils and emerge rosy and happy, he is filled with angelic emotion. He feels more powerful than an Assyrian monarch or a Persian king when he sees a sunset or a smiling dawn. To be good, all he needs is to gaze upon the beautiful. It is by the light of these flames that he writes. His ideas fall into the mind like white pebbles in a shining sea. What sparks! What lightning! What veins of fire! And one feels dizzy, as if flying on the back of a winged lion. He himself feels this and emerges strong. One clasps the book to his breast as if it were a good kind friend, or caresses it tenderly as if it were the unstrained brow of a faithful wife.

He meditated upon the profound. He tried to penetrate the mystery of life and discover the laws of the universe. As a child he felt powerful, and set out in search of the Creator. He returned from his journey happy, claiming he had found Him. The rest of his life was spent in the exaltation that follows such a colloquy. He trembled like a leaf in these expansions of his spirit and this merging with the Universal Mind; and once back into himself, he was fresh and fragrant as a leaf. At birth he was confronted with all the obstacles that centuries of presumptuous men have laid beside the cradle of the newborn. Books are filled with subtle poisons that inflame the imagination and sicken the judgment. He drained all those cups but still walked by himself, barely affected by the poison. It is man's cross that to see well he must be wise, and then forget that he is wise. Possessing truth is nothing more than a struggle between the revelations imposed on men. Some succumb, mere voices of another spirit; others triumph, adding a new voice to that of

Nature. Emerson triumphed, and therein lies his philosophy. His finest book is called *Nature*;[12] in it he surrenders to those exquisite delights, tells about those wonderful strolls, turns with magnificent strength against those who ask for eyes to see, and then forget they have them. He sees man as master, the universe as kindly and submissive, and all that lives emerging from its womb and then returning to that womb; above every living thing he sees the living spirit that will hold man in its arms. He gives an account of himself and of what he has observed. He says nothing about what he has not felt. He would rather be considered inconsistent than fanciful. When he is no longer able to see, he confesses as much. He does not deny that others see, but maintains only what he has seen. If there are contradictions in what he saw, let another comment and point out the distinctions; he simply narrates. All he observes are analogies; he finds no contradictions in nature, looks upon everything in it as symbolic of man, and considers everything in man as also in Nature. He finds that Nature influences man, and that man makes Nature happy or sad, eloquent or mute, absent or present, according to his mood. He feels that the human idea is lord of universal matter, that physical beauty invigorates and prepares man's spirit for moral beauty, and that the desolate soul conceives of the universe as desolate. According to him, the spectacle of Nature inspires faith, love, and respect. For him the universe that refuses to respond to man in formulas responds by inspiring him with sentiments that calm his anxieties and permit him to live a strong, proud, and happy life. And he maintains that everything resembles everything else and has the same objective, that everything touches man, who beautifies it with his mind, that all the currents of Nature pass through every creature, that each man holds the Creator within him and everything created has something of the Creator within itself; that everything will eventually come full circle in the bosom of the Creative Spirit; that there is a central unity in all

12. *Nature*, Emerson's first book, published in 1836, sounded a trumpet to his generation.

events, in thoughts as well as actions. He believes that the human soul, in its wanderings through Nature, finds itself within all of it; that the beauty of the universe was created to inspire desire and ease the pain of virtue, and to encourage man to seek and find himself; that man "carries within him the soul of all things, the soul of the silent sage, the universal beauty to which every part and particle are equally related: the Eternal One."[13] Life does not trouble him; he is content in the knowledge that he labors well, that the important thing is to be virtuous. "Virtue is the golden key that opens the gates of Eternity." Life is more than merely buying and selling and government; it is communion with the forces of Nature and the self-government that these forces bestow. Universal order inspires individual order; joy is certain and is the supreme influence. Therefore, whatever is true about all mystery, it is rational to do anything that will give one real happiness, which is virtue, the best happiness that exists. Life is only a "waystation in Nature." And this is how the eyes of the reader run over these calm and glowing pages that seem to have been written on a mountain-top, by superhuman dispensation and by some divine light. Stimulated with the desire to see these seductive marvels and to roam through the palace of all these truths, this is how one fixes one's eyes upon those captivating pages that shine like mirrors of steel, reflecting glorious images on eyes already smarting from so much light. Oh, how good it is to read when one feels the flame strike the brain; it is like impaling a live eagle! If only the hand were a bolt of lightning and could annihilate the skull without committing a crime!

And death? Emerson is not troubled by the idea of death, for it neither troubles nor frightens anyone who has lived nobly; it is feared only by those who have cause to be afraid. The deserving will attain immortality: dying is simply returning the finite to the infinite. Emerson is not in favor of rebelling; life is a

13. Martí is referring to Emerson's essay, "The Over-Soul." (*The Complete Writings of Ralph Waldo Emerson*, vol. I [New York, 1929], p. 206.) The essay also reflects Swedenborg's influence on Emerson.

fact, and therefore has reason to be; it is a plaything only for imbeciles, but for real men it is a temple. It is better to live and move forward by honestly exercising one's thinking, feeling spirit than by rebelling.[14]

And the sciences? They confirm what the spirit possesses: analogy between all the forces of Nature; similarity between all living beings; a certain equality of composition in all the elements of the universe; the sovereignty of man who knows inferiors but no superiors. Spirit foresees, and belief corroborates. Since spirit is submerged in the abstract, it can see the whole; whereas science, inspecting the concrete facts with the meticulousness of an insect, can see only the details. The fact that the universe may have been formed by a slow, methodical, and analogous process neither proclaims the purposes of Nature nor contradicts the existence of spiritual truths. When the sciences have run their course and known all there is to know, they will probably know no more than the spirit knows today, and their knowledge will be equal. It is true that the hand of a saurian resembles the hand of a man, but it is also true that a man's spirit reaches the grave young and his body old. A man's spirit in its oneness with the universal spirit feels such intense and enthralling pleasures, and in its wake so fresh and powerful a strength, so majestic a serenity, and such a lively need to love and forgive, that this is as truly the law of life for those who accept it as the similarity between the saurian hand and the human hand, even if this truth may elude those who do not accept it.

And the object of life? It is the satisfaction of the yearning for perfect beauty; as virtue beautifies the places it influences, so beautiful places influence virtue. All the elements of Nature have a moral character, for since all of them stimulate this character in man, and all produce it, all must have it. Therefore

14. Martí is paraphrasing Emerson's sentence: "First innuendoes, then broad hints, then smart taps are given, suggesting that nothing stands still in Nature but death; that creation is on wheels, in transit, always passing into something else, streaming into something higher. . . ." (Ibid., vol. II, p. 727.)

truth is one. It is beauty in wisdom; kindness, which is beauty in affections; and pure beauty, which is beauty in art. Art is only a man-created Nature, and it never strays from this interrelationship. Nature kneels at man's feet, showing him her many facets so that he may perfect his wisdom; her wonders, to encourage his desire to imitate them; her demands, to educate his spirit in his labors, his disappointments, and his virtue that overcome them. Nature gives man her purposes, and these are reflected in the mind that governs his speech where each purpose will become a voice. The stars are messengers of beauty and of the eternally sublime. Forests are eternal youth, and return man to faith and reason. The forest fills him with joy like a good deed. Nature inspires, heals, consoles, strengthens, and prepares a man for integrity. And he does not feel complete, is not revealed to himself, cannot see the invisible unless he is on intimate terms with Nature. The universe strikes a man in numerous ways, in the manner of spokes meeting at the hub of the wheel, and the many acts of man's desires cast their influence on the universe like spokes radiating from the wheel's axis. The universe, although multiple, is one; its music can imitate the motions and colors of a snake. The locomotive is the elephant of man's creation, huge and powerful as an elephant. Only the degree of heat makes the water running through the river bed different from the stones the river bathes. And in all this complex and many-sided universe, as if a symbol of the human being, everything happens as it happens in man. Smoke rises in the air like a thought in infinity. Ocean waves surge and swell like affections in the soul. The mimosa is as fragile as a sensitive woman. Every quality of man is represented in some animal of Nature. Trees talk to us in a language we can understand. The night whispers something in our ear, for the heart that went to it tormented by doubt awakens filled with peace. The appearance of truth suddenly illumines the soul, as the sun illumines Nature. Morning makes birds sing and men talk. Virtue, toward which everything in Nature conspires, leaves man at peace, as though he had finished his work, or as a curve that has become a circle and having done so need go no further. The universe is a servant and the human being a king. The universe was created to teach, nourish, delight, and educate man. Confronted with a transient and changeable Nature, man senses a certain stability in himself. He feels both eternally young and immemorially old. He recognizes that what he knows well he did not learn here, and this reveals to him a former life in which he acquired the knowledge he brought to this one. So he turns his eyes to a Father he cannot see, but of whose presence he is certain, and whose kiss, which fills all space and comes to him in the aromatic breezes of the night, leaves upon his brow a flame whose soft pale light confusedly reveals to him the inner universe which is a miniature reflection of the outer one, and the outer one which is the inner universe magnified, the beautiful but fearful universe of death. Is God beyond the earth, or is He the earth itself? Is God above Nature? Is creative Nature, and the immense spiritual being to whose breast the human soul aspires, nonexistent? Did the world in which we live come into being of its own accord? And will it move forever as it moves today, or will it evaporate, and will we, rocked in its mists, come to rest in a delightful, noble, and harmonious merging with a being of whom Nature is only an illusion? These are the thoughts that occupy the powerful mind of this giant of a man whose peering eyes search in the gloom for the divine mind, and find it provident, invisible, uniform, and throbbing in light, in earth, in the seas, and in himself. He feels that he knows what he cannot say, and that man will go eternally through life touching yet never feeling the wings of the golden eagle that is finally to bear him away. This man has stood erect before the universe and has not vanished. He has dared to analyze the synthesis and has not lost his way.

He has held out his arms to enfold in them the secret of life. From out of his body, the fragile container of his winged spirit, he has ascended through painful labors and mortal anxieties to those pristine heights from which the traveler's devotion is rewarded by visions of the starlight-embroidered robes of infinite beings. His body has felt that mysterious overflowing of soul which is a solemn adventure that fills the lips with kisses, the hands with caresses, and the eyes with tears, like the sudden swelling and overflowing of Nature in the spring. And then he would feel that calm that comes from conversations with the divine, and that magnificent kingly courage that the awareness of power gives a man. For who that is master of himself does not laugh at a king?

Dazzled at times by those resplendent books of the Hindus, in which the human creature, after having been purified by virtue, flies like a brilliantly colored butterfly out of his earthly scoria to Brahma's bosom, he settles down to do what he criticized, and to look at Nature through the eyes of others because he has found those eyes to be like his own. And then he sees darkly and tarnishes the luster of his own visions. The fact remains that Indian philosophy intoxicates like a grove of orange blossoms, and makes one want to fly as if seeing a bird take wing. When a man delves into this philosophy, he feels gently annihilated, as if consumed by blue flames as he soars upward. And then he wonders if Nature is not some kind of phantasmagoria, and man the one who imagines, and the entire universe merely a concept, and God the pure idea, and the human being the aspiring idea that will at last come to rest in the bosom of God like a pearl in its shell or an arrow in a tree trunk. And he begins to build a scaffold for constructing the universe. But he immediately destroys the scaffolding, ashamed of the ruinous state of his edifice and the poverty of his mind, for when dedicated to building worlds, his mind seems like an ant dragging a mountain range.

And then once again he senses those vague and mystical effluvia flowing through his veins; perceives how they calm the torments of his soul in the friendly silence of the forest that is peopled with promises; observes that when the mind runs aground like a ship on a reef, foreboding springs up like a caged bird, sure of the sky, that escapes from the shattered mind. In language as inflexible, brutal, and unyielding as stone, he translates these luminous transports, chaste raptures, soothing delights, and joys of the tremulous spirit which captive Nature, amazed at the courageous lover, admits to her embraces. And he announces to every man that, since the universe is revealed to him fully and directly, to every other man as well is revealed the right to see it for himself, and with his own lips satisfy the burning thirst it inspires. And because in these discourses Emerson has learned that pure thought and pure affection produce joys so intense that the soul feels a sweet death in them, followed by a radiant resurrection, he announces to men that only through purity can one attain happiness.

After this discovery, and being certain that the stars are man's crown and that when his fevered brow has cooled, his serene spirit will cleave the air, enveloped in light, he laid his loving hand upon tormented humans, and turned his lively, penetrating eyes upon the harsh and stupid struggles of the world. His glances cleared away the rubbish. He sat familiarly at the tables of heroes. With Homeric language he related the crucial moments in the life of nations. He had the candor of giants. He let his intuition guide him, thus opening to him the refuge of the clouds as well as of the grave. Having sat in the senate of the stars and returned strong, he now sits in the senate of the people as if in the house of his own brothers. He recounts history both old and new, and analyzes nations as a geologist would analyze fossils. His phrases resemble the vertebrae of mastodons, gold-encrusted statues, Greek porticos. Of other men it can be said: "They are brothers"; of Emerson it must be said: "He is a father." He wrote a marvellous book, a summary of human experience, in which he sanctified the world's great men, studying each type. He went to see old England, land of his Puritan forebears, and as a result of that visit he wrote another book, a most powerful book called *English Traits*.[15] He arranged the facts of existence into categories, and made a study of them in his magical *Essays*,[16] giving them laws. All his laws of life revolve around the axis of this truth: "The whole of Nature trembles before the consciousness of a child."[17] He breaks up

15. Published in 1853.

16. Published in two series, the first in 1841, the second in 1844.

17. Martí's translation in Spanish reads: "toda la Naturaleza tiembla ante conciencia de un niño." He is quoting from the poem "Wealth" (*Complete Writings*, vol. II, p. 915) in which Emerson writes:

culture, destiny, power, riches, illusions, and greatness into their component parts, and analyzes them with the skill of a chemist. He allows the beautiful to stand, and demolishes the false. He has no respect for custom. The base is base no matter how much it is esteemed. Man must begin to be angelic. Tenderness, resignation, and wisdom are law. These essays are codes of law. They are overflowing with sap. They have the grandiose monotony of a mountain range. Emerson enhances them with tireless fantasy and singular good sense. He finds no contradiction between the great and the small, or between the ideal and the practical, and he claims that the laws which finally prove their worth, and give a man the right to wear a crown of stars, are the ones to bring happiness on earth. There are no contradictions in Nature, only in man's inability to discover her analogies. He does not deprecate science for being false, but for being slow. Open his books and you will find them spilling over with scientific truths. Tyndall[18] gives Emerson credit for all the science he knows. The entire doctrine of evolution is contained in a handful of Emerson's phrases. But he does not feel that understanding alone is enough to penetrate life's mystery, give man peace, and put him in possession of his means of growth; he believes that intuition finishes what understanding begins, that the eternal spirit divines what human science barely touches. Science sniffs about, like a dog, whereas the eternal spirit leaps over the chasm in which the naturalist stands amused. Emerson was constantly observing, making, like a powerful condor, notes on everything he saw, arranging in his notebooks the facts that were similar, and commenting when he had something to reveal. He had certain of the qualities of a Calderón,[19] a Plato,

---

". . . Which binds the strengths of nature wild / To the conscience of a child."

18. John Tyndall (1820–1893), British physicist, born in Ireland, best known for his researches on radiant heat to which has been given the name Tyndall effect or Tyndall phenomenon.

19. Pedro de la Barca Calderón (1600–1681), Spanish poet and playwright.

and a Pindar.[20] Also of a Benjamin Franklin.[21] He was not like the leafy bamboo whose heavy foliage, poorly supported by a hollow trunk, touches the ground; he was like a baobab or juniper or great genisaro whose many fully leafed branches rise from a sturdy trunk. Scornful of walking the earth, and disliked by judicious men, idealism nevertheless did walk the earth. Emerson has humanized it; he did not wait for science. The bird needs no stilts to reach the heights, and the eagle needs no rails. He outdistances science the way the impatient commanding officer mounts his flying horse to leave behind the plodding soldier loaded down with heavy battle gear. Emerson does not think of idealism in terms of a vague desire for death, but as a conviction of a future life to be earned by a serene practice of virtue in this one. And life is as beautiful and ideal as death. Do you wish to follow his trend of thought? It is like this: he maintains that man does not devote his entire potential to the study of Nature, merely his understanding, which is not the most important part; therefore he does not investigate that study thoroughly. He says: "The axis of man's vision does not coincide with the axis of Nature."[22] He seeks to explain how all moral and physical truths are contained within each other, and how each one contains all the rest, and he says: "They are like the circle on a sphere that contains an infinitude of circles, and they may be added and taken away freely, with none being superimposed upon another."[23] Would you like to hear how he

20. Pindar (522–433 B.C.), Greek lyric poet who developed the Pindaric ode, consisting of triads formed by the strophe, antistrophe, and epode.

21. Martí was referring both to the fact that Benjamin Franklin (1706–1790) was a scientist and philosopher as well as a statesman, and a practical revolutionist who moved slowly and cautiously, a tendency Emerson displayed.

22. Martí is paraphrasing the original (*Complete Writings*, vol. I, p. 23), which reads: "The axis of vision is not coincident with the axis of things, and so they appear not transparent but opaque."

23. Martí is paraphrasing the original (ibid., p. 14), which states that every universal truth "is like a great circle, comprising all possible

talks? This is how: "For the man who suffers, even the warmth of his own fireplace has an element of sadness in it."[24] "We are not made like ships to roll and pitch, but like a house to stand firm."[25] "Cut these words and they will bleed."[26] "To be great is to be misunderstood."[27] "Leonidas wasted an entire day in dying."[28] "Events in natural history, when taken out of context, are as barren as a single sex."[29] "That man is tramping in the mire of dialectics."[30]

His poetry is made out of colossal irregular blocks of stone, like Florentine palaces. It ebbs and flows and crashes like ocean waves. But sometimes it is like a basket of flowers in the hand of a little naked child. It is a poetry of patriarchs, primitive men, and cyclops. Some of his poems resemble groves of oak in bloom. His poetry is the only polemic verse to sanctify the great struggle on this earth. Some of his poems are like rivulets of precious stones, wisps of clouds, or bolts of lightning. Are you still wondering what his poems are like? Sometimes they are like an old man with a curly beard, wavy hair, and flaming eyes who sings as he leans on an oaken staff before a white stone cave; at other times like a gigantic angel with golden wings who plunges from the high green mountain into the gorge below. Marvellous old man, I lay at your feet my sheaf of newly gathered palms and my silver sword!

La Opinión Nacional (Caracas), May 19, 1882

---

circles; which, however, may be drawn and comprise it in like manner."

24. Ibid., p. 3.

25. Ibid., p. 15.

26. See the essay "Montaigne; or the Skeptic," ibid., p. 377.

27. See the essay "Self-Reliance," ibid., p. 142.

28. The original reads: "Leonidas and his three hundred martyrs consume one day in dying."

29. See *Complete Writings*, vol. I, p. 8.

30. Martí is paraphrasing Emerson's expression "the insanity of dialectics," used in his essay on "Race," ibid., p. 434.

Walt Whitman, the Poet

"He seemed like a god last night, sitting in a red velvet armchair, with his shock of white hair, his beard covering his chest, his bushy eyebrows, his hand resting on the head of his cane." This is how today's newspaper describes Walt Whitman,[1] the venerable man of seventy to whom the knowledgeable critics, always in the minority, assign an extraordinary position in the literature of his country and his times. Not since the sacred books of antiquity has there been a doctrine comparable in its prophetic language and vigorous poetry to that of this old poet whose grandiose and priestly aphorisms spring forth like sunbursts from his astonishing and proscribed *Leaves of Grass*.

And why not, since it is a natural book? The universities and scholars have isolated men so they no longer know one another; instead of embracing, attracted by what is essential and eternal, they draw apart, flattering each other like gadabout

1. Walt Whitman (1819–1892), was one of the greatest literary figures in American history, and has often been identified with the American democratic tradition. Born of ordinary people on Long Island, he worked at carpentry, school teaching, and printing, and became an editor of several newspapers which followed the position of the Democratic Party. His *Leaves of Grass* (1855), broke with conventional verse and conventional ideas. His glorification of himself, his body, with intimate details, all men and things, and national destinies, brought praise from men like Emerson as well as scandal. Whitman's *Democratic Vistas* (1871) was a prose testimony of faith in democracy.

women, for purely accidental differences. As a pudding fits its mold, so men are molded by books or by the diligent teacher who exposes them to the current fad or fashion. The philosophical, religious, and literary schools confine men's thinking the way a lackey is confined to his livery. Men submit to the iron like horses and bulls, and then strut about the world displaying their brands. Therefore, when brought face to face with the naked, pure, amorous, honest, and potent man who walks, loves, fights, rows boats—the man who is not disturbed by misfortune but can read the promise of eventual happiness in the grace and balance of the world; when they find themselves in the presence of the vigorous and angelic progenitor Walt Whitman, they run away as if from their own consciences, and refuse to recognize in that vital and superior example of male humanity the true type of their own discolored, cassocked, and stunted species.

The newspaper went on to say that yesterday, when the other venerable patriarch Gladstone[2] had just instructed his opponents in Parliament on the justice of granting self-government to Ireland, he seemed like a powerful mastiff standing unchallenged above the crowd, and those at his feet a pack of terriers. This is how Whitman appears, with his "natural person,"[3] his "nature without check on its original energy," his "myriad youths, beautiful, gigantic,"[4] his belief that "the smallest sprout shows that there is really no death,"[5] with his impressive account of peoples and races in "Salute to the World,"[6] his logic in "knowing the perfect fitness and equanimity of things,[7] while they discuss

2. William Ewart Gladstone (1809–1898), British statesman, prime minister four times: 1868–74; 1880–85; 1886; 1892–94.

3. Walt Whitman, *Leaves of Grass*, vol. I (New York, 1948), p. 430. Poem "So Long!"

4. "So Long!": "Myriads of youths, beautiful, gigantic, sweet-blooded. . . ," Ibid., p. 430.

5. Ibid., "Song of Myself," poem 6, p. 67.

6. Title of poem. Ibid., p. 145.

7. Here Martí paraphrases Whitman's text which reads: "Knowing the perfect fitness and equanimity of things, while they discuss I

I am silent, and go and bathe and admire myself." This is the Whitman who "does not say these things for a dollar";[8] who says "I am satisfied—I see, dance, laugh, sing";[9] who has "no chair, no church, no philosophy."[10] So stands Walt Whitman when compared with those rachitic poets and philosophers; those picayune, one-sided philosophers; those standard, sugar-water, bookish poets: all literary or philosophical fashionplates.

Walt Whitman must be studied, for if he is not a poet in the best of taste, he is certainly the most outspoken, all-embracing, and uninhibited poet of his time. In his small frame house that is almost at the poverty level, there is a black-bordered portrait of Victor Hugo[11] standing in a conspicuous place near the window. Emerson,[12] whose writings tend to purify and uplift, threw an arm about his shoulders and called him his friend; Tennyson,[13] one of those who looks into the origins of things, sits in his oaken chair in England and sends tenderly affectionate greetings to the "grand old man." Robert Buchanan,[14] the spirited Englishman, scolds the North Americans roundly: "What do you people know about literature," he cries, "when you let that colossus of a Walt Whitman grow old without giving him the high honor he deserves?"

The truth is that his poetry, although at first it may cause some astonishment, leaves a delightful sensation of recuperation in the soul tormented by universal disparagement. He

---

am silent, and go bathe and admire myself." Ibid., "Song of Myself," poem 3, p. 64.

8. "I do not say those things for a dollar or to fill up the time while I wait for a boat." Ibid., "Song of Myself," poem 47, p. 110.

9. "I am satisfied—I see, dance, laugh, sing." Ibid., "Song of Myself," poem 3, p. 64.

10. Ibid., "Song of Myself," poem 46, p. 108.

11. *See* pp. 239, 257, 285.

12. *See* pp. 149–67.

13. (Lord) Alfred Tennyson (1809–1892), English poet laureate.

14. Robert Williams Buchanan (1841–1901), English poet, novelist, and playwright.

makes his own rules of grammar and logic. He reads in "the eye of an ox and the sap of a leaf." "The one who cleans the filth from your house, he is my brother!" His apparent irregularity, disconcerting in the beginning, is later seen to possess that sublime order and composition with which mountain ranges stand out on the horizon.

Whitman does not live in New York, his "beloved Manhattan,"[15] his "superb-faced . . . million-footed Manhattan" where he appears when he wants to intone "the song of what I behold, *Libertad*."[16] Since his books and lectures earn him barely enough money for bread, some "loving friends"[17] see to his needs in a cottage tucked away in a pleasant country lane from which he rides out in an ancient carriage drawn by his beloved horses, to watch the "athletic young men" busy with their masculine diversions, to see the *camerados*[18] who are not afraid of rubbing elbows with this iconoclast who wants to establish "the institutions of the dear love of comrades," to see the fields they cultivate, the friends who pass by arm in arm and singing, the pairs of lovers, gay and vivacious as quail. This he relates in his *Calamus*,[19] the extremely strange book in which he sings of the love of friends: "City of orgies. . . . Not the pageants of you,

15. "Crossing Brooklyn Ferry," Whitman, *Leaves*, op. cit. p. 169.

16. "But I will sing you a song of what I behold, Libertad." Ibid., p. 234. *Libertad* is Spanish for freedom. Whitman made considerable use of Spanish words.

17. Whitman frequently used this expression as: "My lovers, my dear friends," Ibid., "On the Terrible Doubt of Appearances" p. 137; "his dear friends, his lovers," Ibid., "Recorders Age Hence" p. 138; "the undiminished faith—the group of loving friends," Ibid., "A Carol Closing Sixty-nine," p. 433.

18. Whitman frequently used the expressions "young men" and "camerados." The latter is apparently a corruption of the Spanish *camaradas*, equivalent to the English *comrades*.

19. A series of fifty poems. Whitman, *Leaves*, op. cit., pp. 131–221. *Calamus* is the name given to sweet flag, a plant growing in moist places and having bladelike leaves, minute greenish flowers, and aromatic roots, which grows in the northern and middle States.

not the shifting tableaus, your spectacles, repay me . . . Nor the processions in the streets, nor the bright windows with goods in them, Nor the converse with learned persons. . . . Not those, but as I pass O Manhattan, your frequent and swift flash of eyes offering me love. . . . Lovers, continual lovers, only repay me."[20] Whitman is like the old men he lists at the end of his proscribed *Leaves of Grass:* "I announce myriads of youths, beautiful, gigantic, sweet-blooded; I announce a race of splendid and savage old men."[21]

He lives in the country where natural man, together with his placid horses, tills the open land under the burning sun; but not far from the amiable and ardent city with its hubbub of life, its varied occupations, its numberless stories, the dust from its wagon wheels, the smoke from its belching factories, the sun that looks down over it all, "the loud laugh of work people at their meals,"[22] "exclamations of women taken suddenly who hurry home and give birth to babes,"[23] "the flap of the curtained litter, a sick man borne inside to the hospital."[24] But yesterday Whitman came from the country to recite before a gathering of loyal friends his oration on that other natural man, that great and gentle soul, "that great star early droop'd in the western sky," that Abraham Lincoln.[25] The cultured New York audience listened attentively and in religious silence to that brilliant speech which sounded at times like the whispering of heavenly bodies, with its sudden trills, vibrant tones, hymnlike flight, and magnificent informality. Those who have been raised on

20. Part of the poem *City of Orgies (Calamus)*, Ibid., p. 141.

21. Ibid., "Songs of Parting," p. 430.

22. Ibid., "Song of Myself," poem 26, p. 85.

23. Ibid., "Song of Myself," poem 8, p. 68.

24. Ibid., "Song of Myself," poem 8, p. 69. During the Civil War Whitman served as a male nurse.

25. Abraham Lincoln seemed to Whitman an answer to his call for a thorough democrat, and he mourned deeply for him. This is from the poem *When Lilacs Last in the Dooryard Bloom'd*, one of the world's great poems, of the series "Memories of President Lincoln" in ibid., *Leaves of Grass*, p. 298.

the milk of the classics, academic or French, may not be able to understand that heroic benevolence. The free and decent life on a new continent has given rise to a hale and hearty philosophy which is spreading over the world in brawny lyric poetry. A calm and soothing poetry of faith and totality is well suited to the largest body of free and industrious men the world has ever known. It rises, like the sun from the sea, inflaming the clouds, touching the crests of waves with fire, awakening the blossoms and nests that drowse in the dense forests along the shore. Pollen drifts on the air, birds exchange kisses, boughs of trees prepare to sprout, leaves look for the sun, and all things breathe out their music; in the language of this hard light, Whitman spoke about Lincoln.

Perhaps one of the most beautiful pieces of contemporary poetry is the mystical threnody Whitman wrote on the death of Lincoln. All of Nature accompanied his mournful coffin to the grave. The stars foretold the event and the clouds became dark with foreboding a month before. In the marsh a gray bird sang a song of desolation. The poet wanders through the saddened fields as if flanked by two friends; the thought of death, and its security. With musical art he groups and conceals and reproduces these tragic elements in a total harmony of twilight. When the poem ends, the entire earth seems to be dressed in black, covered from sea to sea by the deceased. We see the clouds, the heavy moon announcing the catastrophe, the widespread wings of the gray bird. This poem far exceeds Poe's "The Raven" in beauty, strangeness, and profundity. The poet places a bough of lilac on the coffin.

That is his poem.

No longer do willows weep over graves. Death is "the harvest," "the opener and usher to the heavenly mansion," "the great revealer," that which is in process of being, was, and will be again; apparent griefs and contradictions merge in an arduous and celestial spring; a bone becomes a flower. Near to us is the sound of suns moving noisily but majestically through space in search of their final destination. Life is a hymn, and death a hidden form of life. Sweat is holy, and holy the amoeba. Men should kiss each other on the cheek when passing. Embrace in ineffable affection, you living people, and love the grass, the animals, the air, the sea, and pain and death. For souls possessed by love, the suffering is less; life holds no sorrows for us if we understand its meaning in time; honey, kisses, and light spring from the same seed. In the star-strewn black firmament of night, an enormous lilac tree rises peacefully with the softest music above the sleeping worlds stretched out at its feet like hounds!

Every condition of society brings its own expression to literature in such a way that the various phases of literature give a more faithful account of a nation's history than do the chronicles of its historians. There can be no contradictions in Nature; the human hope of finding a perfect type of grace and beauty in love while we are alive, and in the unknown after death, shows that in the totality of life there must be a joyful adjustment among the elements which in our present lifespan seem hostile and irreconcilable. Literature that announces and spreads the ultimate happy agreement between apparent contradictions; literature that, as spontaneous advice and instructions from Nature, heralds identity with a higher peace than the peace derived from the rival dogmas and passions that divide and bloody nations in their primitive states; letters that inculcate in timid souls a conviction of ultimate beauty and justice so deep-seated that the poverty and ugliness of life cannot dishearten or embitter them—this kind of literature will not only reveal a social state that is closer to perfection than any heretofore known, but will happily join the benevolence and reason that these letters will provide to humanity (so eager for wonders and poetry) to a religion it has confusedly been awaiting ever since it recognized the emptiness and inadequacy of its ancient creeds.

Who is the ignoramus who maintains that people can dispense with poetry? Some persons are so shortsighted that they see nothing in fruit but the rind. Whether it unites or divides the soul, strengthens or causes it anguish, props it up or casts it down, whether or not it inspires a man with faith and hope, poetry is more necessary to a people than industry itself, for while industry gives men the means of subsistence, poetry gives them the desire and courage for living. What will become of men who have lost the habit of thinking with faith about the meaning and scope of their actions? The best of them, the ones whom Nature anoints with a sacred desire for the future, will lose, in a painful and unheeded annihilation, all incentive to bear the brunt of life's sordid aspects; and the masses, the common people, the materially minded, the average man, will unrighteously beget a race of empty-headed children, will raise to the level of essentials the faculties intended to be nothing more than instruments, and will perplex the incurable torments of the soul, which delight only in the beautiful and grand, with the bustle of an ever incomplete prosperity.

Aside from other reasons, freedom should be blessed because its enjoyment inspires modern man—deprived from birth of the calm, the stimulus, and the poetry of existence—with that supreme peace and religious well-being that an ordered state of the world bestows upon those who live in it with the courage and serenity of their will. Set your eyes above the mountains, you poets who water the deserted altars with childish tears.

You thought religion lost because you saw it changing form beyond your understanding. Stand up, for you are the priests. The ultimate religion is freedom, and the new cult is the poetry of freedom. It calms and beautifies the present, deduces and illumines the future, and explains the ineffable objectives and seductive goodness of the universe.

Listen to what this hardworking and satisfied people are singing; listen to Walt Whitman. He raises self-assertiveness to majesty, tolerance to justice, and order to happiness. Anyone who lives according to a creed of autocracy lives like an oyster in its shell, for he sees nothing but the prison enclosing him, and in his blindness thinks it is the world. Freedom gives wings to the oyster. And what appears to be an ominous struggle inside the oyster shell turns out in the light of day to be the natural flow of sap in the throbbing pulse of the world.

For Walt Whitman the world has always been as it is today. Should we wish to prove that a thing exists, it is enough to know that it ought to have existed, and when it no longer exists it will cease to be. What no longer has being and cannot be seen is proved by what does have being and can be seen, for all is in all and one thing explains another. When what now exists has ceased to be, it will be proven in turn by what will exist at that time. Infinitesimal things collaborate for the infinite, and everything is in its place: the turtle, the ox, the bird: "winged purposes."[26] It is as fortunate to die as to be born, because the dead are alive: "Nobody can say how calm I am about God and death!"[27] He laughs at what is called disillusionment and knows the fullness of time, accepting it absolutely. Everything is contained in his person; all of him is in everything; another's degradation is his own; he is the tide, its ebb and flow. How can he fail to take pride in himself if he feels he is a living and intelligent part of Nature? What does he care if he returns to the womb that gave him birth, and with the love of the humid earth becomes a useful vegetable or a beautiful flower? After having loved men, he will nourish them. His duty is to create; even an atom is essentially divine if it creates; the act of creation is exquisite and sacred. Convinced of the identity of the universe, he sings the "Song of Myself," weaving the song out of everything—beliefs that struggle and pass away, the man who procreates and labors, the animals that help him; ah, the animals, of which he says: "Not one kneels to another . . . not one is respectable or unhappy . . . they do not sweat or whine about their conditions."[28] He considers himself heir to the world.

Nothing is strange to him, and he takes everything into account: the slow-paced snail, the ox looking at him with its inscrutable eyes, the priest who defends a part of the truth as if it were all of it. Man must open his arms and clasp all things to his breast, crime as well as virtue, filthiness as well as cleanliness, ignorance as well as wisdom. He should blend everything

26. Ibid., "Song of Myself," poem 3, p. 72.
27. Ibid., "Song of Myself," poem 48, p. 111.
28. Ibid., "Song of Myself," poem 32, p. 89.

in the crucible of his heart, and he should be especially determined to let his white beard grow long. No doubt of that: "We have had ducking and deprecating about enough."[29] He scolds the skeptics, the sophists, and the talkers. Breed children instead of grumbling, and add to the world! Believe with the devotion of a pious woman kissing the altar steps!

He is a member of every caste, creed, and profession, and finds poetry and justice in all of them. He appraises religions dispassionately, but believes the perfect religion to be in Nature, the abode of religion and life. When a man is sick he tells the priest and doctor to "go home"; "I seize the descending man and raise him with resistless will . . . I dilate you with tremendous breath, I buoy you up, every room in the house do I fill with an armed force, Lovers of me, bafflers of graves."[30] The Creator is the "Lover divine and the perfect Comrade"[31]; men are "comrades," and the more they believe and love, the greater their worth, although everything that occupies time and space is worth as much as every other thing. Let each man see the world for himself, for he, Walt Whitman, has felt the world in him since its creation, and knows, from what the sun and the open air have taught him, that a dawn is more revealing than the greatest book. He thinks about the heavenly bodies, he desires women, he feels possessed of a universal and frenetic love. He hears a concert rising from the scenes of the creation and the work of man, music flooding him with happiness, and when he goes to the river at the hour of the day when the shops close and the setting sun sets fire to the water, he feels that he has an appointment with the Creator, recognizes that man is fundamentally good, and sees his own head reflected in the water, emitting rays of sunlight.

But who can give an idea of his vast and fiercely burning love?

29. Ibid., "Song of Myself," poem 21, p. 79.

30. Ibid., "Song of Myself," poem 40, p. 101.

31. This is a paraphrase of the words used in Whitman's poem, "Gods," in ibid., "By the Roadside," p. 225.

This man loves the world with the fire of Sappho.[32] His world is a gigantic bed, and the bed an altar. He gives nobility to the words and ideas that men have prostituted with their secrecy and false modesty; he sings and sanctifies what Egypt sanctified. One source of his originality is the herculean strength with which he flings ideas to the ground as if to violate them, when all he wants to do is kiss them with a saintly passion. Another force is the earthy, brutal, and fleshy way he expresses his most delicate ideals. Only those incapable of understanding its greatness have considered that language lewd;[33] with the affected innocence of impudent schoolboys, fools imagine that they have seen a return to those low desires of Virgil[34] for Cebetes, and of Horace[35] for Giges and Licisco, when Whitman uses the most ardent images of human language to celebrate love between friends in his *Calamus*. And when he sings the divine sin in "Children of Adam,"[36] in scenes which make the most powerful images in *The Song of Songs* seem pale, he trembles, shrivels, swells, and overflows, goes mad with pride and satisfied virility, recalls the god of the Amazons[37] who rode through forests and across rivers sowing the seeds of life throughout the land, "singing the song of procreation."[38] "I sing the body electric,"[39] he writes in "Children of Adam"; and to find some appropriate resemblance to the Satanically forceful enumera-

32. The famous Greek woman poet, *c.* 600 B.C., whose poems exalted love of women for each other and made her the symbol of lesbianism.

33. As *Leaves of Grass* grew in size it also grew in notoriety and it was banned in a number of communities for its alleged lewdness.

34. Virgil (70–19 B.C.), greatest of the Roman poets.

35. Horace (65–8 B.C.), Roman poet.

36. A series of poems which are a part of Whitman, *Leaves of Grass*, pp. 114–31.

37. In Greek mythology, a race of women warriors with whom, according to the legend, the Greeks had frequent battles.

38. Whitman, *Leaves of Grass*, "Song of Myself," p. 102.

39. Ibid., "Children of Adam," poem 1, p. 116. One of the most famous of Whitman's lines.

tion in which he describes, like a hungry hero licking his bloodthirsty lips, the various parts of the female body, it would be well to have read the patriarchal genealogies of Genesis in Hebrew, and to have followed the naked cannibal bands of primitive men through the virgin jungle. And you say this man is brutal? Listen to his composition "Beautiful Women," which like many of his poems has only two lines: "Women sit or move to and fro, some old, some young[40] / The young are beautiful—but the old are more beautiful than the young." And this one, "Mother and Babe": "I see the sleeping mother and babe—hush'd, I study them long and long."[41] He predicts that just as virility and tenderness are combined to a high degree in men of superior intelligence, so the two energies which have had to be divided to carry on the work of creation will come together again in that delightful peace where life will find its rest with a joy and solemnity worthy of the universe.

When Whitman walks in the grass, he says the grass caresses him and he feels "all his joints moving."[42] The most restless novice could never find such burning words to describe the joy of his body, which he considers part of his soul, when he feels the ocean's embrace. All living things love him; the earth, the night, the ocean, love him: "You see . . . Dash me with amorous wet."[43] He savors the air. He offers himself to the atmosphere like a trembling lover. He wants doors without locks, and bodies in their natural beauty. He is "Walt Whitman, a kosmos, of Manhattan the son, / Turbulent, fleshy, sensual, eating, drinking and breeding, . . . no stander above men and women or apart from them."[44] He pictures truth as a frantic lover invading his body and stripping him of his clothes in its eager-

40. Ibid., "By the Roadside," p. 259.

41. Ibid.

42. "My joints the limberest joints on earth and the sternest joints on earth," ibid., "Song of Myself," poem 16, p. 76.

43. Ibid., "Song of Myself," poem 22, p. 80.

44. Ibid., "Song of Myself," poem 24, p. 82. The words omitted are "No sentimentalist. . . ."

ness to possess him. But in the clear midnight, his soul free of books and occupations, he emerges whole, silent, thinking about the day well spent, and meditating upon the things he likes best—night, dreams, and death; on the song of the universal, for the benefit of the common man; on the sweetness to "die advancing on,"[45] falling at the foot of the primeval tree with ax in hand, bitten by the last snake in the forest.

Imagine what strange new effect is produced when that language infused with proud carnality celebrates the great love that will bring men together. In one of the *Calamus* poems he names the most intense pleasures he owes to Nature and country; but only the waves of a moonlit sea are worthy of singing his happiness when a friend he loves lies asleep beside him. He loves the meek, the wounded, the downtrodden, even the wicked. He feels no scorn for the great, for he considers great only the useful. He throws his arms around the shoulders of truck drivers, sailors, and farmers. He hunts and fishes with them, and at harvest time he climbs onto the back of the loaded wagon with them. The powerful Negro standing behind his percherons and guiding his wagon calmly through the commotion of Broadway seems more beautiful to him than an emperor riding in triumph. He understands all the virtues, receives all the rewards, works in all the occupations, suffers all the pains, and senses a heroic pleasure when he pauses at the threshold of a smithy and sees the young men, bare to the waist, swinging the hammers above their heads, each in turn letting his fall. He is the slave, the prisoner, the fighter, the fallen, and the beggar. When a slave comes to his door hounded and sweaty, he fills the bathtub for him and offers him a chair at his table. In the corner is his loaded gun ready to defend him, and if they should come to attack him, he would kill the pursuers and sit down again at table as if all he had done was to kill a snake!

Walt Whitman, then, is content. What vanity can grieve him if he knows that eventually a man becomes grass or a flower?

45. "Oh, to die advancing on!" Ibid., "Birds of Paradise," poem "Pioneers! O Pioneers!" p. 225.

Where is the vanity in a carnation, a sprig of sage, or honeysuckle? How can he look calmly at human sorrows unless he knows that above them is an everlasting existence for him who awaits a joyous immersion in Nature? What can hurry him if he believes that all is where it should be, and that the will of one man cannot change the course of the world? He suffers, yes, but looks at that lesser and exhausted self suffering within him, and perceives another self that is above weariness and misery and cannot suffer because it recognizes universal greatness. It is enough for him to be as he is, and he follows the course of his life with serenity and contentment, whether that course has been silent or praiseworthy. With a single stroke he casts aside romantic tears as a useless excrescence: "Not asking the sky to come down to my good will."[46] What nobility in the phrase in which he says he loves animals because "they do not whine about their condition."[47] The truth is that the world is already overflowing with prophets of doom; one must face the world as it is in order not to make mountains out of molehills; give men strength instead of tearfully robbing them of what little is left to them by grief. Do the injured go about the streets displaying their wounds? Not even the doubts raised by science disturb him. He tells the scientists: "Gentlemen, to you the first honors always! Your facts are useful, and yet they are not my dwelling, I but enter by them to an area of my dwelling."[48] "How beggarly appear arguments before a defiant deed!"[49] "Lo! keen-eyed towering science. . . . Yet again, lo! the soul above all science."[50] But it is that phrase, not entirely devoid of the melancholy of the defeated, with which he uproots all reason for envy, where his philosophy completely overcomes hatred, as the Magi command. "Why should I be jealous of my brother who does what I cannot do?" he asks. "He that by me spreads a

46. Ibid., "Song of Myself," poem 14, p. 73.
47. Ibid., "Song of Myself," poem 32, p. 89.
48. Ibid., "Song of Myself," poem 23, p. 82.
49. Ibid., "Song of Myself," poem 6, p. 191.
50. Ibid., "Birds of Paradise," "Song of the Universal," p. 221.

wider breast than my own, proves the width of my own." "Let the sun interpenetrate the Earth until it all be sweet and pure light, like my blood! Let the rejoicing be universal. I sing the eternity of existence, the happiness of our life and the beauty beyond change of the Universe. My signs are the calfskin shoe, the open collar and a staff cut from the woods."[51]

All this he tells in apocalyptic language. Rhymes or inflection? Oh no, in all that apparent chaos of convulsive and superimposed phrases, his rhythm lies in the wise distribution of his ideas into great musical patterns, the natural poetic form for a nation that does not build stone upon stone, but builds with enormous boulders.

Walt Whitman's language is completely different from any heretofore used by poets, and its strangeness and power are well suited to his cyclical poetry and to this new humanity brought together on a productive continent of such promise that they cannot really fit into fastidious or lyrical quatrains. It is no longer a matter of hidden affairs, unfaithful ladies, cowardly discretion, or the sterile complaints of those who lack the necessary energy to cope with life. These are not the times for jingles or bedroom frustrations; an era is emerging, a definitive religion is dawning, and man is being born again. It is a matter of a new faith that must replace the one that has died, and it is coming into being shining with the courageous peace of redeemed mankind. It is a matter of writing the sacred books of a people who, in falling away from old-world ideas, are bringing to the milk-swollen breasts and to the Cyclopean flamboyance of Nature all the virgin strength of freedom. It is a matter of expressing in words the hubbub of throngs of people settling down, of cities at work, and of oceans and rivers harnessed and put to man's use. Will Walt Whitman pair consonants and combine in tame couplets these mountains of merchandise, these forests of masts, these cities of ships, these battles where millions are felled to preserve man's rights, and let the sun, whose limpid fire spreads over the vast landscape, rule over all?

51. Ibid., "Song of Myself," poem 47, p. 109.

Oh no! Walt Whitman speaks in verses that seem bereft of music until, after listening to them for a while, one hears something like the earth echoing to glorious, unshod, conquering armies riding across it. At times his language strikes one as the window of a butcher shop hung with sides of beef; at others like the song of patriarchs singing in chorus with that gentle world-weariness, at the hour when smoke vanishes in the clouds. Sometimes it sounds like a lecherous kiss, a ravishment, the cracking of dry leather splitting in the sun. But his phrases never lose their rhythmic, wavelike motion. He himself tells how he talks: in "prophetic screams,"[52] "a few words indicative of the future."[53] His poetry is a table of contents. A sense of the universal pervades the book and gives it a grandiose regularity running through the superficial confusion; but his disjointed, flagellant, incomplete, and disconnected phrases emit rather than express such images as: "I send my musings over the hoary mountains"; "Earth! . . . Say, old top-knot, what do you want?";[54] "I sound my barbaric yawp over the roofs of the world."[55]

He certainly is not the kind to turn out a beggarly thought in regal finery and send it plodding along weighed down with superficial opulence. He does not inflate hummingbirds to look like eagles; every time he opens his hand he scatters eagles the way the sower scatters seed. One line of poetry contains five syllables, the next forty, and the next ten. He does not force comparisons, in fact he does not even make them, except when he tells what he sees or remembers with a sharp or graphic perfection while always the absolute master of the impression of totality he is ready to make. He uses his art, which he completely conceals, to reproduce the elements of his picture in as disordered a fashion as he observed them in Nature. If he uses

52. "The dirt receding before my prophetical screams," ibid., "Song of Myself," poem 25, p. 84.

53. "To conclude, I announce what comes after me," ibid., "Song of Parting," poem "So Long!" p. 429.

54. Ibid., "Song of Myself," poem 40, p. 100.

55. Ibid., "Song of Myself," poem 52, p. 113.

an extravagant image, it is not inharmonious, because that is how the mind wanders from subject to subject, with neither order nor subservience. And then without warning, as if he had only slackened the reins instead of dropping them entirely, he suddenly takes them up again and pulls in his galloping team of four with the grip of a horsebreaker, and his lines of poetry go galloping along, devouring the earth with every stride. At times they whinny eagerly, like a breeding stallion; at other times, white and frothing, they paw the clouds; sometimes, black and daring, they plunge into the bowels of the earth, and the thundering hoofs are heard for a long while. He sketches, but one might say with fire. He gathers all the horrors of war into five lines as if they were a bundle of recently gnawed bones. All he needs is an adverb to expand or shorten a phrase, and an adjective to heighten it. His method must be large because his effect is large. One could hazard a guess, however, that he proceeds without any method at all, especially in his unprecedented daring in the use of words when he puts the noble and nearly divine ones beside those considered least appropriate or decent. He paints certain pictures without the use of his incisive and ever lively epithets, but employing sounds introduced and then removed with consummate skill, thus maintaining by his variety of techniques an interest which the monotony of one style alone would endanger. He makes the reader melancholy by using repetition, like the savages. His unexpected pauses that run over into the next line change incessantly and without following any rule whatsoever, although some wise order can be found in his modulations, suspensions, and breaks. He can describe things best by means of a storehouse of words, and his logic never takes a pedestrian form of argument or a high-sounding form of oratory; rather, he uses the mystery of insinuation, the fervor of conviction, and the fiery course of prophesy. At ever step we find these words of ours in his writings: *viva*, *camarada*, *libertad*, *americanos*. But what is a better indication of his character than the French words he puts into his poetry with obvious delight, and as if they enlarge his meaning: *ami*, *exalté*, *accoucheur*, *nonchalant*, *ensemble;* he is especially captivated by *ensemble* because he sees heaven in the life of nations and worlds. One word he has taken from the Italian: *bravura*.

Thus, celebrating muscle and boldness; inviting passersby to fearlessly put their hand upon his shoulder; listening receptively to the songs in things; discovering the gigantic fecundities and delightedly shouting them to the world; gathering up seeds, battles and celestial bodies and making them into epic poetry; pointing out to the astonished times the shining hives of men spreading over America's mountains and valleys, brushing with their bees' wings the hem of freedom's garments, a freedom ever on guard; shepherding the friendly centuries toward the still waters of the ultimate calm—Walt Whitman stops at the rustic tables of his friends to be served champagne and some fish from the first catch of the dew-drenched spring. Having shown the world a sincere, loving, and articulate man, he awaits the happy time of casting off the material, the time when, given over to the purifying air, he will perfume and germinate its breezes "unencumbered, triumphant, dead!"[56]

El Partido Liberal (Mexico), 1887
Dated New York, April 19, 1887

56. Ibid., "Songs of Parting," poem "So Long!" p. 432.

Longfellow[1]

Now the celebrated poet sleeps in his grave as in a cold urn. No longer will he peer from his window at the children playing; the leaves hovering about and falling; the snowflakes, like butterflies, dancing jovially in the air; the trees stooped by the wind as men are stooped by sorrow; the bright sun so warming to a limpid soul; those slight visions of subtle wings that poets see in the air; that solemn calm that floats on the blue hills; the wheat fields; the stately trees like incense over a vast altar. Longfellow[1] is dead! Oh, what company good poets are! What gentle friends they are even when we know them not! What benefactors they are when they sing of heavenly things and console us! How soothing they are when they make us cry! How they push and uplift us when they make us think! How they fill our souls with soft music when they sorrow and pluck the air and make it sing as if it were a lyre and they held the secret of playing on it!

Life left his body like a departing bird. They clothed him in black. They kissed his generous hand. They gazed on his broad forehead as on an empty temple. They laid him in his satin coffin and on his body placed a humble bouquet of wild flowers. They dug a hollow under a majestic elm. There he sleeps!

1. Henry Wadsworth Longfellow (1807–1882), American poet, whose famous *Hiawatha* (1885) treated the Indian sympathetically, though on a sentimental level. Longfellow was little connected with the reform movements but his *Poems on Slavery* (1842) helped the antislavery cause.

How beautiful he was in life! He had that mystic beauty of good men; the wholesome color of those who are chaste; the magnificent arrogance of those who are virtuous; the goodness of the great; the sadness of all who live, and the craving for death that makes life beautiful.

His chest was broad, his gait was sure, his courtesy was genuine, his countenance was indescribable. His gaze was warm and caressing. He had lived among literary cliques which is no small merit in a man of his stature. His studies served him as a crucible, which is as it should be, and not as fetters as studies serve many others. He had in him so much light that the reflection of other lights never blinded him. He was of those who give of themselves, not of those who take from others. Some crows croaked at him, as crows always do at eagles. Some envious men nibbled at him with their green teeth. But teeth cannot bite into light. While glancing anxiously into the sky, he fixed his eyes on the high clouds and the tall mountains, and shed peace by describing beautiful things which are calming. He saw the beautiful land where men work, and that other land which is more beautiful still, where perhaps men also work.

He had no desire to rest, as he did not tire; but having lived long he had the desire a son would have who has not seen his mother for a long time. At times he felt the soft sadness of one who sees moonbeams far off in the black shadows, and at other times he felt a hurry to end it all, or doubt as to life hereafter. The fear of knowing himself filled his eyes with lightning. Then he would smile at having conquered himself, as a man who has tamed an eagle.

His poems are like resounding urns or Greek statues. To the frivolous eye they seem small, as everything great seems at first sight. But then, as from Greek statues, the soft charm of harmony and proportion emerges from them. In the bottom of those urns no rebel angels combat among burning clouds; nor do we hear winged laments arising that fly like wounded condors with dismal glance and scarlet breast; nor do we see tender lovers, stretched in a flowery vale and lulled by their gentle kisses and the swaying oat stalks; his poetry is rather a vase of myrrh from which human essences ascend fragrantly as an homage to what is high. The long-lived poet sang of Finns and Norwegians, of students from Salamanca, or Moravian nuns, Swedish ghosts, picturesque colonial things, and of wild America. But these diversions of the mind, though beautiful, do not represent well the poet's soul, nor are they his real creation, as are those wanderings of his eyes and spiritual exaltations and long, tender dialogues with nature, who was as his lover's betrothed, for whom she donned her finest garments and to whom, sure of his love, she showed the treasures of her splendid beauty. Then from his lips, born to song, emerged the harmony of song. Thus did he look out through his window-panes on evening, not as one who feared night, but as one awaiting a tardy bride. To him little boys were flowers, little girls roses, and he was to them an old wall on which they could climb.

The thought of being lost like a wavelet in a boundless sea filled him with apprehension, and he rebelled, asking himself what might be the use of so much sorrow and the reason for so much martyrdom, but he felt pity for himself and others and kept this sorrow from his fellow men. He would have them live like Hector, not like Paris, with gratitude, not wrath, and know the beauty there is in sorrow, in death, and in work. He did not incite men to unfruitful wrath, but to the brave cultivation of themselves. It was his belief that since we have a soul we should live by the soul and not by vanity, and neither by buying nor selling pleasure, for real pleasure cannot be bought or sold. Life to him was a mountain: to be alive involved the obligation of carrying a white banner to its summit. He lived in peace, far from the noisy market place, midst murmuring bowers and where under a spreading chestnut tree a sturdy blacksmith toiled, sparks flying from the forge like kernels of golden corn while thoughtful groups of school children stopped to watch.

Now he has died serenely as a wave that disappears at sea. The children bear his name. The tall, ornate, and cozy armchair made from the blacksmith's chestnut tree, given him by the children, is now empty. The grandfather clock which survives the watchmaker who made it, the warrior who counted by it the hours of battles, and the poet who praised it, still moves on lazily. And when, more like the voice of vengeance than the words of consolation, the religious chant which reminds us that we come from dust and to dust return resounded over the open grave. Nature, in whose bosom her beloved now rested, seemed to show her displeasure by lowering on the newly opened tomb a strong wind which bowed the elm's high bough, and whose voice repeated, as a consolation and a promise, Longfellow's noble lines: "Dust thou art, to dust returnest, / Was not spoken of the soul."[2]

Earth was thrown into the grave; it snowed; sadly, silently all found their way back to the city—the poet Holmes;[3] the orator Curtis;[4] the novelist Howells;[5] Louis Agassiz,[6] the son of the sage; gentle Whittier;[7] and tremulous Emerson[8] in whose lean visage could be read the solemn, majestic concentration of one who feels his head already bowing toward the pillow of the unknown!

La Opinión Nacional (Caracas), April 11, 1882

2. "A Psalm of Life" in *Longfellow's Writings*, vol. III (Cambridge, Mass., 1886), p. 21.

3. Oliver Wendell Holmes (1809–1894), American physician, poet, essayist, and contributor to the *Atlantic Monthly*, father of the famous associate justice to the U.S. Supreme Court, Oliver Wendell Holmes, Jr. (1841–1935).

4. The reference is probably to George William Curtis (1824–1892), essayist and editor of *Harper's Weekly* for many years.

5. *See* pp. 18, 29, 189.

6. Noted American naturalist.

7. John Greenleaf Whittier (1867–1892), anti-slavery poet.

8. *See* pp. 149–67.

Mark Twain[1]

In spite of his reputation in the world of letters, Mark Twain is not a major luminary; but he shines with his own light, a rare quality today, and deserves his renown, which is great in both Europe and America. He was not led to a living by the hand, or given a good and handsome wife, or provided with a house and coach, as were the pampering customs in our lands just as soon as the young gentleman of the house left the halls of learning wearing the red or yellow doctoral hood.

He started out as a printer,[2] but adventure whispered into his ear and he became a Mississippi river boat pilot;[3] his face still shows that fresh and ruddy look. He took his pen name, "Mark Twain" on the Mississippi because he was captivated by the

1. Samuel Langhorne Clemens (1835–1910), better known by the pseudonym Mark Twain, was one of America's greatest novelists and a world-famous humorist. But he was also a leading social critic, and a vigorous opponent of imperialism. Unfortunately, this aspect of Twain has usually been ignored. *See*, however, Philip S. Foner *Mark Twain: Social Critic* (New York, 1958).

2. The death of Twain's father when he was only twelve years old forced the boy to leave school in order to earn some of the money on which the widow and her children might live. He was apprenticed to a printer in Hannibal, Missouri, and became expert at his trade.

3. In 1857, on the way to New Orleans by boat, Mark Twain apprenticed himself to a river pilot. He served a year and a half as an apprentice and two and a half years as a licensed pilot on the Mississippi, a river that has been called his university. Afterward he wrote *Life on the Mississippi*.

original. "Mark Twain," the pilot would often call out when a depth of two fathoms was sounded. And as soon as he began telling, in his uninhibited joking manner, what he had seen of the world, and drawing out the real man from the man of appearances, he signed his name with the Mississippi cry: "Mark Twain." Then he traveled as a secretary to one of his brothers through the mining country where people went to bed upon a lode of gold and awakened with a dagger in the heart.

He has been in factories of angry workers where the country is being forged; with those who make mistakes, who fall in love, who steal, who live in solitude and populate it; with those who build. He was fond of wandering about, and no sooner had he seen man in one place than he would leave him, eager to see him in another. He has a habit of blinking, as if to see better, or to prevent people from divining his thoughts by his eyes. He knows men and the efforts they put into concealing or disguising their defects. It amuses him to tell things so that the real man—hypocritical, slavish, cowardly, lascivious—falls from the last sentence of his story the way a clown's *polichinela* tumbles out of the hands that are playing with it. And Twain peers into his sentence to watch the real man fall.

He draws with charcoal, but with swift and certain lines. He understands the power of adjectives—those adjectives which economize sentences—and piles them upon a character so that the man being depicted begins to move as if he were alive. His confidence in description has come from his habit of observation. There are credulous and ardent souls who see everything in the light of their own flames, or through the film covering their own eyes—see everything as nonsensical, enormous or deformed, false or confused. Then there are other souls, like Mark Twain, who are incredulous because of being experienced, and quieted down perhaps on account of their sufferings; and these see everything in natural size, no matter how impossible it is at times for them to divine, like defects in their own quality, the wings of things. His travel books have given him fame and a profit of four hundred thousand dollars.[4] He tells his witticisms

4. After publishing his first book, *The Celebrated Jumping Frog of Calaveras County, and Other Sketches* (1867) and following a very suc-

grudgingly, as it were, and produces them with no intention of causing harm.

He has no desire to school himself, so that men will not hide away and conceal their character from him, character which he brings out and for which he lies in wait with the skill of a good hunter. He must have the incurable melancholy of all those who know men deeply, and I believe he does have it. He married a wealthy woman[5] and has been to the Sandwich Islands, through Europe, Egypt, and Palestine. His pen is inevitably moved by the mad and the hypocritical. His wit derives from the originality and gross vitality of his own life. He has put them into practice for a long time with simple folk, and he must have been a madcap among them, for the common people appear in all his pages. He has more of Kock than of Chamfort. But over and above those men he has an exquisite sense of nature, for had he been favored by more delicate paint brushes he would have produced some glorious copies. His own person, making jokes and scoffing, diminishes his vivid pictures.

For anyone who reads Mark Twain's description of Athens by night, there is no need to go there if one would rather not, for it is described so glowingly that one can see it; nor is there any need to go to the pyramids. He undertakes to tell how, standing atop one of them, one of the guides wagered that he could descend from there and climb to the top of the next pyramid, and then return to the one upon which they were standing, all within ten minutes. And the swift Arab starts running; Twain

---

cessful Cooper Union lecture stint, Mark Twain sailed on the *Quaker City* with a party of excursionists bound for the Mediterranean and the Holy Land. The reports which he sent back were published in *The Innocents Abroad* (1869), a book which made him a national figure, and brought him both a reputation and a fortune.

5. During the voyage Twain had become acquainted with a young man named Langdon who had with him a miniature of his sister, Olivia. Twain almost fell in love with the picture, and on his return, he courted Olivia Langdon until he won her over. They were married in 1870 at her father's house in Elmira, New York.

describes him descending hurriedly, turns him loose on the burning sands below. Now you see him as a dog, now as a dove, now as a fly, now you see him no longer, just a wild black dot climbing riotously up a pyramid, reaching the summit, waving, coming down and starting to run again. Now he touches the base of the pyramid, now returns like the wind, now he is at the top again and has won his bet. The ten minutes have not yet gone by. In a scant twenty lines Mark Twain tells this whole tale, and although he does not describe it thread by thread, one can sense the magnificent solitude, the burning sun, the Great Pyramid, the distance between it and the others, the whirling sands, and the burnoose floating out behind the guide.

Mark Twain writes novels, not yet well put together. As if unwillingly and in an offhand manner, he recites incidents from his life or episodes from his books; he trudges off stage into the wings as if bored, speaks his piece to the public as he might do to his own children to entertain them and then be free of them. In these recitations he adds to the wittiness of his thought that which produces an irresistible contrast between his comical and exaggerated portrayals and the ill-humored, nasal, and imperturbable tone of voice he uses to recite them. He achieves no effect with brief jokes, but draws them out and dilutes them for the sake of the lot of them, because his pungency lies not in felicity of expression, which is usually violent when he strives for it or expands it; rather, it lies in the justice of his criticism and in his manner of opposing appearances to feelings. Wandering about and appearing unexpectedly has always pleased and been useful to him, and this method and tendency of his is revealed in the titles of his best books: *Innocents Abroad*, *Innocents at Home*, *A Tramp Abroad*, a method which surely leads to an extremely ingenious slingshot.

Sometimes he picks up an avalanche of witticisms and sets them to dancing upon an atom, with the marvelous skill of a balancing act. The *Figaro* of Paris revels in his books, translating and celebrating him not for the purity of his style, because he knows his people and has no desire for delicacy, but for the subtlety of his observation.

He wears his shock of white hair long; his eyes show experience, depth, and roguery; a long, aquiline nose presides over a martial mustache; the rest of his face, of a healthy color, he keeps cleanshaven. He thrusts his head forward as if scrutinizing; he carries his shoulders high as if he has decided to shrug them forever. Such is Mark Twain, or Samuel Clemens, the foremost American humorist.

Knighthood was once in fashion, and outside of the *Quixote*, nowhere was it better treated, nor thrashed and trounced more effectively or in so novel a manner, than in the book which was written with the force of a natural man, by the perspicacious and indignant humorist, Mark Twain.

He lives in his castle because his home in the town of Hartford, surrounded by oaks and bordered by a lake, looks like a castle; but he earned it with his brains, describing in *Roughing It* the rustic characters seen with his own all-absorbing eyes in hospitals and fights and mines and on rivers, and in *The Innocents Abroad* and *A Tramp Abroad* whose rough-hewn wit found men laughing from London to Cairo. He has a countryman's hand and smokes his tobacco in a pipe, but one can discern in those books a man able to see for himself, his wisdom refined by long and severe hardship, and a love for the unfortunate. With the most cultured and relaxed skill, moved by the disorder he sees, by the injustice which exasperates him, and by the highborn who keep riding on the backs of the poor, he finally created this book about *A Connecticut Yankee in King Arthur's Court*.[6] In it, by means of the simple device of contrasting the free Yankee with the castle lords of the Round Table, and with anger bordering at times upon the sublime, he makes clearly evident the disreputable way by which some men desire to lord it over others, eating from their wretchedness and drinking from their misfortune. And so skillfully does he develop his theme that the salient character of that age of kings and bishops, peasants and

6. *A Connecticut Yankee in King Arthur's Court* was published in 1889 at a time of sharp class conflict in the United States between capital and labor.

slaves, proving to be a picture of what is beginning to be seen in the United States, is more than a mere copy. And virtuous men, armed by nature in hunger and solitude, are scourging with the lash of apostles, appearing with a pen as a spear and a book as a shield, to overthrow those castles built with the dollars of the new knighthood. There are paragraphs in Mark Twain's book that make one want to set out for Hartford and shake hands with him. He has hoisted a flag for men, and men will be grateful to him. The *Quixote* will be readily acceptable in libraries, and with it the *Connecticut Yankee*. There are visors and leather shields in both, and the two books resemble one another in magnificent mockery, but the *Quixote* is what it is, a wise and sorrowful portrayal of man's life, and the *Connecticut Yankee*, invigorated by indignation, is a battle in cowboy style—with lariat and revolver like those of its hero—against Sir Lagramor, in behalf of the majesty and crown of free and simple man. The plot fits into a thimble: a factory foreman, in an encounter with a rebellious worker, is hit in the head with a crowbar. When he regains consciousness, with his skills of the present-day Yankee, electric and hustling, he finds himself in the court where all knowledge resides in Merlin, with the vault of heaven the mitre, the loves of Launcelot and Guinevere the kingdom's morality, and the will of powerful King Arthur the government. Those travels of the king, incognito, and the Yankee who has defeated Merlin and is now prime minister, over the scaffold-studded slopes of the infamous castle, through peasant villages and the fields of plowmen, into the hut of smallpox that was cursed by the Church, with the chains of slaves sold to the highest bidder! That joust of "Slim Jim," dressed in the tights of a gymnast, astride his prairie nag and armed with only a pistol at his belt and a lariat swinging in the air—that joust against the iron tower rushing upon him, the great Sir Lagramor, Merlin's protégé, who falls backward, his horse's silver-studded trappings flying in all directions, his arms and legs pointing skyward, the lariat around his neck, and his buttocks in the sand! That site wired for electricity where "Jim" and his fifty-two young men—fifty-two youths of dawning courage with truly marvelous spears never seen before, win a battle against twenty-five thousand defenders equipped with the helmets and suits of armor of knight-errantry. And the language the essence of Yankeeism.

Twain takes everything typical and expressive in the vernacular, and talks with "Jim"[7] in Yankee and with Merlin and King Arthur in the speech of the chronicles.

La Nación (Buenos Aires), January 11, 1885

7. "Jim" is also the Negro runaway slave in what is Mark Twain's greatest novel, *The Adventures of Huckleberry Finn*, one of Twain's greatest characters. But the book was published after Martí's article appeared.

Louisa May Alcott[1]

There is no reason to go searching among the new nations for those imitative and "hack writer" kinds of literature taught in the typical schools by mummified professors. "And who is that secretary of yours who makes so many mistakes?" a Chicago journalist was asked. "He's an imbecile who speaks eighteen languages and knows six life sciences. You give him the end of a Latin verse and he'll tell you if it's from Juvenal[2] or Persius[3]; but don't ask him where human life is going, or how to influence it, or how to derive happiness from it, or how to travel the world without tripping over one's neighbors' calluses and bunions; that is science, my friend, not to trip over bunions!"

It was certainly not that kind of scientific literature that gave fame to the writer who has just died: Louisa May Alcott. Her name is surely not known in our countries, as neither was that of her father, the philosopher Bronson Alcott[4] whose old age she maintained so decently with the product of her work. And her

1. Louisa May Alcott (1832–1888), second daughter of Amos Bronson Alcott, whose novel *Little Women*, founded on her own family life and published in 1868, became a phenomenal bestseller.

2. Juvenal (Decimas Junius Juvenalis) (55–127 A.D.), most powerful of all Roman satirists.

3. Aulus Persius Flaccus (34–62 A.D.), Stoic poet, philosopher, and writer of Latin satires.

4. *See* pp. 47–53 in *On Education*, volume 3 of the collected writings of José Martí, ed. Philip S. Foner (New York, 1979) for essay on Bronson Alcott.

work was remarkable. The main thing was to live rather than study. She lived a poor life in the country, near Thoreau the hermit naturalist, and Hawthorne[5] the novelist of the spirit, and that white eagle called Emerson. She lived in a modest house as oldest daughter in a home to which her philosopher father brought little bread, and where what her mother earned in the town by teaching manners and sewing was decreasing so much that Louisa, engrossed in reading pretentious books, stopped writing all those letters to Victor Hugo, Milton,[6] and Goethe, to teach in a neighborhood school where she was dearly loved because of her talent for inventing stories. She sent them to the newspapers by the dozens, just in case they should want to print them, and finally one of them seemed good to a certain compassionate editor who paid her five dollars, and ten for the second, until one snowy day upon returning from her lessons she came upon a poster on which was printed, in very large letters: *Bertha*, a new novel by the author of *The Rival Primadonnas*. The whole family went in a procession to see that poster, the principal language of fame, and tore off shreds of it which her sisters are still devoutly preserving.

But in vain did Louisa May Alcott write imagined novels, with more invention than observation and full of reminiscences and literary imitation. "She'll do something," said those who knew her, but with twenty books written she still had not done it; until, her noble heart touched by the sufferings of the wounded from the Civil War, she enlisted as a nurse, saw death, and found this language: "Around the stove, the enormous red stove, were gathered—stretched out, fallen on an elbow, lying one against another—the most unhappy men I have ever seen; thrown out of joint, their clothes in tatters, pale, with mud up to their knees, with blood-caked bandages from days past, many huddled in their blankets, their coats at their

5. Nathaniel Hawthorne (1804–1864), novelist and short-story writer and one of the first great imaginative writers in the United States.

6. John Milton (1608–1674), one of England's finest poets, author of the epic poem *Paradise Lost* (1667).

feet or without any coats, and all with that weary look that proclaims—rather than the silence of the cities or the commanding officer's dispatch—the defeat. I sympathized so deeply that I dared not talk to them. I was dying to be of some use to the most miserable ones." And this is how, in *Hospital Sketches*,[7] she tells the hospital stories: "the meals were brought in and I gave some food to one of the most severely wounded, and then offered some to the man beside me. 'Thank you, lady, but I don't think I'll eat again; there's a bullet in my belly. But I do want a drink of water if you're not too busy.' I started walking very quickly, but the buckets had just been taken away to be filled, and they took a long time to be returned. I did not forget my wounded man and went to him with the first pitcher. He seemed to be asleep, but something in his pale and tired face made me put my ear to his lips. He was not breathing. I touched his forehead. It was cold. Then I realized that, while I was waiting for the water, another and better nurse had given him a more cooling medicine to drink and had healed him with a caress. I spread the sheet over that man whose sleep could no longer be disturbed by any noise, and half an hour later the bed was empty."

Since then, and enlightened by tenderness, Louisa May Alcott wrote only the truth. She did not make use of her imagination to fabricate, but to compose, which is her true craft; and of course what she knew about literature was very valuable to her, not for building houses out of cards daubed with legends and mythology—with one column Greek, another Hindu, another German, and another Latin—but for disseminating what was her very own, the things she saw and knew from close at hand, with that naturalness, sense of proportion, and good taste which are the eternal and useful lessons learned

7. During the Civil War, Louisa May Alcott was a nurse in the Union Hospital at Georgetown, where she rendered efficient service until her health broke down. Her letters to her family, in a revised form and under the title, "Hospital Sketches," were published in the *Commonwealth* in 1863, and later in the same year brought out in book form. They excited widespread interest, and were followed, in 1864, by her first novel *Moods*.

from the study of good literature. Louisa May Alcott then told about her life as a child, the lives of her sisters, the life of that good father who ate no meat, of her mother who raised her like a flower, and of her neighbors in the town of Concord—a refuge before, and even today, of the brightest and happiest souls among the Pleiades of Bostonians in whom were rooted equally the love of man and the love of letters. But she did not tell it in the first person, for that might have deprived the narrative of freedom and charm; rather, by arranging the incidents around a propitious plot and contriving real characters in an imagined and always simple action, she created, with all the strength of someone who had lived a typical albeit original childhood, the new novel of the American child. Especially of the American girl. There is no city home nor country home that does not have a copy of her *Little Women*,[8] *Little Men*,[9] *Work*,[10] *Eight Cousins*,[11] *Lul's Library*, *Under the Lilacs*. Louisa's entire life is in *Little Women* and *Work*, for she is that "tomboy of a Jo," and she is that "success of a Christie." So salutary and vigorous are her books that not only do children read them with delight, but the older person who begins one cannot set it down. *Little Women* has sold by the hundred thousands, *Little Men* not far behind. Life sparkles in them without vain images or coarse descriptions; virtue gradually enters the soul as one reads, the way balsam enters a wound.

José Martí, *Obras Completas*
(La Habana, 1964), vol. 13, pp. 193–95

8. The first volume of *Little Women* was so successful and its popularity so great that she promptly produced a second volume in 1869. Both were translated into several languanges and had phenomenal sales. From this time on she was able to make her family financially independent.

9. *Little Men* was written in 1871 during a sojourn in Europe.

10. *Work*, published in 1873, recounts her own early experiences.

11. *Eight Cousins* was published in 1875; *Lulu's Library* (3 vols.) in 1886–89, and *Under the Lilacs* in 1878.

Aboriginal American Authors

Such Indian writings as we know, the fragments that escaped the episcopal hands of the Landas and Zumarragas, are informed with the splendor of the *samán*, the elegance of the palm, and the brilliance and variety of the flora of the American uplands. The rays of the Persian sun do not shatter in richer hues against the silver saddles and precious gems of the paladins of tempered sabre and silk tunic than those abundant and vivid colors rendered by the Indian phrase, ample and pliant as a robe. Who that has read an account of battle or title of property of the Guatemalan Indians will deny it? The *Mahabharata* is more sententious; the *Schahnameh*, more grave; the prophesies of Chilam Balam of Yucatán are more serene and profound; the odes of the Mexican Netzahualcoyotl, more sublime; the dramas of Peru have more passion, the *Apu Ollantay*, perhaps the Uska Pankar; the traditions of Tingal shimmer like a tunic spangled with diamonds. But the legends of the Quiche and Zutugil are like a brook, like a young stallion of winged gait and flaming mane, like a magician's rope that grows upon itself in endless coils, like an ocean newly formed that sparkles in pure, virgin light, like a chattering troop of Indian girls tinkling with little blue bells, and warriors in plumed headdresses cavorting under the blazing sun of a summer morning, or a river of jewels, as if a maiden had set her thoughts adrift on the limpid waters of a forest stream. The tremendous "Jonatin," the handsome Alvarado, surprised them while they quarreled among themselves and conquered them. The despot laughs in the shadows when a people become disunited.

Literature is simply the expression, form and reflection of the vital spirit and natural setting of the people who create it. How, then, could our indigenous literature run counter to this universal law, and lack the beauty, harmony and color of the American scene? We who love the Indians as one loves a broken lily are not the only ones who see this. The purpose of these lines is to report the publication of an interesting book in which a North American author discovers these qualities in the fragments of pre-Colombian literature that we know, and in all the literature after the conquest in which the native genius demonstrates its richness and character, both in the native languages, and the language of the *conquistadores*. What institutions were Tlaxcala's! What warriors, Mayapán's! Teotitlan, what schools! What a circus in Copán! Mexico, what workshops, plazas, and aqueducts! What temples in Zimpoalo! The Andes, what highways! What does it matter that we come of fathers of Moorish blood and fair skin? The spirit of a people resides in the land in which they live and is drawn in with the air one breathes. One may descend from fathers of Valencia and mothers of the Canary Islands, yet one feels the blood of Tamanaco and Paracamoni run hot through one's veins and regards as one's own the blood of the heroic, naked Caracas warriors which stained the craggy ground of Mount Calvary where they met the armored Spanish soldiers hand to hand! It is good that canals be dug, schools built, steamship lines organized, good that we keep abreast of the times and in the vanguard of the beautiful human march; but if we are not to fail from the lack of a living spirit, or the pursuit of false values, we must drink deeply at the springs of the Nature into which we were born, which is strengthened and animated by the spirit of men of all races who spring from its soil and return to it. Politics and literature prosper only when they are a direct expression of their people. The American intelligence is an Indian headdress. Is it not yet apparent that the blow that paralyzed the Indian, paralyzed America? Until the Indian marches again, America will limp.

There are excellent Americanists in the United States, and Daniel G. Brinton[1] is among the best. He has just published a study he read before the Congress of Americanists in Copenhagen last year containing all that is known of indigenous works. He demonstrates how broad, adaptable, and flexible was the vocabulary of the aborigines. He discovers a powerful literary capacity in them, and vigorously points it out. Since they dealt in living impressions, their need for expression was immediate. They like to narrate, and they did it with both abundance and grace. Color was always essential to them, and an indispensable part of their stories. An ingenuous soul and vivid imagination are the hallmark of what we know of the Indians. Their relish for symmetry and ornament is apparent in their manuscripts, as in their ruins. The Greeks have their Atriums and Niestes, and easily swayed Europa; the Indians also had theirs, and their feuds between rival houses and families, which, to judge by the scant pages translated from their letters and symbols, are told with greater flourish and passion in their parchments and tablets than the rivalry of Atrides and Pelopides in the glorious Greek romance. How august, the Illiad of Greece! How brilliant, the Indian Illiad! Homer[2] shed golden tears; the Indian verses are palm fronds, alive with hummingbirds.

Brinton's book contains not only facts and deductions, but a list of documents: he has included an appendix cataloging all the works that are known and considered of authentic indigenous authorship. The Indian in the North, subjected to a struggle for survival against wild beasts and the cold, had little time to leave a painted or written record of his life; a poor people, constantly at war, and on the march toward the warm lands, they wrote more with the arrow than with the quill. But in the tropic lands, where all men will eventually seek a haven, the poetry that

1. Daniel Garrison Brinton (1837–1899), pioneer of anthropology in the United States whose *The American Race* (1891) was the first systematic classification of the aboriginal languages of North and South America.

2. Greek epic poet.

springs from repose and imagination, which is sumptuous in lands of natural richness, flowered in all its magnificent colors. Nature placed a wondrous mantle on America's shoulders! The world will witness an imposing spectacle the day it discovers its strength and awakes. What silver fringes, our rivers! Our mountains, what roses! What embroidery, our thoughts! Our souls, what eagles! Nature placed a wondrous mantle on America's shoulders!

The Hour (New York), 1880
[written in English]

Modern French Novelists

The years immediately following the disastrous war of 1870–1871 are a period of unusual barrenness in one field at least, of French literature. With their beautiful country lying prostrate at the feet of the conqueror, the French people, struggling for their very existence, had more serious things to occupy their minds than the amusement of reading novels. The relation between demand and supply, applies to literature with equal force as it does to commerce. But with the return of peace, prosperity, and security, the literature of fiction received a fresh impulse and the world has been supplied from Paris during the last six years with numerous novels, which, as regards variety of subjects, boldness of speculation and realism of description, surpass the productions of any previous epoch.

Among these *post-bellum* authors there are two, namely, Zola[1] and Alphonse Daudet,[2] who have principally attracted the attention of the world and, if the number of the editions of their works be a criterion of their merit, may claim the first rank. But this popular success is the only thing which these two men have in common. The observing, poetical and artistic Daudet is far removed from the poet of the sewer. Daudet's popularity is based upon a feeling of gratitude for the delightful offerings he gives us. He combines the keenest knowledge of the human

1. Emile Zola (1840–1902), French novelist and critic, the forerunner of the Naturalist movement in literature.

2. Alphonse Daudet (1840–1897), French short-story writer and novelist.

heart with a humor worthy of Thackeray and clothes his creations in the brilliant, fiery language of which the French are masters. Zola owes his fame to what is lowest and saddest in man's nature. The *Assommoir* has gone through nearly eighty editions and has been translated into nearly every European language, including Greek and Roumanian, and of his last work, *Nana*, forty thousand copies were ordered of the publisher before it appeared.

Daudet's fame dates from his *Fromont jeune et Risler ainé*. *Jack*, which followed, is a most pathetic, but almost unbearably sad story of a child's suffering. *Le Nabab* marks the zenith of his glory, and his last work. *Les Rois en Exil*, shows no decrease in the writer's powers.

French fiction of today may be divided into three classes—the novel, descriptive of purely French manners and habits *(Roman de Moeurs)*, all after the fashion of Balzac,[3] the great prototype; the boulevard and salon novel, and the popular police, blood and murder novel. Always leaving Daudet and Zola, who occupy places of their own, out of consideration, the highest place in the first class is due to Hector Malot,[4] who may be considered as the legitimate heir to Balzac's inheritance. He possesses some of the latter's best qualities and is superior to him in many respects. He is more humane, more trusting; he believes there are some good, unselfish people in this world, who are not fools and weaklings, and his villains are not so hopelessly abject and lost as those whom Balzac represents. His best works, *Le Mari de Charlotte*, *La Fille de la Comédienne*, *La Belle Madame Donis*, are written in a superior style, with a certain *noblesse oblige* tone. His men and women are people one would like to know; they are of our own flesh and blood and, with all their faults, healthy and natural.

3. Honoré de Balzac (1799–1850), French novelist, universally recognized as a genius in the novel, whose vast lifework was arranged under the title *La Comédie humaine* (The Human Comedy) in which he claimed to be explaining man to himself. His prodigious output included some 40 novels.

4. Henri Hector Malot (1830–1907), French novelist.

Ferdinand Fabre[5] must be mentioned in this class. He has chosen a subject for his fiction which would soon become tedious in the hands of a less gifted writer. The heroes of Fabre's stories are those poor, devoted country priests, "Monsieur le Curé," who play so important a part in French provincial life, and of whom outsiders know little or nothing. He introduces some delightful types; the kindhearted, easy-going old *curé*, who does not trouble himself about the *Syllabus* or papal infalibility, is a patriarch in his little parish, the temporal and spiritual adviser of his flock, and who always looks with a vast amount of charity upon the failing of the simple souls entrusted to his care. Then we have the ambitious young ascetic, fresh from the seminary, eager for action, who even dreams of the mitre and crook and sees in the buxom, rosy-cheeked village girls temptations which the devil has thrown in his way to be fought against with the courage of St. Anthony. Then there is the man who has missed his vocation, who might be a Humboldt,[6] a Talleyrand[7] or a Wellington,[8] if he had been placed in a different sphere of life. All these types are interesting and lifelike, and it is a matter of astonishment that so little is known of this distinguished writer outside of a limited number of readers in France.

The Hour (New York), 1880
[written in English]

5. Ferdinand Fabre (1827–1898), French novelist, considered founder of the French regional novel with his studies of country life.

6. Alexander von Humboldt (1769–1859), German explorer and scientist, internationally famous for his study of earth sciences and originator of ecology.

7. Charles Maurice de Talleyrand (1754–1835), French statesman and diplomat prominent under all the different regimes that ruled France in the late eighteenth and early nineteenth centuries.

8. Duke of Wellington (1769–1852), British conqueror of Napoleon at the Battle of Waterloo, later prime minister of Britain (1828–1830).

Heredia[1]

Ladies and gentlemen:

It is with pride and reverence that I am beginning to speak from this post which I would gladly have surrendered, due to its extreme difficulty, to anyone with more ambition than mine and less physical fear—anyone could have taken this job from me were it not for the needs of the homeland which requires me to be in this position today. I would gladly have given up this post, I say, were it not for the fear that he who has awakened an unquenchable passion for freedom in my soul—as in the soul of all Cubans—may rise from his seat of glory beside the sun, where he reigns face-to-face, and accuse me of ingratitude. The world has much splendor and many honors which men solicit with alarming eagerness and incredible humiliation; I do not seek more honors for myself, for there is no higher honor than that of having been judged worthy of gathering into my mortal words a hymn of tenderness and gratitude from these womanly hearts and manly breasts—a hymn to divine Cuba—and of sending our thoughts with it, thoughts still veiled in public shame, to the mountain peaks where his unfading genius waits, perhaps in vain, with thunder at his right hand, the waterfalls at his feet, the storm clouds shaken by the primitive winds of creation, and his face still bathed in the tears of Cuba.

1. José María Heredia (1842–1905), Cuban poet, brilliant master of the sonnet, whose poems in that form were exquisite miniatures. His 118 sonnets and some longer pieces were published as *Les Trophées* (1893).

If people consider me discreet, nobody will expect me to demean this occasion—one of gratitude and tribute—merely to win fame as a learned and punctilious critic, by examining the origins and elements of literature alone; this would be improper to the festivities at hand and to the state of our spirits. With but a single glance, a man can see for himself the various critical moments of Heredia's existence and the difficult and encyclopedic times of world jubilation and change in which it was his lot to live. Nor will I usurp, for a display of pedagogy, the time in which his own stanzas, like flower-bedecked spears, must come here to courteously and passionately bow to Cuban woman, ever faithful to genius and misfortune, and suddenly casting roses upon the ground to repeat before men—confused in these times of little virtue and tempting interests—the following lines, magnificent as slaps in the face, in which Heredia predicts that:

If a nation dares not break
its heavy chains with its own hands,
that nation can remove its tyrants
but never can be free.

I do not come here as a judge to examine how his classical and French training, his passionate soul, and the times, accidents, and places of his life come together in him; nor how his boyhood odyssey and father's teachings quickened his genius. I shall not judge which of his famous lines are his own and which are reflections; or point out with a pitiless finger the time when, his soul deprived of high callings, he repeated his foremost ideas in less fortunate cantos because of a habit of producing, or the need to express himself, or gratitude to people who sheltered him, or political obligation. I come here as a desperate and loving son to briefly record, with only the notes which glory orders set down, the life of which he sang with disregarded majesty to woman, to danger, and to palm trees.

Heredia was born in Cuba where those palm trees are tallest, in indefatigable Santiago. And they say that starting from childhood—as if the spirit of the extinct race were whispering its complaints to him and lending him their fury, as if the last gold of the plundered country were burning in his veins, as if in the light of the tropical sun life's entrails were being revealed to him by some supernatural favor—the virile anathema, the pithy word, the resonant ode were springing from the lips of that "wonder child." Heredia's father, with his great store of knowledge and the inspiration of affection, put before his eyes the elements of the earth, the movements of humanity, and the events of nations, all in an orderly manner and with comments. In the robes of a judge he protected that precocious son from the fever of genius. He taught him to love Cicero,[2] and because of his artistic and harmonious nature he loved Cicero more than either Marat[3] or Fouquier Tinville.[4] His father taught him the importance of things and the need of urging them forward impartially and establishing them with moderation. The Latin he studied with the teacher Correa was not the diffuse Latin of Seneca,[5] or the wordy Latin of Lucan,[6] or that of Quintilian,[7] full of trimming and spangles; it was the Latin of Horace[8]—sheer beauty, more beautiful than the poetry of the Greeks because it has their elegance with none of their crudity—new wine straight from the grape and perfumed by the few roses that this life produces. Don José Francisco taught his son Lucretius[9] in the morning, Humboldt[10] at night. The father and

2. Marcus Tullius Cicero (106–43 B.C.), statesman, scholar, lawyer, writer, and Rome's greatest orator.

3. Jean-Paul Marat (1743–1793), leading exponent of radical elements in the French Revolution, who was assassinated. *See also* pp. 54–62.

4. Antoine Quentin Fouquier-Tinville (1741–1795), French revolutionary lawyer, public prosecutor during the Reign of Terror.

5. Lucius Annaeus Seneca (55 B.C.–39 A.D.), famous author of Latin work on declamation.

6. Marcus Annaeus Lucanus (39–65 A.D.), Roman poet and republican patriot, grandson of the elder Seneca.

7. Marcus Fabius Quintilianus (35–96 A.D.), Roman writer, famous for his work on rhetoric.

8. *See* p. 226.

9. Titus Lucretius Caus (1st century BC), Latin poet and philosopher, famous for his long poem, *On the Nature of Things*.

10. *See* pp. 207, 216.

his after-dinner friends dropped their books in amazement. Who was that boy who drew everything to himself? Child, have you ever been a king, or Ossian,[11] or Brutus?[12] It was as if the boy had seen battles among the stars, because their radiance shone in his face. That voracious genius threw tempestuous sparks and seethed like a volcano. Rotund and essential words flowed from those nine-year-old lips, divining the laws of light or commenting upon the Trojan wars.[13] With shining eyes he foresaw the martyrdom to which men who were denounced by the splendor of virtue submit to the genius who dares to see clearly at night. His poetry was the pride and religion of the household. In order not to interrupt it, his mother silenced all noises. His father propped up the poorly constructed rhymes. They opened all doors to him. To enable him to see well when writing, they gave him the strongest light in the parlor. Others have had to compose their first lines of poetry amid spankings and mockery in the light of a restless glowworm and a collaborating moon! . . . Heredia's poetry ended upon his mother's lips and in the arms of his father and his father's friends. Heredia's immortality began in that strength and self-confidence which, as a constant lesson from his strict parents, gave the boy the household's affection.

His father was a judge and a person of counsel and benevolence for which reason, in addition to his American birth, he was chosen to establish peace in Venezuela where Monteverde, with the chance assistance of nature, had defeated Miranda, too wise for a war in which the attack is more necessary and wins more battles than does wisdom—in Venezuela where the creator

11. Ossian, Scottish Gallic name for Oisin, the Irish warrior-poet of the Fenian cycle of heroic tales. Largely the invention of James Macpherson, the Scottish poet who "discovered" them in 1762.

12. Marcus Junius Brutus (85–42 B.C.), a leader of the conspirators who assassinated the Roman dictator, Julius Caesar, in March, 44 B.C.

13. Trojan Wars were the legendary conflict between the early Greeks and the people of Troy in the twelfth or thirteenth centuries B.C.

leisure of theft, luxury of blood. His father carried a tortoise shell cane bought with his earnings as a judge and a new lawyer in a vile society, and so did he. The one who lives from infamy, or only passively nudges it, is himself infamous. Abstaining from it is not enough; it must be fought. To look calmly upon a crime is to commit it. His youth invited Heredia to love affairs; his father's favored position and his own fame as an extraordinary young man brought clients to his writing desk; in the homes of the wealthy he was heard with amazement to improvise forty stanzas upon forty different lines of poetry. Out in the streets they would say, "That fellow is Heredia!" And when he passed by, lovely heads would gather in the windows and whisper, as the sweetest of rewards, "That man is Heredia!" But glory increases the misfortune of living when it must be bought at the price of complicity with infamous behavior. There is but one certain glory—that of the soul contented with itself. It is pleasant to walk beneath the mango trees at the delightful hour of dawn when the world seems to have been just created, and the sun appears out of nothingness, with its army of chattering birds, as on the first day of life. But what "iron hand" weighed down upon his heart in the Cuban fields? And what bloody hand in the heavens? Kisses were thrown to him from the windows, he was applauded in the homes of the wealthy, and the practice of law oozed gold; but when leaving the triumphal banquet, the eloquent drawing rooms, the happy appointment, does the whip not crack and ask clemency of a heaven which lends a deaf ear to the mother whose cries for her beloved son want to choke her with lashings? It is not the slave who is the despicable one, nor he who was once a slave, but the man who sees this crime and fails to swear, before a skilled court of justice which presides in secret, until slavery and every vestige of it is abolished from the earth. And America freed, and all Europe crowned with liberty, and Greece itself returned to life. And Cuba—as beautiful as Greece—thus lying in shackles, a stain upon the earth, a prison surrounded by water, the remora of America? If among living Cubans there are not enough soldiers for honor, what are the snails doing on the beach, snails that fail to call dead Indians to battle? The uselessly moaning palm trees, what are they doing instead of commanding? The mountains that do not stand in close ranks to cut off the paths of those who pursue the heroes, what are they doing? Heredia shall fight upon the land as long as there is a foot of it left, and when there is not he shall still fight standing in the sea. Leonidas of Thermopylae, Cato of Rome, pointed out the road for the Cubans to follow. "Come now, Hernández!" Heredia's voice wandered from scaffold to scaffold, from Estrampes[17] to Agüero,[18] from Plácido[19] to Benavides,[20] until one day, in the darkness of night, among a hundred arms upraised to heaven, it thundered at Yara.[21] Then it became discouraged and there is still someone who tells us, when the sun is behind the clouds, that it shall disappear. Are perversion and misfortune so rife among Cubans that Heredia's voice can be silenced by the weight of his people killed by their own hands?

It was at this time that he came to New York to receive the buffeting of cold. He was unaware when it pierced his side because he found some consolation in being away from the moral laziness of his country; although he never forgot it in those now powerful cities where, if there was no prevalence of a well-informed republic that desired his generous soul, freedom did prevail in a region worthy of it. He immersed his thoughts in the depths of history; in wonder he studied the colossal skeletons; stiff with cold beside his fireplace, he meditated upon the epochs that shone and then died out. His sublime mind grew to gigantic proportions in the solitude; and then, like one

17. José de Estrampes, painter.

18. Juan Miguel Agüero, Mexican architect.

19. Plácido was the free Negro poet in Cuba, whose real name was Gabriel de la Concepción Valdés, and who was executed during the scare associated with the suppression of the slave conspiracy of 1844.

20. Juan Benavides, Ecuadorian painter.

21. Grito de Yara was the cry for the outbreak of the Ten Years' War in Cuba, the first war for independence, issued on October 10, 1868.

who discovers his very self, he saw those ages of water break up into light and plunge headlong to his feet—prodigious Niagara humbly revealing its mystery to him. And with one leap of the mind that adolescent poet of a disdained people found the meaning of a Nature that could not be understood so majestically by its own inhabitants in centuries of contemplation.

Mexico is a land of refuge where every pilgrim has found a brother. From Mexico came the wise Oses to whom Heredia, with the gravity of a senator, used to write those epic letters of his youth. In a Mexican house he would read to himself, at a table adorned by a blue vase filled with jasmine, the gallant poem on "The Virtue of Women." President Victoria[22] summoned him to share in the triumph of the liberal constitution, more laborious than complete, for he did not want to see that volcanic flower come to naught in the snowy tomb. What could have detained Heredia at Niagara where his sincere and prophetic poetry failed to find the accents needed to bring about freedom? Mexico is beginning the bloodiest and most courageous ascent, among the ruins of the Church and with an inert race behind it, that any people has completed. Without direction or education or any tutor but the country's own character, Mexico was on its way to the heights, marking every range pole with a battle, and every range pole higher than the last! If the still tender tree of liberty languishes in the shadow of the Church, a generation comes singing, its courage overflowing at the foot of that thirsty tree. Heredia went to Mexico where the great Quintana Roo adorned the Castilian lyre with flowers of the oak. And when Heredia saw those hospitable yet warlike beaches again, those valleys so like the deserted mansion of an Olympus awaiting its redemption, those mountains which in the absence of their gods are like overturned urns, those summits which the sun in its course tints with chaste silver and amorous violet and living gold—as if creation wanted to show its favors and special tenderness to its preferred nature—he believed that that was the place, not the egoistic north,

22. Felix Juan Manuel Fernández Victoria (1789–1843), Mexican president and leader in the fight for independence.

where he could find in freedom the selfsame solemn order of the plains guarded by the volcano sentinels. He climbed with the nimble feet of a man in love to the solitude where the dead kings uselessly begged the heavens for their aid against Cortés, at the time when "fountains of light" were bursting open in the tenebrous cavern; and rather than to the world's great, his respects went to the mountains that rose like spectors but awakened no fear in him in the eloquent moonlight.

Mexico treated him kindly, as it knows how to do, gave him the gold of its hearts and of its coffee, sat in the togaed chair to judge that foreigner who was familiar with history as well as with laws, and who put the soul of Volney[23] into the epode of Pindar.[24] Magistrates are truly magistrates there where in the air itself splendor and repose go hand in hand. Heredia was proclaimed a natural magistrate, with no objections to his youth, and seated at the table like a brother. The courts there have persons in exalted positions, and the country's orators gave him the floor and accompanied him with palms. Poetry has pontiffs there, and everyone sought to take his arm. Lovely women are also there, tremulously exhaling their aroma when the poet went by. He fought the liberal "Yorkists" so the murderous "Scotsmen" would not get rid of the republic. He wrote, sang, argued, published, and poured out his heart in payment for Mexico's hospitality, but failed to feel beneath his feet that stability of his native soil which is man's only complete possession and a common treasure which equalizes and enriches everyone, and which, for personal happiness and general tranquility, must never be yielded or mortgaged or entrusted to another. Nor did he have the strength of his native soil; nor the pride with which virtue prevails in his country; nor could he expect any virgins or strong men to shed tears at his hero's grave, or place one of his country's palms upon the earth that would cover him. What is the matter with that poetry of his which

23. Contantin François de Volney (1757–1820), French historian and philosopher.

24. Pindar (518–446 B.C.), greatest of the Greek choral lyricists.

gave out regal sounds only when he was thinking about Cuba? And when he attempted another theme but that of his pain, or of the sea that carried him to Cuba's shores, or of the hurricane with whose force he wanted to attack the tyrants, it turned out like a judge's poetry—difficult and slothful, reminding one of big wilted flowers and faded tapestries—and not, as when his mind was upon Cuba, crowned with flashes of lightning.

His personal vanity failed to sustain him, because being of great worth, and for the very thing he served, he was not one of those men of myrrh and opopanax who declare their own value by displaying breast buttons for all to see, and hire the air to noise them about, and the sea to sing their glory, and consider the heavens their lunch and eternity their wine. No, he was a genius of a noble republic, and when indignation disturbed him or when he thundered against the slavish of the world and of his country, he was looked upon solely as a king. There are two classes of men: those who go about on foot, face to the sky, begging for the consolation of modesty to descend upon them, who live by tearing out their flesh with their teeth to obtain a little more bread or a little less, and rising above the tomb of their honor to go about wearing a diamond ring; and another class of men who kneel and kiss the cloaks of the world's great. In Heredia's country when he dedicated his tragedy *Tiberius* to Fernando VII, he thought in scalding phrases; in his country when he depicted in exemplary scenes the death of "The Last Romans," his thoughts were imposingly simple. No no, it was not the Romans who filled the poets's mind, now turned away from its most cherished hopes. For the sake of his country, and of the greatest country in our America, he had wanted the free republics to hold out their arms to the only nation in the emancipated family which was still kissing the feet of the enraged master. "Liberate America," he ordered, "go and rescue the island placed by nature as your porch and sentinel!" The continent was still pawing the ground—covered with foam, eyes flashing, flanks throbbing—from the run in which San Martín and Bolívar had carried their banners of the sun; may the liberating horse plunge into the sea and with a single onslaught of its chest throw the insecure despot out of Cuba! And Bolívar was already putting his foot into the stirrup when a man who spoke English came from the north with government documents, seized the horse by the bridle, and said to Bolívar: "I'm free, you're free, but that nation which will be mine because I want it for myself cannot be free!" And when Heredia saw freedom a criminal, and as ambitious as tyranny, he covered his face with his stormy cape and began to die.

He was already prepared to die of his own accord; for when greatness cannot be employed in the work of the charity and creation that nourish it, it devours the one who possesses it. Embittered by exile, that frenetic and chivalrous soul with such strong desires found no work in life's usual occupations, for when he saw that his first love was false and slavish to man, saw that genius was intimidated, virture impotent, and the world bereft of heroes, he wondered why his temples were throbbing, and he even tried, in a misplacement of purity, to free them from their bony prison. With the fall of an ideal humanity which promenades in splendor, the cup of death at his lips, for the sake of the stanzas of his youth he stood up, pale and sick, no longer strong enough except for the reflective poetry and artful drama that sparkled only when he was moved by the memory of his country, or by his horror of the turmoil of tyranny, or by his hatred of "infamous intrigues." He lived in the sun and abominated those who went about with their backs for hire, sharpening their tongues in secret to aim them at the pure in heart. If in order to live one had to accept with a docile smile complicity with flatterers, hypocrites, the harmful and the vain, he was loathe to smile or even to live. Why live if one cannot move across the earth like a comet across the sky? He felt like a deserted beach, like the shores of the sea. His tempestuous heart, tender as the heart of a woman, suffered under the domination of a bully or of the insolent like a flower under a horse's hoof. He took pity upon his horse, to the point of weeping with it and asking its forgiveness, when in the sudden start of a run he bloodied its flanks; and why did nobody take pity upon him? What good is virtue if the more one sees of it the more it is mortified, and there is a conspiracy, so to speak, among men to take the bread out of one's mouth and the soil from under one's feet? Enough of the traitorous glances of those who come like colored arrows whose points are smeared with curare; enough of those stern looks and abrupt letters and lukewarm greetings to darken his day. He needed nothing less than "universal tenderness." The indigent and monotonous house exacerbated his pain instead of calming it. His joy lay in affliction. He could not even think of his country, for there it was, the despot standing, the whip cracking, and every Cuban kneeling! From that weight of useless greatness, from idle passion and a vile life, this poet who no longer found any comfort upon earth except from one constant friend, was dying, painfully weaving his final verses. The knees of all those who bend them weighed heavily upon the heart of this honorable genius!

Even in his most polished poetry, which had to have something of the boudoir in those times of Millevoye[25] and Delille,[26] one notes the vehemence and simplicity which contrasts so handsomely with the natural pomp of the stanzas—to the extent that when an idea comes to nothing because of a poor subject or a false theme, the reader is deceived for quite some time by its thundering imperiousness before he realizes that the stanza is empty. The heroic temper of Heredia's spirit gives his lines constant loftiness, and the liveliness of his sensitivity takes him from one impression to another with the happiest of interruptions and compromises. From his earliest years he had been speaking a language at once exalted and natural, his greatest poetic invention. He imitated Byron's[27] love of horses, but whom did he imitate in his ode to Niagara[28] and to the Hurricane and to the Teocalli, and in his letter to Emilia and his

25. Charles Hubert Millevoye (1782–1816), French poet.

26. Abbé Jacques Delille (1783–1813), French poet and classicist, considered at the time as the "French Virgil."

27. George Gordon Byron (1788–1824), one of the great English Romantic poets, who died fighting for Greek independence.

28. *See* pp. 308–27.

lines to Elpino and those of the Invitation? He can be compared only to Sappho,[29] for she is the only one with his ardor and disarray. With a turn of phrase, in a dignified manner, and with grand effect, he left incomplete the lines of those sorrows which must not be profaned by discussion. He derived more effect from a sensitive manner of writing than from garish rhetoric. He looked for no comparisons in what he did not see, only in objects of nature which everyone could see and feel the way he did; nor had he a "beadwork" imagination—troublesome and useless—which creates vain and insignificant entities; he had a durable and obliging imagination consisting in highlighting what he depicted with the proper comparisons or allusions, and in exhibiting the captive and vibrant harmonies of nature. In his free and resonant prose itself there is a continuation of that broadwinged flight and movement at once rhythmic and unbridled. His prose has frequent gallicisms, in keeping with his times. There is much of Alfredo in his Hesiod, and many lines could be better than they are, just as when an eagle flies close to the sun, it has an occasional ugly feather. Hairdressing shops are where one has beauty spots applied; but who, when he is not holding a compulsory professorship, will spend his time going tooth and nail after the admirable work, vibrant with anguish, when there is really not enough time for charity and admiration?

Nobody depicts his torment better than he in the serious and ingenuous lines he wrote "on his birthday" when he described

> *the cruel state*
> *of an ardent heart without inamoratas.*

In his manner of loving a woman it is obvious that nature was short of blood to put into the veins of that Cuban, and put in lava instead. He loved freedom and his homeland as he loved Lesbia and Lola, the "beauty of sorrow," and the Andalusian María Pautret. It was a pure and honorable love which offered

29. Sappho (610–580 B.C.), celebrated lyric poet of Greece, famous for the beauty of her writing.

to his inamoratas in Olympian poetry a timid rose, a cool reed; and he took them for promenades where the turtledoves cooed, looking out for them respectfully. There was something of our peasants' artificial behavior in that outrageous lover who bent his knee and placed at the feet of his beloved his song with a golden hilt. He did not love in order to set his heart fluttering, but to stabilize it and consecrate his ardent youth. Walking with Lesbia at the age of sixteen, he trembled like every lover when her blond curls brushed against his forehead. Because he could not find a sensible woman he complained to the moon, which is very knowledgeable about these things. He loved furiously. He probably expired for love. He was unable to deal with the tumult of his love-stricken heart. No one defeated him in love, no one. With his great poetry he ennobled the most childish aspect of love, and the sweetest: the giving and withdrawing and giving again of his hands, the not knowing what to say, the sudden blurting out of everything. He would leave a ball like a star-crowned king because he had seen the one he loved there. Any man who danced with his beloved was unworthy—devoid of feeling and unworthy. Cuba applauded the object of his love, Catulus sent her the girdle of Venus, and the gods of Olympus were envious. He trembled beside Emilia in the romantic days of his persecution in Cuba, but the young man's nobility was more powerful than seductive solitude. He endured by escaping from himself at the side of the poor "rose of our fields," who bent before him, dazzled, like a flower before the sun. He suffered to the point of pining away, and was proud that his brow showed a lovesick pallor. Who doubts that the object of one's love embraces the entire universe? He was no longer fond of beauties, for since one of them deceived him he discovered that the world is vile; yet he could not live without them. Why was it that women were unable to tenderly love that man who was all that captures and seduces a woman's superior soul: sensitive, fearless, chivalrous, vehement, and faithful—and in addition to all those qualities, handsome? Why were they unable to love that meek and unhappy man who put a rug under their feet and then suddenly straightened up before them like an exasperated sovereign? And what is life's power and its only wellspring but the love of woman?

Weary of those fond encounters and the power they gave him, he raised his renewed thinking to the heights of nature, and he who had wrapped his song to Lola in rose petals saddled his swift horse an hour later, looked up at the turbulent sky bareheaded, and in the brightness of the lightning ventured to escape into the darkness of the night. Or when the ship's watch, straddling the broken mast and blinded by the lightning, refused to challenge the storm. Standing at the bow, the invisible stirrups impatient at his heels, his eyes happy and sparkling, Heredia saw the mist spread over the sky and the waves prepared for combat. Or when evening invited man to meditation, with a firm step he would climb the mountain which night had covered with darkness; and at the summit, while the stars were lighting up, he would think about the course of nations and surrender to melancholy. And when there was no mountain to climb, he saw out of his inner self the world being born and ending, as if it were there at his feet, and how the spirited and triumphant ocean was spreading its immensity over him.

One day a devoted friend, one solitary friend, held out his arms and entered the room of a constable from Havana, and there, sitting upon a bench awaiting his turn, his small and noble hands already transparent, a final glow in his eyes, was the poet who had been brave enough for everything but to die without seeing his mother and his palm trees once again. He left there trembling upon the arm of his friend. When he regained his freedom at sea, encouraged by his mother's kiss, he again found, to take leave of the world, the words with which he had astonished it in the early years of his youth; and in the silence of night he flickered out like a weak lamp in the valley where the sun-gilded summits of Popocatepetl and Iztaccihuatl keep a perennial watch. There he died, and that was the appropriate place to die for the man who, to be a symbol of his country in all things, bound us, in his voyage from cradle to grave, to the nations which creation has given to us as companions and brothers. Through his father he bound us to Santo Domingo, seedbed of heroes where, in the bleeding mahogany trees, in the plaintive cane fields, and in the invincible forests, the heart of Guarocuya, oozing knowledge and decrees, is as if still alive. Through his boyhood he bound us to Venezuela where the crumpled mountains seem like blankets rather than folds of land—blankets left behind by the heroes when they went to heaven to give an account of their battles for freedom. And through his death he bound us to Mexico, immense temple built by nature so that the terrible and final justice of America's independence might be consumed, as in former times the sacrifices in its teocallis, upon the crests of its steps of mountain ranges.

And if the possible disappearance and the future of his country is symbolized even in the disappearance of his remains, which cannot be found, then, oh immortal Niagara, there is still one useful stanza of your superb poetry needed! Demand, oh Niagara, of the One who giveth and taketh away, that every nation upon earth shall be free and just; that no nation whatsoever shall employ the power obtained by freedom to take it away from those who have shown themselves worthy of it; that if any nation dares to lay hands upon another, let not the sister nations of the abandoned one aid in the robbery without bursting out of your borders, oh Niagara!

Not my words but the voices of the torrent, the prisms of the falls, the plumes of color springing from its breast, and the rainbow girdling its temples, are proper homage to the great poet in his grave. There, before the conquered marvel, is where one must go to salute the conquering genius. There, invited to admire the marvel's majesty and meditate upon its crashing din, arrived not a month ago the envoys whom the American nations sent to assemble in winter to discuss the world of America and to hear the crashing thunder of the falls. The son of Montevideo stood up and cried "Heredia!" The man from Venezuela, remembering its glorious infancy, cried, "Heredia!" . . . The Cubans in that gathering, as if unworthy of themselves and of him, cried "Heredia!" All of America cried "Heredia!" And the statues of the Mexican emperors tipped their stone hats to him;

Central America saluted him with its volcanoes, Brazil with its palm groves, Argentina with its seas of pampas, the distant Araucanos with their spears. And we guilty ones, how shall we salute him? Give us, oh Father, enough virtue for the women of our time to weep for us as the women of yours wept for you; or make us perish in one of the cataclysms you loved, if we fail to learn to be worthy of you!

Francisco Sellén

Poetry is certainly not what occurs merely by virtue of its name; it is the heroic and virginal aspect of one's sentiments arranged so that it flows in ringing tones and carries one along like wings. Or it is the select and subtle part of the human soul, and the soul of the earth with its harmonies and dialogues, or the good order of worlds in which sublimated man is annihilated or excels. The one who makes an ant begin to walk, with a soap bubble upon its back, is not a poet. Nor is the one who goes out upon his balcony, in bowler hat and cutaway coat, to serenade the Middle Ages with a bouquet of parchment flowers; nor the desperate role-player who denies a purpose to Nature because he feels his own life to be aimless. Everyone who puts politics and sociology into verse is not a poet; a poet is one who sheds enlightenment and fragrance, from a heart streaked with blood like a hyacinth, or beating within it as upon a martial drum and unafraid of the beat, he calls the world to faith and victory and moves men heavenward where he goes from echo to echo, soaring to the drum roll. Poetry is poetry and not a meat and vegetable stew, or an exercise for flutes, or a rosary of blue beads, or a madwoman's patchwork shawl made out of scraps of silk and stitched with pessimistic thread, to show the world she is a lady of fashion who has just received the latest styles from Germany or France.

All America has read Francisco Sellén's poetry, for he is the tireless artist who lets no day slip by "without a line of verse," nor believes that there is any greater pleasure than silently complying with his duty, beyond which there is no true poetry, and spreading the cult of the beautiful idea. A son of that land bled white who desperately atones for an iniquitous abundance; a son of Cuba whose inexperienced heroes were given time to err by the indifference of an insensitive continent, Sellén could not return to where every leaf is an accusation, and the belted and spurred overseer, with Phryne upon his knee, serves poisoned wine in creole goblets. Nor could he take from his shattered life—a life he offered to his country in her tragic hour—the poetic energy of those who live upon their native soil without the affliction of breathing borrowed air and without the solitude so frightening to loving hearts. And since the only way to be a poet of one's oppressed country is to be a soldier, he did not decry his exile by grumbling childishly, nor did he set up a shop for rhyming where he rhymed everything that came into his head—today an ode to charity and tomorrow a rhapsody to a mockingbird. But since the sources of his own poetry were shut off or interrupted, he kept the hopes of his genius alive with other people's poetry.

One day it was Ibsen,[1] another Blumenthal;[2] one month the Greeks, another the Russians. He studied Khayyam and then Horace. Hidden away in the high Himalayas or upon the banks of the Arno, he would read the original and follow it throughout literature, from one copy to another. He was not a random reader who takes from his desk everything brought by the daily post, and behaving like a poetic dandy promenades the latest models from journal to journal—sometimes in tears, wearing dalmatic and breeches, his blond toupee crowned with daisies and forget-me-nots; sometimes prophetic, with bright red lips, mascaraed eyes, dark suit of austere cut, a piece of junk in his buttonhole and a glass of absinthe in his trembling hand. No, he would read selectively, at times considering the principal quality

1. Henrik Ibsen (1828–1906), Norwegian playwright, creator of the modern realistic drama and one of the greatest influences on the theater of all times.

2. Oskar Blumenthal (1852–1917), German dramatist and wit, founder of the Lessing Theater in Berlin.

of each literary genre in itself, or in what it took from the others, at times studying the passions common to all of them, in order to note how to state them, and their stories, at times comparing the poets of one frame of mind, or one period of history, to see how the light was reflected equally from different glasses. This he did until he found that man's thought is like trees whose roots are few and whose leaves are many, and that man is simple and individual, as is shown in his literature where the romantic and the real are seen at the same time, the only difference being the literature put into the imagination, through individual themes, by the country and times of each poetic composition. He saw eternal simplicity and the demise of pomp.

He heard better music from the vague and essential than from the weakened and academic. In the art of the imagination fable and allegory seemed more proper to him than polemic and discourse. He carried within him the kind of twilight inherent in those who know all they have to know about the world, and whose faces shine with the light of the future. Why is there a sun if he did not have one in his own country? Nor was the sun real if he did not have it in his own life. Since "Intimate Book," a work written in his youth, he knew that one must travel the earth in rapid flight, because from every grain of dust an enemy rises to bring down, by hook and arrow, everything born with wings. He began to put his love into the silent stars, and eagerly studied the languages of those nations of perpetual snow whose blue and white poetry soars to the sky in nights that are eloquent with groups of flirtatious women with golden hair falling down their backs. Neither was he to sing of his sorrows, for such continuous complaining is like taking away one's sex. Nor was he to serve his country bonbons or baskets of strawberries when his country, upright among the corpses, was pointing out to the impassive world, with its wasted hand, the feast of crows. And his hateful, buttressed, routine life upon the shores of the hostile Hudson was not by any chance to give him that brief and immortal bloom of enlightenment with which the poet, matured by grief, embellishes his soul. Nor is the inflated and garish, erysipelatous Castillian employed in poems the precise and radiant language from which poetry must speak.

Thus, in search of the honest and ideal, Sellén became so dedicated to the German, where man's entire work is translated, that he lived year after year immersed in matters relating to his art as if forgetful of self and as if he were not a poet eager only to put before the public what he considered beautiful, and to work to perfect his poetry and test it in the sunlight until he left it in its natural colors. This was an arduous task, because the German is rose-colored and blue, and the Castillian yellow and deep scarlet, and the moonbeams slipped in and out between his fingers so that he could never find a way to imprison them in his lace. He was captivated first and foremost by Heine,[3] who lived with his heart stabbed, for everyone suffers from dagger thrusts. He was captivated by Geibel[4] because of his tenderness and intensity, and translated him with brotherly care. The invincible Goethe moved him less than the etherial Uhland,[5] and the loyal Hartmann,[6] and the pitiful and forsaken Kerner.[7] One day he would work with the subtlety of Von Arnim,[8] another with the ardent Freiligrath,[9] or with Bodestedt[10] who was made for the firm Persian quatrain, or with Simniock whose words were coins, or with Rüchert[11] who wrote with

3. Heinrich Heine (1797–1856), German poet and prose writer, famous for his lyric poetry and biting satire in prose.

4. Emmanuel Geibel (1815–1884), German poet and dramatist.

5. Ludwig Uhland (1787–1862), German romantic poet, author of historical ballads and lyrics.

6. Hartmann von Ane (1170–1220), German poet, master of the court epic in Middle High German.

7. Justinus Andreas Kerner (1786–1862), German poet and spiritualist.

8. Ludwig Achim von Arnim (1781–1831), German romantic novelist and poet.

9. Hermann Ferdinand Freiligrath (1810–1876), one of the outstanding German revolutionary poets of the nineteenth century.

10. Friedrich Martin von Bodenstadt (1819–1892), German poet and scholar.

11. Friedrich Rückert (1788–1866), German poet, translator of Oriental poetry.

roots. He chose to expose them to view rather than expose himself. He wanted to give comfort and spread pure beauty throughout the Spanish-speaking world. And he translated so continuously that to judges who do not delve deeply, he seemed like a born translator carrying an empty casket and filling it with everything he found along the way. They lost sight of his efforts to master the language, or his passion for an essential and enduring poetry, or his honesty to hold his tongue until he had something to say. Why should one not praise, without fear of appearing to be an easily pleased critic, this vigorous poet who emerges safely from all the literary forms, and sings with the faith of a lover the eternal spirit of Nature, in stanzas built upon his heart?

The book is called *Poems*, and there are few of them in it, for genuine poetry, in which the whole of life at times shows only a single facet, is like a diamond. The first thing that attracts one's attention is the modesty with which the poet presents his writings, as if they were mere students' essays and not works of art in which every composition lives independently, and all of them together ring out the world's final peace and angelic glory, like a chorus of different voices. The poet divides his book in two parts: "Before the War" and "After the War," like a tree trunk split in half by lightning. And there is not one Cuban who does not go through the world in this way: split in two by lightning. Ever since his youth Sellén has been self-controlled, going to his heart for inspiration, to the earth for agony, and to repose for passion. From his earliest attempts he put aside fear. He hardly ever hoped or desired. His "Desires" are imitated: his nature is not to desire, and therein lies his greatness. "Smoke and Ashes" is illusion; he trembles from "what I need to move ahead"; he wants to "forget all that exists"; he imagines the sky to be quieter than it is, and envies it because it is calm "while the storm rages in my breast"; but "if you suffer, be still"; if you weaken, look at your home, at your child in whom your own life continues, at the solemn evening, and turn your hand to the plow! Anyone who reads his song to "The Butterflies" will love all things, for it is like the play of a rainbow, a beautiful sorrow, that remains in the soul! For him everything has spirit and pain;

he suffers for everything and for everything "I open my heart to the infinite." Seeing flowers makes him want to become a lightning bolt and climb heavenward to drink of flaming water and descend upon the world with outspread wings "lavishly shedding torrents of happiness, light and freedom." Never, never will he talk about his sorrows for fear of prostituting them, and because a man should talk about his sorrows only if they can benefit and comfort mankind. What he desires is death: "eternal dawn," "the voluptuous bed." The first stanza of "Hymn to Death" seems to ascend at nightfall from gigantic lilies, like a flock of virgins. Death roams the world upon fragrances, like an aerial queen. Death is an affable lover, not a ravenous witch. The world is going to open "like an immense flower." He considers the Virgin Most Merciful with Christ in her arms, as Death receiving mankind. And the bird of Storms—almost sublimely symbolic, its plumage black and its song prophetic, piercing the overcast and huddled in the mist—serenely intones, in the brilliance of the lightning flash, the funereal hymn to those who "died in the sea."

In love with an image, he errs here by repeating in it what he said in the previous one, or he discredits a natural picture with a metaphoric word, or he completes the stanza with a rubber stamp rhyme, or he weakens the poem with a facile epithet, or, with the deceptive authority of prosody, he gives a diphthong more value than it musically and logically deserves. But although sometimes unsure in this first part, the style proceeds in waves and masses from one color to another, and these colors soar when he sings "River Waves," or they hum, whirl, and stop out of breath like the frenzied, whirling couples in "A Dance in Cuba."

And what of the second part written in the sunset of his life? From the maelstrom of men, freer in the blue air because of long and restricted life in prison, "The Captive Condor" appears from mountain to mountain, ripping the mists with his beak, flapping his wings among the smoke and lava, crowning his head with lightning, flying among the suns to see which of them is greater, his or the sky's. A victory hymn rings out; the mountains are perfume censers, the stars steps; the stanzas, with truth upon their backs, climb from cloud to cloud like young girls with their amphoras. From the heights this magnificent poet proclaims universal brotherhood; in the epic dawn new faith descends upon the world's spirit. Everything throbs and sings; the human heart, which is one with the star and the flower, fills with ineffable tenderness; the beauty of sorrow enhances the face and purges the storm or Nature, like the flame of the consumed tree trunk, the flame of death that purifies and transforms and breathes forth life, joyful and new. Everything throbs and sings. And the essential and absolute poet, in his vision of the greater spirituality, suffers gently like myrrh in the censer, and surrenders to the life-filled air which carries him—in its soaring and whirling, with its ascending aromas and disengaged souls—to where upon a pinnacle of light, like jewels returning to a broken crown, the twinkling stars fit into their sockets.

Continuous and sensitive pain, by which man knows himself and is ennobled, purifies and exalts the spirit that clings to it as to true salvation, and the cross that drew blood from men becomes the anchor that moors the purified soul in an eternal snug harbor. As with the effect of fire upon quartz, which makes beautiful gold ooze from its smoking fissures, so the perennial pain of flame discloses life's reality among the falling dross. It doubles the toil of punishment for the rebellious soldier who wishes to climb to the heights without having felled the mountain tree with his own hands, or arduously fashioned the steps. Pain beats and knocks to the ground the lazy man who wants to go, in top hat and coach and without paying the toll, through the gate leading from the world's unhappiness to perpetual happiness, and knocks him down again each time he rises to his feet. It comforts those who suffer fearlessly and take pleasure in their suffering, insinuating into the purified soul the certainty of serene eternity and the kinship of all creation. With a feeling of solemnity, pleasant as music, the world begins filling with pure forgiveness spread by the soul and by pleasure.

Every sorrow brings its own bundle of firewood that feeds the bonfire with faith in the spiritual and successful aspect of the zenith of universal life to which all things ascend by means of trials, and of which this present life is merely a harsh and preparatory fragment. A vague and happy familiar feeling, so to speak, and a tenuous but lofty splendor follows the rudimentary doubt, childish discontent, or satanic turbulence, and vanishes among the clamor, lights, and hymns. The alienated soul opens to an invisible sun like the lilies of the field. And groups of worlds, breathing soul, pass by to the spontaneous and continuous chords of the universal lyre, at times slow and serious, at times strident and trembling with fear. And in their glorious march, and in the function and harmonies of their elements, the pain-seasoned poet glimpses, for the time when wisdom achieves perfection, the triumphal song of the final epic poem.

Sellén believes in "Preexistence," a poem well known both in Spanish and English, for in some other life, whatever it might be, he proved this: "words are useless for explaining what can be perceived only by the soul"; in "Pantheism" he salutes in this world the "glorious love feast of the early Christians that is still in progress, the mysterious and eternal glass from which drink all present beings and all who have been." In "Transformation" he entones with the joy of spring "the powerful anthem that has been resounding since the dark beginnings of time"; in "Meditation," the spirit departed, he sees in the glare of mournful comets "the empty earth" rotate, grown cold. In "Aspiration" he dares not state, with the rigor of wisdom, the things that Nature sings to him in her resolute voice, but begs the stars, "tormented by immortal desire, to take him in their bustling nightly rounds to the palace of the infinite, to the great abundance that spills the immense cascade of diamonds." His eagerness, however, is no longer that longing, forgivable in youth, to be saved from suffering by death, and to flee to where there is no suffering. Inevitable pain flourishes in his life, and he begins to call it "the only thing that is eternal and true." But later he loves his pain because it makes him brother to every living thing, and he discovers the beautiful truth of comforting others, for although it may not seem so it is more characteristic of man to give comfort than to receive it. This is apparent in the fact that a person's joy in receiving good is less than when he does good. Sellén suffers until he inadvertently falls into imitation suffering, and bids goodby to the "sun of illusions" in an "Autumn Afternoon," or he becomes sad because he fails to see the month of May in himself when he publishes his "Spring Morning" in its entirety. But his grief is not ornamental like that of professional doubters who cannot see that in creation everything affirms and persists, and who go away as soon as the maid serves the wine and pastry. Nor does he copy from the French their pessimism translated from the German; rather, in the happiness that springs from his own grief like the dawn that follows night, and in the celestial purity left in his soul from obedience to duty and knowledge of the natural, just like pure air blowing in the heights, he learns without violence, and with the unanimous testimony of all that exists, that the eternal is both desirable and beautiful, and that one must court pain instead of running away from it, for he who renounces and masters himself goes from this life into the joy of a majestic and divine freedom of will where the spirit, united with the universe, loses the notion of and the desire for death.

His is not the dismal eternity of Leconte de Lisle,[12] nor does he consider the living as "incurable imbeciles" as does Leopardi. He does not proclaim the finality of death and the futility of living as does Louisa Ackermann. Instead, he leaps impulsively from his sorrows to the universal peaks, a flame upon his helmet like the legendary warriors. His stanzas are feathered with plumes from the bird of paradise whenever his poetry sings of the radiant and eternal universe. "There is a soul in all things." "The note of a forgotten song reveals to the soul its previous existence." "The world is harmony, a flame that is never extinguished." "Life proceeds from sun to atom, and from man to star." All is life and light and movement.

12. Leconte de Lisle (1818–1894), poet, leader of the Parnassians, and known as the foremost French poet, apart from Victor Hugo, until the rise of Charles Baudelaire.

In his more personal poems, which are in the minority, this majestic concept of creation persists, and "its trees are like its soul"—roots driven into the earth but branches in the sky. Like childhood memories, he sings about "the gulf current" in grave and copious lines of poetry to justify this daring image by the volume and nobility of the words. When he goes to the "Sea-shore," for him "the origin of life," it is not like a dishevelled rhapsody for setting to rights his odes on the drum, nor is it academic pomposity with the congregation out in front, as in a theater, for people to look at one another and say how fine it is and that Pindar has come back to life. No, it is to sink into his noble silence and invite it to plunge downward upon "those dreadful Gehennas and infamous slave prisons."

He loves the ox just like Carducci,[13] and sings about it in a sonnet resembling a Japanese window, delicate as the finest cabinet work, through which one can see, carved out of the blue, the blossom-covered ridge of hillocks with their green valleys, and there in a pleasant cluster of trees by the peasant's house, like a golden seed. For him Helios is "divine," and his poetry aspires to a Grecian beauty that captivates by reason of the whole and abhors the exaggerated line. But his is not the Hellenism[14] of that "second son" who transposes the idylls of flute and cloven hoof into the tongues of today, and starts going to the silk hat and dress coat satyrs; rather, it is that wise agreement between language and ideas where the idea is not dressed up in a three-tiered skirt edged with passementerie, but is as smooth and imposing as a good statue—that art of stripping the subject of all that fails to help and enhance it, without putting into every detail so much color that the description is disfigured by it, or so little that the description appears distorted or limited. For what is eternal about the Greeks is not what we are told of Atis and Cybele;[15] it is the harmony and

13. Bartolomeo Carducci (1560–1610), Spanish painter.

14. Hellenism referred to the devotion to or imitation of the culture of the ancient Greeks.

15. In Greek mythology, Cybele was the wife of Cronos and the mother of the Olympian God.

deliberation by which they acquired the fullness of beauty. Sellén's understanding of Hellenism is not like that of the others who carve the marble but forget to give it blood; in Sellén's poetry—beautiful as the frothing, leaping colt that pulls its head away from the tamer—the romance constituting and animating the verse flows along impetuously and unexpectedly.

He is not a single note poet who sometimes plays it in war, sometimes on the gaita, and sometimes on the flageolet; he expresses passion, the essence of poetry, as his state of mind desires—whether gentle and contemplative, like fire smothered in the embers, or flickering like a tongue of flame, or flowing downward like waves of lava. His love is not a cipher written in the sand, but a hieroglyph carved upon a pyramid: "she who loves him is like a new temple receiving its God"; when they kiss, lightning springs forth and the world begins to sing praises. When he eulogizes pagan love, the pagan is himself; he is young India when he sings the Indian *areito*. His dramatic ballad "The Fugitives" deserves to figure among the very best of Castillian poetry because of its stanzas that rise and fall with the waves like the ship in which the young couple slips away, or it trembles like the chin of the father pursuing them. In the duel between the brothers, the startled stanza gallops along and startles the reader, and with the dead rider's horse it follows the murderer into the grave. When describing "the tropical night," he does not set about disrupting the scene by intruding his person like the personal poets; rather, the person appears where he should, which is in the art of painting the picture so that it produces sound, mystery, and terror, at times by means of groups of accents vaguely disposed to sudden congestion, at times by means of the similarity of the phrase to the incident or object he describes. And if what he loves makes him suffer, he will take revenge in "unjustice" by kissing the hand, or writing, with a grandiose love, "The two waves": man and woman, together through the world, holding hands through the world—two who have suffered! He is not a man to complain of the burden like a boudoir lover, and walk over the rest, sucking upon souls and leaving them strangled at the edge of the road. He accompanies them hand in hand, singing in his grief a song of courage, and if they tire of walking, taking them upon his back. He has a sensitive adoration for his country and loves the poor man, although he does not go about saying so in white necktie and starched shirt front, with a glass of sugar water on the table, like so many who go out to be charitable in verse, and who are professional sufferers, as if almsgiving in public were not always ugly, in verse or in any other way.

"He will descend from heaven itself to lavish the poor man with happiness." In the hour of struggle he offered his life to his country. And when singing the praises of his country, his eight line stanzas "To the Memory of Heroes" give off smoke like a funeral pyre. His ten line stanzas "To Cuba" weep like grieving mothers. He hides a sword among the flowers in "Song of Waiting." His "Song of War" darts from hill to hill like a prancing horse. His patriotic verse glistens like polished guns. But he never diminishes the dignity of his most sensitive feelings with verbose pomp.

Thus does this poet school himself with more than an occasional reflection from his readings, for he is a poet free from erudition, and he shines through his original poems in an age where there were as many mixtures as there are now, where nations copy other nations to excess, without confining themselves to draw from a study of those others the knowledge of man's identity by which nations still in the process of emerging must improve and mix together. But absorbing all that theory—whether out of curiosity or sterility of inventiveness or intellectual dependence—he comes to the market place surfeited.

In America one suffers from this more than in any other nation, for the Spanish speaking countries receive nothing from Spain except warmed-over food, and because of the ignorant and mixed population they inherited they still do not have a national character able to do more in behalf of poetic innovation than the literature where the impatient genius of its sons is nurtured and accomodated. Bécquer's genius has already met its end the way a portrait is put aside when one knows the beautiful original; and that of Nuñez de Arce is going to meet its end because new faith is dawning and careworn doubt must not prevail, so that through merit alone it may wear a less dazzling cape than the cape of romanticism. Now, with a desire for the contemporary, the accessibility of language, and the laudable urge toward perfection, what is beginning to prevail is French influence, which in these days of transition does not have much to say. Therefore, while new ways of thinking consolidate, they polish and perfect the form, and at times carve in precious stones the fine, small-faceted containers into which they empty all the grace and color they can find in the ancient. Or they rhyme, for ostentation and amusement, the fashionable, lace cuff pessimism so typical of unemployed writers in a city rich in literature. Poets of imagination cannot see this from afar, or those who live with an aesthetic spirit in decayed or not yet well developed nations fail to take this seriously because of their hopeless lives.

For Sellén the danger was greater, because ever since boyhood he had gone from Petofi[16] to Gogol[17] and from Firdusi[18] to Hugo, and because he had had a permanent home in the United States where his poetry was influenced by the mystery of Poe,[19] the prophetic ode of Emerson, and the revolutionary rhythm of Walt Whitman. In addition to all, the poet lives an immaculate life with his hidden sorrows, heeding the universal song and proclaiming, with a vague but ardent faith, an empire of happiness, the force of virtue, and the world's spirituality.

This is not to say that others here may not have found "the soul of things" from Lucretius, or that what Sellén repeats has not been said before. Everything has already been said; but

16. Sandor Petofi (1823–1849), great Hungarian poet and revolutionary.

17. Nicolai Vasilievich Gogol (1809–1852), Russian novelist, author of *Dead Souls*.

18. Firdusi (941–1020 A.D.), Persian poet, author of *Shabnamah* (*Book of Kings*), Persian national epic.

19. Edgar Allan Poe (1809–1849), American poet, critic, and short-story writer, considered father of the mystery story.

every time a thing is sincere, it is new. To verify is to create. What the world makes grow is not the discovery of how it is done, but the effort each one puts forth in discovering it. So let us not look upon a tree as plagiarism, for men have been seeing trees all their lives! And is not every man alive a plagiarism? He who takes from himself what others have taken from themselves first, is as original as they. Tell the truth you feel, and say it with as much art as possible. In poetry emotion is the main thing, as a sign of the passion that moves it, and it must not be warmed-over or something remembered, but a jolt of the instant, and a breeze or an earthquake from one's entrails. In poetry what is left for later is lost, since the principal thing in poetry is neither understanding nor memory; it is a certain state of spiritual confusion and tempestuousness in which the mind functions merely as an aid, putting and taking away, until the music is able to contain what comes from outside of it. Here Sellén errs at times, although not much, as when he says: "Farewell to Youth" in some alexandrine lines composed of old sorrows, or when from his past memories he writes "Calm." This poem did not turn out so well as other poems of his, for in poetry as in painting one must work from a model; or when in "The Sea" one observes that certain lines were weak because they were not inscribed upon the rock as they should have been, with a hand moist from the flying chips. But Sellén, an honest poet, usually waits for the time to rhyme, with neither violence nor an eagerness to be seen, and stops as soon as his emotion stops. Poetry must have its roots in the earth and a basis in reality.

Cloud castles vanish. Without emotion one can be a sculptor in verse or a painter in verse, but not a poet.

What gives Sellén a character of his own and a right to consider himself among the best, however, is the novelty of working his poetry as the art it is, and of struggling with his emotion, assisting it or paring it down until it takes a suitable form. Art does not lie in becoming too familiar with the hiding places of the language, or in scattering violent or archaic words among the lines. There is no art in tarnishing the natural beauty of the poetic idea by crowning its head with a mitre of ostentatious stones as if it were a Russian bride; it lies in choosing words so that with their frivolity or stateliness they enliven the poetry or give it an imperial pace. The words may whistle or hum, or whirl and creep and move with the idea, spreading and fighting or weakening and cooing, or end like sunlight in a sky aflame. What is said need not be said by thought alone, but by the poetry with it; and if by its accent and length the word fails to suggest the idea within it, then the poem is at fault. Every emotion and every hour of the day has its own poetic foot. A state of love requires dactyls, wedding ceremonies, anapests, jealousy, iambics. Marshy ground full of rushes is depicted by stanzas frivolous as waving wheat, and the trunk of an oak tree by phrases that are wrinkled, contorted, and profound. In the language of the emotions, as in the Greek ode, one must hear the wave upon which it breaks, and the wave that answers, and then the echo. Art does not consist in contrivance or ostentation; it consists in a language conforming to the occasion described; in the poem coming out of the oven in one piece, as genuine emotion delivers it, and not full of holes or lacking outlines, later to be stuffed with empty adjectives, in the torture of the library, or have its corners patched with stucco. For the sake of keeping the primitive impression unchanged, Sellén has left a prosaic line here and there, something his skill has enabled him to do so well, and has endowed it with wings as every line of poetry must be endowed, for it is an aerial art in which mere reasoning, or contrived turns of phrase, or clamor have no place. He still prefers Latin elegance to creole roots. The forest is still "a shady place," he has a "thirst for the unknown," and *esperanza* (hope) rhymes with *lontananza* (distance). But even in this second part there is little catalectic or hypermetric poetry; the lines follow obediently where the poet leads them. The lively, happy language seems to be filled with breezes and fresh air when he describes "Daybreak," or vagueness and sluggishness in "Autumn Afternoon," or darkness and luminosity in "Cuban Melody." "Sapphire suns appeared out of silent chasms like squadrons"; "the great canopy of sublime gems"; "wants to merge with the brilliant and adamantine sphere"; "it will bind silken garlands of flowers to the wheel of time." Whenever his stanzas "To L. . ." are read, he seems to rise through the air like the fragrance of a gently shaken rose bush. These lines show by example all that proceeds from the idea in an arrangement of words, which in the art of writing is decisive, and only the ignorant ignore or scoff at it. The poems skip about like water lilies when air from the lake frolics with them. The poem moves on, chastised and fleeing, when a wild dog moves on. Every picture carries words of an appropriate color; for there are weak words such as the rose-colored or gray, and radiant words, and humid words. The blue seeks some rapid and vibrant accents, and the black others that are obscure and extended. A tone is obtained with certain words that with others would render the idea false and without strength, because this tonal art in poetry is nothing less than saying what is meant so the meaning is achieved and made to endure, or not saying it. Therefore Sellén, who is master of his tongue, ponders the accents, reducing or accumulating them so that every one of his compositions cajoles the eyes and ears at the same time, thus reaching the imagination by both roads. He pours the poem, or waves it, or furls it around the flagstaff. And when he wants to describe the multiple aspects of Nature in "Pantheism," he puts into each line the right epithet and the substantial noun that belongs there. Each stanza is a new aspect, mild or terrible, and the rough after the smooth. He calculates everything with orchestral subtlety so that one tone runs through the diverse tones, and the different tones, all bound to a single expression, break with the force of a choir in the final canticle, and the simple colossal music of the Universe prevails in this poem as in all his poetry.

And if something more were needed, besides decorum and his agile inspiration, to explain the energetic simplicity and intimate charm of this poetic art, it would be the noble peace to which, by the narrow stairway of virtue, the ever victorious poet has arrived. Those who know him say that his emigrant's table has no trout bellies to offer the accomodating newsmonger, and that there is no new tunic in his wardrobe for the ill-clad critics. They say that after his work is finished, he spends every evening among his books, placed in rows with the careful attention of a lover, in the room where his wife suffers in the grip of poor health. She gazes upon him and doubts that his spirit is that of the man he is, but believes it is the spirit of the flowers in her window that he himself waters for her before leaving for work. They say that slender threads of blood flow silently out of his stern and immaculate heart, and that his exemplary life has been dedicated to kindness and sacrifice.

El Partido Liberal (Mexico), September 20, 1890

Julián del Casal[1]

Such a beautiful name, which at the bottom of his sad and silken poetry seemed rather like some romantic invention rather than reality, is no longer the name of a living man. This pure spirit, this tender and timorous affection, the ideal course of this life, this melancholy love for the beauty absent from his native land—because literature can be clothed in mourning or prostituted only in a country without freedom—are now nothing but a handful of poems printed upon wretched paper, as wretched as the poet's life is said to have been.

His spirit lived from beauty, from the etched crystal of Japanese delicacy, from the color of absinthe and of roses fresh from the garden, from perfect, exquisite women adorned with silver finely wrought; and he, like Cellini, put Jupiter upon a saltcellar. Abhorring the false and pompous, he died because of a frail body, or the sorrow of living, with his graceful, loving sense of fantasy, in a servile and disfigured nation. Pleased with art for having enjoyed the art of France so intimately, he could be said to have been adopted, though reluctantly, by that worthless poetry with which in recent years the goldsmiths of Parisian verse amused the empty ideals of their changing times. There is still some worthwhile poetry in this world, if one gets along with it in a dignified manner; all is the moral courage with

1. Julián del Casal (1863–1893), Cuban poet, close friend of the great Nicaraguan poet, Rubén Darío.

which one faces and overcomes life's apparent injustice. As long as there is one good thing left to accomplish, one right to defend, one honest and powerful book to read, one corner of a mountain, one good woman, one true friend, the sensitive heart will be strong enough to love and praise the beauty and order of life, odious at times because of the brutal wickedness with which greed and vengeance deform it. That triumph is the seal of greatness. Antonio Pérez spoke this truth: "Only great stomachs can digest poison."

Julián del Casal is very well known and loved throughout our America, and now we will hear the eulogies and grief. The fact is that in America the new people are in full bloom, demanding some weight from prose and some quality from poetry. They want effort and reality in politics and in literature. They became tired of presumptuous, empty and undeveloped politics, and of that false lustiness in literature that was so reminiscent of Cervantes' madman's dogs who were driven away. This literary generation in America is like a family, for it began with the imitative quest, and is now in the free and concise elegance, the sincere and artistic expression, brief and chiselled, of personal feeling, and direct, creole wisdom. For these laborers poetry must be sonorous and swiftly moving. Since poetry stems from the emotions it must be as delicate and profound as the note of a harp. One need not state rarities, only the rare instant of a noble or pleasing emotion. And it was that kind of poetry, so praised and loved by Americans, that Julián del Casal wrote. Then there was another reason why they loved him: the sad and whimsical poetry with its lofty rhyme that he received from France he transformed into the natural expression of the limited fondness that such a delicate artist must have felt for that country so dear to his heart. For France is a country where a hidden or confessed awareness of the general humiliation leads everyone as if intimidated or veiled, with neither the taste nor the power for frankness and the graces of the soul. Poetry lives from honor.

This poor poet died before we were able to know him. It is the way all of us go in this poor land of ours, divided in two with our energies strewn over the world, living without individuality among alien souls, and with the foreigner sitting in the armchair of our own people! We exasperate instead of loving one another. We arouse jealousy instead of building roads together. We love one another as if through prison bars. Truly it is time to put an end to this! The sad young Julián del Casal has died. His poetry remains. America loves him for his honesty and purity. Women weep over him.

Patria (New York), December 31, 1893

Charles Darwin[1]

Darwin was a grave old man who glowed with the pride of having seen. His hair fell over his shoulders like a white mantle. His forehead terminated in the craggy brows of one who has often closed his eyes to see better. His gaze was benevolent, as it is in those who live in fruitful communion with Nature, and his hand, soft and affectionate, was made to care for birds and plants.

He had created about him a living miniature of the universe he carried in his spacious mind: here a mound of moist earth in which to observe insects preparing the vegetal layer, there a family of plants eloquently arranged to show the elaboration of a flowering plant from a plant initially barren of flowers, and beneath that bell jar, a tiny island of the coral that had revealed to him the master work of the lowliest organism. Off in a corner of his garden, he kept the group of voracious plants that subsist on tiny insects, like that terrifying African plant that spreads its brightly mottled leaves on the ground and suddenly, as a lion grasps a man, enfolds its prey in the broad, liplike leaves that crush and drain of blood like the boa, and drop their lifeless victim to the ground once they have satisfied their fatal hunger. In this, as in the power to attract, fascinate, and crush, the shrub, the tree, the lion, and the serpent all go together in human life.

One often came upon him seated beside his crowded, picturesque greenhouse, diligently jotting down notes, or drawing

1. For other references to Darwin, *see* pp. 21, 245–56, 269.

up lists paralleling the habits of humans and quadrupeds in an effort to discover new evidence to add to the dawn of reason in simians in support of his theory that the human species descends from that hairy quadruped with ears and a pointed tail, denizen of the trees, in which he thought to see, in his solitude populated with hypotheses, the origin of man. Or one might find him in his handsome study filled with bones and flowers, and that benign light that illuminates rooms where honest thought takes place. Standing before his book shelves, he would leaf respectfully through the works of his father, a poet of science who studied the loves of plants with fervor and tenderness, and the essays of his grandfather, who burned, as he did, to wring living answers from the mute earth. Gathering together his major works, which are humble in style, faithful in observation, and fanciful in theory, he would set aside space for two, and place the rest side by side on the shelf, starting with the *Origin of Species*. That is the work in which he maintains that living beings are capable of change, adaptation, and improvement, and of transmitting to their offspring their improved existence. From this, drawing analogies down through the scale of living beings, which are all analogous, he concludes that all the animals that populate the earth descend from four or five progenitors, and the myriad, varied plants from four or five others. These primary species, in constant struggle for survival with others of their kind and different species, have developed and improved, producing offspring ever superior to themselves, which, in turn, endow their offspring with new superiority. From this successively improving, unbroken line of creation, the *monera*, which are albuminous mass without form, and *bathybius*, which is living protoplasm, have evolved into magnificent man. This law of creation, which assigns to each being the faculty of overcoming its rivals in the struggle for existence by its powers of adaptation, and of transmitting its adaptations to its offspring, is the now famous law of natural selection, which today inspires the easily dazzled, novelty-seeking theorists, whose eyes travel swiftly but do not penetrate the surface, influences the German philosophers, who consider it infallible and carry it to extremes, and illuminates the hidden recesses of the earth to noble students engaged in the eternal quest for truth with what the exaggerated theory has of basis in faithfully observed facts. Next to the *Origin of Species*, whose appearance[2] caused as great delight and amazement in the thinking world as that of the *Animal Kingdom* of Cuvier,[3] wherein epic and novelesque things are told, or the *History of Development* of Von Baer,[4] whose lightning flashes illuminated the wonders of the shadowy unknown, or the geological works of Sir Charles Lyell,[5] which reconstruct forgotten worlds, Darwin's gentle hand placed *The Descent of Man*. In this work, he maintains that an intermediary hairy animal must have existed as a link between the simian and primitive man, a theory which moved large numbers of men, unprepared to respect the liberty of sovereign thought and the efforts of a sincere and dedicated investigator, to unjust anger, which error never arouses in those who have the strength to overcome it. To be sure, the similarity between all living beings proves they are similar; it does not follow that certain beings evolve from others. To be sure, there is a similarity between the intelligence of man and other animals, just as there is a similarity of form; this does not prove that animals develop spiritually by stages that parallel the progressive evolution of form. While this thesis will cause no alarm among those who maintain that the spirit is an outgrowth of the material being, there is cause for alarm in thinking that things as beautiful as the affections, and as sovereign as thoughts, spring, like flowers, from the flesh, or as exhalations of the bone, from the perishable body. The

2. Darwin's *On the Origin of Species by Means of Natural Selection* appeared in 1859 and was a major challenge to fundamentalism in religion.

3. Georges Leopold Frederick Dagobert Cuvier (1769–1832), French naturalist. His *Le Règne animal* was published in 1817.

4. Karl Ernst Von Baer (1792–1876), German naturalist, especially noted for his researches on embryology.

5. Sir Charles Lyell (1797–1875), leading geologist of Victorian England, and a friend and supporter of Darwin.

human spirit is horrified and outraged at the suggestion that man's barbarous sufferings are for nothing, and that he is the contemptible toy of a magnificent madman, who amuses himself by lacerating the flesh of his creation with burning irons that leave wounds no one will ever heal, and kindling in this thirsting mind, ever a tinderbox, flames whose impious tongues consume the brain they lick and scarify.

Nature, moreover, does not reveal a spiritual superiority corresponding to successive stages in the evolution of form. Anyone who has visited the rivers of Brazil has seen the manatee cow, as loving as a human mother, carrying her brood on her back as she swims; he has seen that the American monkey, while further removed from humans in form than the African monkey, is closer to man in intelligence. The tiniest spider constructs a web to catch insects, which it repairs in a twinkling if a thread parts, that resolves the problem of the nonagon in a manner that has not yet been revealed to man. Is it that the science of the soul has gone mad, closing its eyes to the laws of the body that moves, harbors, and enslaves it, and is the science of the body equally mad, denying the laws of the radiant soul, which opens the sky to the minds of men and canopies, guides, and glorifies thought?

Thought can cause the skull to burst. It can cleave the earth with golden warmth, and cover the burning sands of the Sahara with a sea of fresh water. A cold skull benumbs thought for the earth, and the whirling sands of the Sahara can smother the body which harbors the spirit of a hero. Life is twofold. Whoever studies life in simple terms goes astray. Dear reader, please forgive this idle tongue of mine that always turns to serious things!

We were in Darwin's study, and we saw him there putting to one side what the harsh Flourens and Haeckel, who venerates and supplements him, and the respectful Kollicker have said of his works, and filling a space in his book shelves with others of his volumes: *Insectivorous Plants*, which seems a collection of fantastic tales; *The Effects of Cross- and Self-Fertilization in the Vegetable Kingdom*, which draws from itself the elements of its life; *The Different Forms of Flowers on Plants of the Same Species*; *The*

Power of Movement in Plants, where marvels, tricks, and mysteries are disclosed of trees, shrubs, and algae, which in the season of courtship select a portion of themselves to seek out the desired mate in her remote abode; *The Structure and Distribution of Coral Reefs; The Geological Observations on the Volcanic Islands:* his monograph on the animals of the family *Cirripedia*, filled with revelations and surprises; and his final book, *Formation of Vegetable Mould Through the Action of Worms*, which moves one to gratitude, for the tenderness that is revealed in his ineffable love of the small, and the new grandeur he imparts to science, always a pleasing subject for the mind. He tells in this book how the selfless little worms prepare that portion of the soil from which the vegetables later spring, scented and heavy with fruit, for the shelter and nourishment of living beings.

Scattered among his books was abundant evidence of the high place he held in the world's esteem—diplomas, medals, and honors from Prussia and England, titles of honorary membership in the Academies that scoffed at him until recently, and degrees from the universities which may question his theories, but count his innumerable and diverse discoveries, which by their number are like a forest that entraps and bewilders, among the greatest, most honest, and most admirable of human conquests. And what of those two works for which he set aside space on his shelf? Well, did you not know? The genius of that man flowered in America: he gestated in our lands; our marvels bestirred him; our luxuriant forests molded him; he was awakened and brought to his feet by our potent nature. He came here as a young naturalist with an English expedition that set sail for the oceans of Africa and America. He discovered himself in the presence of our nights, which moved him to respect; he sat on our peaks, amazed by the surrounding beauty; he showered praise on the inert Indians that a romantic and avaricious people scythed in their first flowering; and he seated himself in the middle of our pampa among our antediluvian animals. Here, on our shores, he gathered the precious stones, hard as conch and of fine enamel, that so marvelously imitate elemental plants. Patiently digging and scraping, he observed how the ocean created the valleys of Chile, which still abound in marine fossiles, and how the level lands of the pampa were deposited grain by grain at the primitive mouth of the ancient Pista River. He studied basaltic lava flows in Santa Cruz, petrified forests in Chiloe, cetaceous fossils in Tierra del Fuego, and observed how slowly the land of America rose in the east, and how Lima on the west has risen eighty-five feet since men first arrived there. He noted that all the lands of America, both to the east and the west, have risen evenly and gradually, and not by convulsions, or by starts. All these things are told in his *Geological Observations in Parts of South America* in the simple language, not of the autocrat, but of the modest student. His other book is a delightful romance, in which serious things are told in a bright and airy fashion. The gallantries of the gaucho go coupled with observations on the habits of insects, and the appearance of horses in the old America with the manner of breaking horses today. He is a scholar on horseback, who dismounts to examine the strings of blue beads which the Indian girls of the highlands wear on their wrists as bracelets, or to remove the jawbone of the fetid puma whose pelt bears the claw marks of the condor. There is no note of presumptuous arrogance in *The Diary of the Investigations in Geology and Natural History of the Countries Visited by His Majesty's Ship Beagle, under the Command of Captain Fitz Roy, from 1832 to 1836*, nor of the deplorable fancifulness of the impassioned scientist who refuses to admit those natural facts which are in conflict with his theory, exaggerates those which support it, and finds facts in his imagination to supplement the real facts when it is to his advantage. The book is not majestic, as it might have been, but it is pleasing. It is not profound, but it is honest. There is no trace of the fanatic who lays violent hands on the universe or importunes it with impatient gestures. There is only the serene observer who rigorously reports what he saw. In matters of the mind, he sees only the surface of things; he does not see deeply into men, and they and their rich world do not greatly arouse his curiosity. As for the affections, he sits down with veneration in the shade of the white-trunked trees deep in the Brazilian jungle, and he wields a branding iron against those who abuse slaves in his sight. But he sees the slaves only as miserable devils. He is a tower of strength who is too little disposed to be charitable toward weaklings. For in addition to having been born in England, which makes men proud, for it is like entering the world in the cradle of Liberty, Darwin was a contented youth with a fresh, eager spirit who knew nothing of that science of forgiveness that comes with a long or a hard life. Sadness makes the soul old and wise before its time.

Whether traveling with his pack horses, or camped in a rude hut, he surveyed the land, buried his hand beneath the bark of trees, lowered himself into deep caves, scaled flowering mountains, and collected insects, bones, leaves, seeds, sands, shells, potsherds, and flowers; he compared the teeth of the new horse of the fertile pampa with the gigantic jaws, capable of girdling trees, of the monster horse of the primitive pampa, which became extinct, perhaps from hunger among the suddenly withered trees on which it fed, perhaps from thirst beside the great, dry bed of the dying river. He coupled facts, drew comparisons, and made an index of all the animals whose remains he was able to find in the various layers of the earth; he noted how the native races of animals prospered and grew, and how those brought in from other lands weakened and degenerated; how there are plants that have something of the reptile, minerals that have something of the plant, and reptiles that have something of the bird. He offers piecemeal in this work the things that were later to appear in the *Origin of Species* cast by reflection into a structural unity. He traversed luxuriant America on horseback; he saw valleys that seemed freshly risen from the primeval slime; he saw rivers gliding like the Lethe; he sailed beneath canopies of butterflies, and canopies of thunder; he witnessed a battle between lightning at the mouth of the River Platte; he saw the ocean glow, as if showered with stars, for are not the phosphorescences the Milky Way of the oceans? He saw the velvet night that fills the heart with starlight; he savored coffee in the roadhouses of Brazil, which are our inns; he saw Rosas laugh his terrifying laugh; he crossed damp Patagonia, desolate Tierra del Fuego, arid Chile, and superstitious Peru. One expects the appearance of a gigantic monarch when one enters the Brazilian jungle, and the apprehensive spirit seems to see him approach in a great, green cape, broad as a mountain slope, crowned with pleached saplings, his beard tangled in long vines, clearing a path through the thick cedars with hands as shaggy as the hide of an old bull. All the jungle is a firmament, with garlands of green moss festooning the trees. Playful deer graze together on one side, while on the other, myriad ants form living mounds that are like hummocks, or those mud volcanoes of Tocuyo which Humboldt saw; now, almost from under the traveler's feet, the sly *tucutuco,* of the pointed snout and ribboned tongue, springs on the crawling mound; now one comes upon a clump of cassava trees, whose flour nourishes men, and whose leaves refresh the weary pack horses. The terrible vampire sinks its sharp teeth in the horse's neck and bleeds the beast, which utters a soft whinny, rather than a neigh; the swift hummingbird flits past on transparent wings that glitter and vibrate. There is a clearing in the forest, dripping from a recent rain, and the foliage, kissed by the sun, gives off a steaming vapor that rises like a column of smoke; in the distance the splendid mountain emerges wrapped in a veil of mist. Mangoes and cinnamon trees entwine branches with the useful breadfruit, the *jaca*, which casts a black shade, and the spreading camphor tree. Graceful is the mimosa; elegant, the fern; thick-bodied, the vine.

The eyes of the irritated glowworm burn in the deep of the night with the living fire that noble anger brings to a human face. The base cuckoo, which lays its eggs in the nests of other birds, croaks its song. Another day is born, and one must kneel atremble before the solemnity and color of Nature. After Brazil, Darwin saw Buenos Aires. The wild deer would stop beside the path to see him pass, looking at him with gentle, trustful eyes, as ingenuous as children, the brave American deer, that have no fear of the musket's report, but flee aghast when they see that the bullet of the stranger has wounded a tree in their forest.

The trip is like a fairy tale; this day they warily avoid the

Indians; the next night they see the eyes of the wrathful jaguar burning in the night as, irritated by the coming storm, he sharpens his strong claws on the trees; yesterday was a day of breaking horses, hobbling a hind leg to a foreleg, and to these the rebellious, curb-bitted head, and setting them walking, sweating and hobbled, with the saddle on their flank and the rider in the saddle, across the torrid plain from which they return panting and conquered. Lunch is with Rosas, whose campaign tent, like a feudal lord's, is a buffoon's court; dinner is with gauchos, the slender, hot-blooded gauchos, who tell how the tyrant of the pampa—who bends trees, and tames wild ponies by placing his hand on their flanks—orders men stretched like drying hides, hanging hand and foot from four stakes, on which they sometimes die.

Darwin saw the sacred Wailechu tree, from whose threads, which are its winter leaves, the pious Indians hang the bread they carry, the cloth they bought for the house, or the flute with which they while away the hours of the journey, because human nature takes joy in giving, and because that thorny tree, standing at road's end of a most difficult journey, is a symbol of health to the Indian. He gives his garments and horses, expecting in return that his pack horses will never tire, and that he will never know misfortune; the tree means so much to him, that if he does not have something to give, he will draw a thread from his woven poncho and hang it from a thread of the tree.

And beyond, what a magnificent surprise! Gigantic rodents, spectators of other worlds; remains of megalosaurs; bones of the megathere sloth, a predecessor of the great American horse. The haunches of those mountainous beasts! What claws, the size of tree trunks! They would sit at the foot of those gigantic trees, and clutching the trunk, bring down the branches to their mouths with the rending sound of a mountainside giving way. The travelers stirred up an ostrich's nest, and learned to their sorrow that the ostrich attacks without hesitation whoever touches its nest, whether the enemy is on foot or on horseback. A jaguar passes with a roar, trailed by a band of foxes, just as the Bengal tiger is followed by jackals, for the fox is the jackal of

America. Or a herd of the proud cattle of the pampa surprises the traveler with their elegance and alertness, for the herd is like a crowd of mischievous schoolboys. There are the peaceful Indians of the highlands, who glitter like genii of the plain on their horses with silver-studded trappings, which they guide with strong, invisible wire reins; the sunlight glints from the shiny stirrup, the jeweled halter, the heavy spur, and the knife handle. There, also, the eunuchs of the plain, the shepherd dogs that tend the sheep.

The road becomes indistinct, and the land turns sad; the gaucho looks back at the receding pampa like a lover who longs for a last glimpse of his sweetheart. The peaceful *guanacos*, jealous of their females, graze in a herd; when they feel the hour of death approaching, they turn, like the men of Tierra del Fuego, toward the place where all the *guanacos* of their herd before them have gone to die. Suddenly, a shudder runs through the herd, and the *guanacos* flee; bounding after them with a roar comes the fierce puma, the lion of America, who prowls from fiery Ecuador to dank Patagonia, and does not whimper when he feels himself wounded: brave American lion! Beyond, there are dead *guanacos*, with vultures hovering, like the puma's crown, for crumbs from the lion's feast.

The travelers advance silently; the shrubs are thorny; the plants, stunted; stones are dry; the ravenous rodents of the forest slake their thirst with drops of dew. That was how Darwin saw the Patagonian desert.

And how black Tierra del Fuego! Little sun, much water, endless marshlands; everything murky, everything mournful, everything damp and sad. The trees without flowers; the plants, alpine; the mountains, eroded; the valleys, almost fetid; the atmosphere, blackish.

The natives materialize like divinities from the marshes, their hair tangled, their faces streaked with white and red, their backs covered with *guanaco* hides leaving the rest of their brown bodies naked. After some observation, the man gradually emerges from the beast. They beat the breasts of their visitors, as if to let them know they trust them, and bare their own chests in turn for the visitors to return the salutation. They have shamans, tribes, and remarkable memories. They regard murder as a crime that will bring down the furies of the elements on their bowed heads. They have heard of the devil, but they say the devil is not there. They know of love and gratitude, which is to know a great deal.

From that land the traveler went by ship to Chile where the hills bear the scars of the quest for gold. No longer was the industrious Englishman accompanied, and his great scientific collection borne, by the romantic, dangerous and happy gaucho, radiant and detached as a beautiful Satan, but instead, by the vain *guaso*, with his heavy spur, white boots, black or green puttees, baggy pants, red *chiripá*, and coarse poncho. They passed the bald mountains, dotted here and there by clumps of green forest, like emeralds cast among ashes, crossed the shaky bridges suspended over murky Maipu, with their treacherous footing of dried hides and wooden rungs, and the floating islands of Taguatagua, which are great clumps of old roots continually sprouting new roots, on which the travelers crossed from shore to shore as though in a comfortable launch. On the slopes of those bare mountains, the traveler read Molina, who sang the ways of the animals of the land, and Azara, whose work is a treasure, and the good Acosta, who revealed unsuspected things about the Indies. He made a special trip to see at first hand the pale miners in their long shirts of dark, uncarded wool, their tanned leather aprons, their brightly colored sashes, and jaunty red hats; he saw with a start the miserable ore bearers, who are men and seem beasts, even dying monsters, until they drop their huge loads, which weigh upward of 200 pounds, and set off on their return journey laughing and joking, even though they eat meat only once a week.

Now the traveler was leaving Chile, and now he was at the nitrate mines of solitary Iquique; yet swimming before his eyes, like a permanent, radiant vision, were the valley of Quillota, where living is a joy; the green, peaceful *llanos*, which seem morning's natural habitat; the wild bamboo trees, which sway like thoughts in the mind; the snowy Andes, which the soul makes warm and golden, and the setting sun dresses in flame. His mind thus charged, the youth returned to Europe. Not a day without work, and no day's work without return. He turned these memories over in his mind, and in his mind's eye, he could see all the animals of the globe walking side by side. He recollected, more with the disdain of an Englishman than with the insight of a deep thinker, the barbarous natives of Tierra del Fuego, the rude African, the agile Zealander, and the new men of the Pacific isles. Since he does not see man in his compound character, nor thoroughly grasp that it is as important to know whence comes the sentiment that moves him and the reason that guides him, as the ribs of his chest and the layers of his skull, he hit on the thought that there was only a short step separating the Fueguian and the simian. Others look desperately toward the sky, their eyes filled with grief's sweet tears. Darwin, with clear eye and inquiring hand, free of the desire to know where we are going, bent over the earth with serenity of spirit to discover whence we come. There is truth in this: nothing should be denied that has a place in the solemn spiritual world, neither the noble impatience with life, that is relieved ultimately by giving of oneself to life; not the ineffable colloquy with the eternal, which bestows on the spirit the strength of the sun and peace of the night; nor the certainty, real because it provides real joy, that an afterlife exists in which there will be no ending to the profound joys, that with a glimmering of the truth, or the practice of virtue, fill the soul; but when it comes to the construction of worlds, no better answer can be had than from the worlds themselves. He saw well, who saw this, despite his errors, which stemmed from seeing only half the being; who spoke to the dumb stone, and received an answer; who entered the palaces of insects, the bowers of plants, the bowels of the earth, and the workshops of the seas. He has earned his repose where he rests: in Westminster Abbey, beside heroes.

La Opinión Nacional (Caracas), July, 1882

Modern Spanish Poets

The sun is the father of poetry and nature is its mother. In the land of Spain, warmed with sunlight and shaded with orange trees, where women glow like burning lava, where flowers perfume the air, where even ruins smile, and the dawn sparkles, where poppy-laden fields look like lakes of blood, where cosy little cottages nesting in rose-dotted foliage seem to burn their inmates in happiness, where the English go every year to thaw their souls, frozen in the humid atmosphere of his native isle, where iron Goth conquered, the fiery Moor loved, and the steel-knit Roman built, where the soil like a captive beauty vanquished its conquerors, where the soul of an African fires a Caucasian body, where painters have only to shake their brushes in the air to fill them with gay colors—in this land poetry gushes from the heart as pure as a mountain stream. It is as much a product of nature as a jessamine or a honey suckle. In all countries the fruits of the soul are analogous to the fruits of Nature. In England, land of fogs, the poet is Browning; in France, land of thought, the poet is Victor Hugo; in Spain, land of flowers, the poet is Zorrilla.[1] You might as well try to reproduce on canvas the perfume of the rose, or the luminous mist or vapor of light that envelops everything in that land of gold, as to translate Zorrilla's verses.

1. Juan Zorilla de San Martín (1855–1931), famous poet of Montevideo, most noted for a long historical verse epic, *Tabaré*, published in 1886.

But in this beautiful land thought is fighting with Nature. The lightnings of civilization have startled the lovely Diana of the South. The shadows of coming anxieties have fallen upon a people who have never raised their hands except to salute a king or a lady, to brandish a naked sword in defense of their honor, or to pick ripe fruit from a yielding tree.

The Spaniards are beginning to understand that in the universal march of progress they too must keep step. It is not enough to own the Alhambra and the Alcazar: they must know how to honor them. They begin to see that they can neither remain Arabs or become Bohemians. Since the entire world is reasoning, and steam factories are taking the places of immense arsenals, they too must reason with the world, work with the factories, range themselves with those who think like Herbert Spencer, frown like Heine, doubt like Byron, and despise like Leopardi. With their Spanish hands they must strike the chords of the human lyre. They have always believed too much and worked too little. For them the poetry of both doubt and industry is a product of the brain alone.

It has no heart. It is imported and imitative. Although illuminated by flashes of sunlight, it lacks warmth. Its majesty of intelligence is imposing, but the voice of nature and the charm of spontaneity are wanting. It is not captivating, for it shows no outburst of feeling. Humanitarian songs will not enrapture those who furnish both ideas and the forms in which they are expressed. An Arab will recognize his own steed although the saddle may be changed and the body covered with ornaments of gold.

Moreover, progress cannot be sung in the language of poetry. The story of human progress is told in harbors filled with shipping, factories crowded with workmen, towns blackened with the smoke of forges, streets choked with drays, schools overflowing with children, and trees loaded with fruit. Poetry is the language of the beautiful: industry is the language of the strength. People may sing in the morning or in the evening, at dawn, and at night when the soul seeks repose: but during the day they should work. Work is dry and difficult poetry, and the Spaniards still detest it.

Spain is the country of dreams. In its rich soul idleness is natural. The South is a natural cemetery for souls blackened in the smoke of the forge. Seen in another light it is Olympus itself. All its men are not gods but its women are certainly goddesses. From them the country draws the inspiration of song. She has always had two great schools of poetry, one typical of her monarchical society, theocratic, inquisitorial, loyal, amorous, and warlike, and another typical of her soil, ever green, covered with a sky ever blue. The shattered smoking ruins of the old society are yet to be transformed into the new elements of the democratic epoch. The poetry of nature, however cannot alone move the hearts of a world when the bitterest conflicts are waged on the most obscure battlefields. Two giants, the past and the future are struggling in the present. Soldiers cry "En Avant." They have only time to ask each other where they live and then they die. Everybody is trying to find a passageway through the dusthidden ruins. There is no time to stop and look at the beauties of nature, the great soother. One of the great sources of poetry is dry, and the other is insufficient. The land of Don Pedro and of Phillippe will sing true poetry when a new society is established and unanimous repose allows people to leave their dreamy souls in boundless nature. A time of transition demands great efforts. Individual griefs, always a fruitful source of poetry, pass unnoticed amid the great sorrows of humanity. The dreams of the imagination are useless when there is need of the intelligence that thinks. Out of this struggle between song and an epoch of trouble there has sprung a poetry harrowing and bitter, weak but true, clouded with seductive sadness.

It is like the poetry of exile—exile from the land of the soul sung in the heart of its native land. It is the poetry of Musset,[2] of

2. Alfred de Musset (1810–1857), one of the most distinguished poets and dramatists of the French Romantic movement.

August Barbier,[3] of Baudelaire,[4] souls born to believe, bewailing the death of their faith. Loving pomp, these poets despised illegitimate grandeur. They were inconsolable because they were compelled to live without real splendor to love. They were kings without kingdoms—exile gods. But their complaints, somewhat French, a good deal German, and a little Russian, are not Spanish. People feel sorrow more keenly in the place where they are born. Where sorrow is the muse it is best sung where there is the most suffering. In Spain the feudal system was not so hard, nor monarchy so despotic, nor the people so badly treated, nor intelligence so impatient, as in France and Germany.

It was not in the land of the Isabellas that the old world was shaken, overthrown and conquered. It was not in Spain that Reform was preached, that a family of kings was killed, that priests were slaughtered, that the currents of life were revised, and that men were brought to the same level under a hecatomb of masters, and a hecatomb of serfs. Lions with the heads of serpents, immortal ideas, spurred by vengeance, and justice posed as a fury, are not Spanish. The revolution in Spain was slower, less bloody, and more benign than the revolution in France. Punishments were less cruel, and passions less embittered. As the old regime was not so terrible, the new regime is not so impatiently demanded. Vengeance and anger, daughters of revolution, do not precipitate the political redemption of the Spaniards, and they will not bring about those cruel reactions which so many times have retarded the progress of republican ideas in France. The disappearance of everything that has been revered is not so sudden as it was in France. It is a gradual and tranquil disappearance. The nostalgia of the past, a source so rich in poetic ideas, has not been felt so keenly. In France a new era flashed from the ruins of a magnificent catastrophe like dazzling lightning from the blackest of clouds. Superb terror,

3. Auguste Barbier (1805–1882), French poet whose best work, *Les Iambes* was published in 1835.

4. Charles Baudelaire (1821–1867), French poet, precursor of the symbolist movement, best known for his *Les fleurs de mal*, published in 1857.

melancholy, desperation, burning menace, and vengeance, the need of faith and grief for its loss, and that essentially human evil of loving with the heart that which is already despised by the intelligence, have been hardly felt in the land where the Tagus rolls its golden pebbles, and the angry current of the Duero files the sharp rocks of its shores. Exalted souls, inspired with a love of the great, not finding it at home seek it abroad. Through the contagion of reading and outburst of sympathy with European misfortunes, they finally fancy these misfortunes their own.

The yearnings of their own burning souls seem to be yearnings of their own people. Poetry is the work both of the bard and of the people who inspire him. The collaboration being lacking in Spain, the poet looks elsewhere for wrongs of which to sing. He quenches his fervent thirst in foreign literature in an atmosphere above the atmosphere breathed by the Spanish people, although not above the intelligence of the educated classes. Hence it happens that the literature of Spain today is not a Spanish literature.

Poetry is durable when it is the work of all. Those who understand it are as much its authors as those who make it. To thrill all hearts by the vibrations of your own, you must have the germs and inspirations of humanity. To walk among the multitudes who suffer, with love in your heart, and song on your lips, you must hear all the groans, witness all the agonies, feel all the joys, and be inspired with the passions common to all. Above all, you must live among a suffering people. Whatever the power of the poet, they must enjoy, bless, curse, hope, and condemn, before he can find the vigorous songs which enliven all hearts, usher in great events, and live forever. Without these conditions the poet is a tropical plant in a frigid atmosphere. He cannot flourish. And in Spain how many roses die in their buds! They lack a grateful air. Public life is too confused. Nobody knows whither he is drifting. To be a poet, unless you become the poet of the battle, you must wait until the battle is finished.

The Spanish poets who are now attracting the most attention in Europe, are poets of the battle. Echegaray has dramatic talent bordering upon genius. In lyric verse, among a multitude of men of letters, Campoamor, Núñez de Arce, and Grilo, are already famous. Echegaray[5] is a devil, luminous and original. Campoamor is a happy man who writes profoundly; Grilo is a Horace, revealing a melancholy life filled with dream-winged griefs and imaginary wrongs in supple language humid with tears and morning dew; Núñez de Arce is the poet Deputy of the Cortes, all the more poet because he is a Deputy.

There is also a long file of youthful writers, anxious, fervid and strong, with souls undoubtedly poetic, but tormented by a lack of the ideal. With such a want the most courageous genius, unable to create a people, chokes and dies without glory.

The most famous work of Nuñez de Arce[6] is called "Los Gritos de Combate" or "Battle Cries." Verses ought to contain the idea by which they are animated. They are forms in which an idea is expressed. The clothing is sometimes so beautiful that it conceals the absence of the idea. The verse is simply stamped by the charm of the senses. The flesh, like poetry, has its rhythm, its clearness, and its repose, and with the admirable logic of the productions of nature in form it always gives the character of the land of its nativity.

Michelet[7] called the poems of Hindustan "A sea of milk." Spanish poetry is a flowing stream, a caressing woman, a lattice partly open, an orange tree with fragrant white flowers. It is a dreaming Arab, a fighting Norseman, a coal-eyed Moor. Read Lope and everything says "Love!" "Fight with each other!" and "Die for the King!" Read Zorrilla—the poet who owes nothing to foreign literature, and who is today almost forgotten in his own country, and you will find only the command to love. Kings and duels were already driven from the verses of Spanish

5. José Echegaray y Eizaguirre (1832–1916), Spanish dramatist, considered to be the outstanding playwright of Spain in the last decades of the nineteenth century.

6. Gaspar Núñez de Arce (1834–1903), Spanish poet, playwright, and statesman. "Los Gritos de Combate" was published in 1875.

7. Jules Michelet (1798–1874), one of France's great Romantic historians.

poets. The voluptuous poetry that seemed to arise from the flower beds of Andalusia and the poems in stone—Generalife, Alcázar, Toledo, and Córdoba—named by the old Moors are not the poetry of Núñez de Arce. With him ideas seem borrowed. The form is too precise. It has the regular clink of the hammer upon the anvil. You recognize the workman. He sweats over his work, tortures his ideas, drives them into verse with blows, files them, burnishes them, and leaves them as a sculptor leaves his image of marble when he thinks it formed and finished. Such labor is not productive of the best results. Inspiration has wings, and in the midst of such rude work it flies away.

Its absence creates finished verses without poetry. You have not the limpid river, sparkling and beautiful in which round shoulders gleam and the lids of dark eyes are closed, over which flutter filmy-winged butterflies and rosy-billed doves, and upon which swans of snowy whiteness glide toward the magnificent land of dreams. Ah no! After reading the magnificent "Misere" of Núñez de Arce—his angry epistles, his sonnet cursing Voltaire, his sombre legends, and his austere, almost ascetic poems filled with pictures of churches, with naked walls of empty castles, of cavaliers torn by remorse, of doubting priests stricken with anguish and of the misfortunes of living poets, you throw down the book and murmur—"Shelley,[8] Musset, Leopardi,[9] Byron!" Your heart does not feel the cheering warmth that remains after reading the verses of a true poet, nor do you feel upon your forehead the cold air that is fanned by the wings of a genius. Núñez de Arce is a man of thought. He knows the music of his language, he understands its century, and he tries to be its poet, but nature did not give him strength for the task. When you read his "Vertigo" you remember "The Corsair" and "Lara." Read only the title of one of his poems "La Selva Oscura" and with Dante you repeat: "Selva salvaggia ed aspra e forte."

8. Percy Bysshe Shelley (1792–1822), famous English Romantic poet.

9. Giacomo Leopardi (1791–1837), Italian poet, noted for his superb lyric poems.

His poem on Luther,[10] "La Vision de Fray Martín," is doubtless the work into which he has put the greatest care, force, and originality. While making of the priest the personification of the actual state of the human soul, he has tried to paint the rebellious spirit that, like a child struggling at the very threshold of life, smashes a vault peopled with beloved shades, and standing on its ruins weeps for the shadows that flee in the crash that he has created. Marching forward and looking backward Núñez de Arce really desired to paint the present European century with its regrets and pains. Portions of his poems have the vague monastic air and the lugubrious light of a chilly old convent. The breath of a real doubt stirs the whole of it. After reading it the heart is unmoved. There is not the irresistible "élan," the interior movement of the wings that always follows the reading of the work of a great soul. You do not think, speak, and soar aloft. You remain upon the earth. You cordially salute the thinker, but you feel that he is beside you, and not as all great poets should be, above you.

Don Ramón Campoamor is a German poet born in Spain. He is an adorer of the beatiful, a hater of the coarse, an aristocrat of thought. His verses are as elegant as his smile, his salon, and his gloved hands. Aged man that he is, he writes something like a grandfather, and he has the right to do so. He has a friendly handshake and friendly counsel for everybody. He is loved for his natural dignity, for his broad and negligé versification and for the independence of his talent. With him thought laughs at the verse. He will not torture a splendid idea with a new syllable. He says that force is irregular. Both Hercules and Homer slept. Rough lines bring to notice harmonious ones. In this century of liberties all sorts of chains must be broken, even the chains of romance. We must speak naturally. We must take sounds just as they are produced in the air, without order, without preparation and without religious periodicity. Charm comes from the unexpected. Form is beautiful, but when it

10. Martin Luther (1483–1546), German biblical scholar, linguist, and founder of the sixteenth century Protestant Reformation.

conflicts with an idea, the idea should be preferred. Poetic thought flies and shines like a butterfly. Shall we cut off the butterfly's wings to make him fit in a verse? Núñez de Arce would cut them. Campoamor would not. The latter revels in his inaccuracies. He excels in such liberties. His goodness of heart and his contempt of form have produced a charming mixture. Even in speaking to children he is a poet nobleman. Notwithstanding his years he is as fresh as a seed in spring. Through all his doubts his faith can be seen. Behind his despair appears his hope. At first, like others he loved what was great. He dreamed of poetry and then made it. His ideas were too expansive and too untamed to be enclosed in a classic mould, and he had not the strength to create a new mould for human thought. . . .

New York Sun, November 26, 1880
[written in English]

The Pampa

The gaucho crosses the plain at full gallop with a wary backward glance over his shoulder. His warrior horse, ears pricked and sharp-eyed, springs forward on slender forelegs that stem from its powerful chest like pointed lances. The poncho, caught about the saddle stock, flaps blue and gold in the breeze. The gaucho is of those born to the saddle; he guides his companion with his knee more than with the reins. He wears blue pants and a white shirt, a red kerchief at his neck, and a soft, narrow-brimmed hat held snug to his head by a strap under his beardless chin. This is the frontispiece of *The Pampa*,[1] a book on the Argentine published in Paris by the Frenchman Alfred Abelot.

It is not a shameful book on coarse paper with pre-Raphaelite prints, but as handsome a book as comes from the press, with pages that invite the reader, and delicate sketches that present in all its tenderness and ferocity the life of the pampa, that awesome and melancholy plain crowned to the north by the tropical palm and luxuriant carob of Brazil, and bounded to the south by the sullen hills of Patagonia. There, the hard life under the open sky, with saddle and sheepskin for gear and gable, and everywhere the horizon broken only here and there by an

1. *La Pampa*, a territory of Argentina, bounded on the north by the provinces of Mendoza, San Luis, and Córdoba, on the east by Buenos Aires, on the south by the territory of Río Negro, and on the west by the province of Mendoza. Agriculture is the chief industry, but stock raising is also carried on extensively.

ostrich's silhouette. There the *pulpería*, the club of the desert, with its gin and conversation, teamsters and song, hub-bub and trade, wakes and verse. There, in the sea of grass, the chase with the balled lariat, the *boleada;* the *baques*, tracking the deadly Indian by his trail through stone and water; the fight between the soldier posse and the gaucho outlaw, who gives them the slip, parrying their bullets with the point of his knife. There the Indian on horseback, who raises his sons to exterminate the white invader and the horses that are his livelihood and fortune—or die under hoof as the riders, guns blazing, raze the Indian wigwams. There, the primitive life, and a whole epoch dying now under the wheels of the locomotive.

In those 700 leagues of solitude, which reach to the gates of the university cities, there still exists an untamed, natural caste of a motley Spanish and Indian tradition, children of the castle and the wigwam, reared on horseback and schooled in bloodshed, who descended on the city, lance in hand, to unseat their despoilers from authority—the frock-coated bureaucrats, the land surveyors, the *botavacas*. *La Cautiva* of Esteban Echevarría[2] and *Celiar* of Magarinos Cervantes relate in verse the life of those centaurs; their courtships in the saddle with their "*china*," and the duels to the death between those knights of the knife, of leonine soul, and regal presence. Rafael Obligado describes that life in his colorful verse. The great Sarmiento,[3] in the work of a founder of nations, *Civilization and Barbarity*, paints the bloodthirsty monk, Aldao, and the "tiger," Facundo Quiroga.[4] Now Abelot presents the pampa that is disappearing: the last wake, the last *pulpería*, the last gaucho outlaw, his poncho wrapped around one hand, his flashing blade in the other; the last *mate*

2. Esteban Echeverría (1805–1851), Argentine poet who introduced romanticism into South American literature.

3. Domingo Faustino Sarmiento (1811–1888), educator, statesman, and writer, first civilian president of Argentina (1868–1874), author of *Life in the Argentine in the Days of the Tyrant, or Civilization and Barbarity* (1861).

4. Juan Facundo Quiroga (1793–1835), Argentine caudillo who ruled as a tyrant.

sipped at daybreak while squatted in a circle around the fire before the horse race, the roundup, or the chase with the *bolas*. "Pampa" is the horse that does not shy from a tiger; "pampa," the dog that breaks the leg of the running ostrich with one snap; the Indian girl, whose head is turned after a month in town by the beaded necklaces and red shawls, no longer wants to be called "pampa"; "luluhuu!" cries the naked Pampa Indian riding after the lank-haired *guanacos* with the balled lariat whirling over his head. The pampa is the poem of the man who rises at daybreak as in the Golden Age; who wrests the hunting ground from the puma he kills with his bare hands; who copies trees, battles, or clouds on hide with the point of his knife; who sings his songs, the *triste* and *cielito*, under the stars; who slashes the face of whomever offends him or challenges his place, and sinks at the feet of civilization, hamstrung by the plowshare. Why read Homer in Greek when he still lives, roaming the American wilderness with the guitar over his shoulder?

The Pampa is not a thick book, which it could have been if the author had simply set down the salient and characteristic aspects of that natural existence with art, but without comment, so that it revealed itself, and the character of its inhabitants became manifest from the environment that surrounded and educated them. The prompter is as annoying in books as in the theater. The important thing is what is seen, not who sees it. Art demands objectivity of an author. It is like the appearance in the Chinese theater of the stage manager in clogs and shirt-sleeves, shifting the properties among the gossamer princes and winged generals while the dance of fury or the swordplay are in progress. The shortcoming of this well-intentioned book is that the author introduces his secondhand, preconceived opinions into the testimony of the facts, which is what the reader looks for in a book. These are times for men to think for themselves, needing and demanding facts on which to base their judgments, without literary frills and useless digressions; there is justified impatience at the complacent, gratuitous intrusion of the judgments of others. There are books of a discursive and personal character that collapse when the opinions of the author are not well premised, and whose charm resides in the art with which his reasoning is employed as argument, and the subtlety with which he sways and persuades the reader toward the desired view, never offending his sight with clumsy pomposity or his reason with dogmatism. What men want to know is what life teaches, and it is infuriating not to be permitted to see life as it is, but through spectacles of this or that hue. Despite all that is being written today, the literature that is useful and strong is still in swaddling clothes.

It is true that the author of *The Pampa* relates what he saw in the manner of a witness, and expresses himself with ease, honesty, and that spirit of nature that makes us all one, in the words of the English poet. But his subject matter is so interesting and lively—the stagecoach carrying gentlemen, country girls, and criminals all together is so noisy; the race between the high-strung horses is so hotly contested; the sixth sense of the *rastreador* on the trail of the "Black Wildcat" is so uncanny; so dazzling, with the sun setting in the distance and the blood quickened by the *mate*, is the return of the hunters from the *boleada* with the ostrich hanging from the saddle stock, or the pelt dripping blood down the horse's flank; so picturesque and novel the battle in which whoever wants a lance to fight takes it from his enemy with the *bolas*, that it is jarring when the French gentleman appears in his smoking jacket, seizes the bridle of the lathered horse with its rider in a white shirt and red headband like a Greek runner, and turns loose on the open plain the latest metaphysical concept, or removes from his lips the silver *bombilla* with which he sips the strong, bitter *mate* to utter the unpardonable artistic and philosophical anomaly of yoking Darwin and Haeckel with that free life, which must be approached with a mind as untrammeled as itself. One does not renounce one papacy to embrace another!

Where he could, and should have seen the heroic aspects of primeval society—the primary combat between man and beast, the pervading sadness and violent pleasures of the nomad life, the submission of the rootless lancers to the cunning and Herculean captain, the conflict between the raw, yet powerful gaucho hordes and the cultured, legalistic cities, and the final triumph of a beautiful, useful civilization over a dazed barbarity—he sees heredity variations, selections, and reversions. He follows a theory, which is like walking blindfolded. He sees only primitive barbarity and a ferocious instinct in the Indian, descended of generations cowed and butchered by the white man, who gathers his children around the bound white captive that they may mete out the Indian justice that the earth of their fathers—stained with blood by the invader—cries for. He attributes the gaucho's traffic in blood, which he considers a relish for gore, to an animal crudity and an outcropping of the bestial in human nature, without recognizing this as a consequence of the gaucho's life as a slaughterer, for, in civilized communities, he is always to be found in the stockyard, wedded to his knife; he forgets that bravery is a quality which all men like to display, anxious as they are to demonstrate prowess and manliness; human blood is red, no different from the bull's; if the bull falls under the knife through no offense of his own, what then of him who offends the punctilio and vanity of the savage? His theories lead him into pitfalls of his own making, such as declaring that the closer man is to the primitive state "the greater his passion for gambling and drinking"; he thinks, in keeping with his naturalist theories, that gambling, which is simply the violent, uncultured form of hope abounding in societies of cravat and casino, is a throwback and a periodic reappearance of the barbarian.

The attraction of the bottomless pit, the vertigo caused by the sea and heights, man's constant endeavor to fathom the absolute, to transcend and diffuse himself, he regards, with scholastic blinders, as a return to the chaotic thinking of the primitives. One has only to see the world in graduated social stages identical to one another at the same level of evolution, modified only by place and environment, to have at one's command a great and ample philosophy which comprehends every social development and permits one to enjoy them all, never being saddened, like our Frenchman, because the carnivals of the Buenos Aires of yesteryear, when ladies and gentlemen engaged in ferocious water fights, are becoming a thing of the past. Changes are a matter for concern only when they are produced by factors not native to the country, and run counter to the enduring and nourishing characteristics that are the salt and leavening of a country, and without which its personality is soon sapped. Why seek to convert into local peculiarities things that are common to all societies in their early stages? The Argentine gaucho[5] has wakes; so does the Canary Islander and the Irish peasant. On the pampa, a dead infant is dressed in holiday clothes, and in Colombia, in golden slippers, for the road to Heaven has sharp stones and the mother pleads that her child not bruise its feet. The hunters of the pampa make their meat into charqui; so do the North American Indians. The gaucho of Choel-Choel knows no law; the Yankee cowboy knows no law. Fired with gin at the *pulpería*, the gaucho fills the air with shots and is ready to take on the house to see who is the best man, and the Colorado miner, when the whiskey goes to his head, makes the tenderfoot dance to the tune of his revolver. The gaucho outlaw counts his dead as an honor, and the *llanero* of Uputa in Venezuela told the teacher: "Mister teacher, what I like is to hear the crunch when I bury my knife in a man's back."

Whoever knows the unsubdued, wandering Arabs, knows gauchos. Are not the towers of the pampa forts the same as those of North Africa? Man is one, and order and unity are the changeless, irrefutable laws of Nature.

These limitations of prejudice, as harmful when they stem from the passion for science as from ignorance of it, are mitigated in the author of *The Pampa* by the fact that he is clearly a good man, which is the first condition of true intelligence. It is apparent that his sincere heart compels him to love those things which he condemns in theory as bestial. He says he likes the *pulpería*. The gauchos, in all fairness, "are good people if one knows how to treat them." The "Black Wildcat" swore death to the justices of the peace, and he killed five in one knife fight. But

5. Natives and pastoral nomads of the Chaco, in the Argentine Republic, expert horsemen and cattlemen who wielded the lariat and the bolas with great skill.

the justices stole his beloved horse, which was his "credit," his silver-trimmed saddle and bridle, and his girl. The author is "sorry" to see the gaucho disappearing. Who will ride out with him now for the pure love of the fight against the cunning Indian, and who will secretly leave the kerchief with the last *mate* leaves hanging from his saddle stock? Who will make him a present of the still warm pelt of the tiger—"because he would have liked it for himself"—killed and skinned with the same knife that disposed of a "weak-sister" in an argument? These gauchos are good people. A *china* catches their fancy, and they swing her up behind them, galloping off to live where the sky is a jewel-box, with a single diamond by day and a thousand gems at night. They have the habit of the knife and hate the dandy from the city. But when the poet Echeverria, pale and sickly, traveled among the gauchos, they would doff their hats and rise when he spoke to them, whispering to each other: "This is no dandy! This is a poet." Good people, those gauchos!

We first see them in the book at a wake. The horsemen arrive at the *estancia* of a wealthy landowner of the region, and tie their horses to the hitching rail, for to pass beyond the rail on horseback would be a discourtesy dearly paid. The little angel has died in his fourth year and the neighbors are holding a wake to celebrate his journey to Heaven. The rain is pelting the roof outside; there are flashes of lightning and claps of thunder. inside, clasped together in an *haberna* or face to face in the dextrous steps of the *zamacueca*, sweethearts dance in couples and cross themselves each time they pass in front of the chair atop a pedestal of boxes where the infant is seated, surrounded by thirty-six wax candles, with the old, gray-haired gaucho on one side, strumming the guitar, and on the other the dry-eyed mother, her hands folded in her lap. Celebrations are few and far between on the pampa, and the keeper of the *pulpería* hires the dead child from the penniless gaucho, who gratefully rents it out to him so the little angel may have candles, and go to Heaven in proper fashion, with song and a wake.

Morning comes. Squatted in a circle around the dung fire, the gauchos sip the steaming *mate*. The saddle and sheepskins spread on the ground have served as a bed for a short sleep.

Now the saddle gear, with its folded blanket, its leather pad to keep out the dampness, wooden saddle, bound stock and frame in leather, silver stirrups, and sheepskins, ceases to be a bed and becomes a saddle again. The girth is of leather and the overgirth of wool; the bit and bridle are in the Moorish style, of silver and tooled leather; wherever he can insert the point of his knife, the gaucho carves flowers, leaves, heads, and whimsies. He tucks his baggy pants into his horsehide boots and pulls on the *chiripá*, tied at his waist in the manner of a short, outer loincloth; he slips the poncho over his head and pulls his hat down over his eyes. The party of gauchos is setting out as a posse on the trail of an assassin who killed the "Old Cowpuncher," a venerable gaucho who was the pride and glory of the region, for he could tell you in a wink where any *estancia* lay, how far it was to the next one, or how many days off the Indians were. The *rastreador*, who has studied the welter of hoofprints at the door of the old gaucho's ranch, sets out at the head of the group in search of the assassin who fled eight days before, riding through the high grass, doubling back on his tracks, taking to the river, and returning to dry ground in a stony place to give no clue of where he left the water. The posse arrives at a town where a fair is underway, with wagons, tents, knots of traders, and strings of horses. The *rastreador* approaches a teamster showing a horse to a circle of traders. "This is the horse," says the *rastreador*, looking at the hoofprints in the mud. And it was. The assassin had traded with the teamster. They return to the point of the trade; the horse, left to its instinct, picks up the trail of its master and presently the *rastreador* drops his hand on the assassin's shoulder. He confesses. Who can withstand the *rastreador*? Even on cobblestone streets the sons of the gauchos can tell if the priest rode past on his mule, or if the horse of the tax collector has passed through, or if the teacher went out wearing rope-soled shoes or boots; they can read in the trampled grass the number of horses in a herd, which are mares and which are colts; it is useless for the fugitive to go on tiptoe, or gallop away to a far off place and continue on foot, for before the year is out the impassive *rastreador* will have picked up the trail.

If a hunt with the *bolas* is organized, who will not stay to see it? It is supposed to be for ostrich and antelope, but the wealthy gauchos are trembling because the hunters are just as likely to send their *bolas* whirling after a horse that catches their eye, or a brindle steer, "for love of the hide." The *boleadores* ride to the gathering place on their horses, in holiday trappings. The morning sun begins to streak the sky. The water for the *mate* bubbles in the kettle. The lean dogs lick their chops. The hunters mount. Off they go to the four winds in search of game! They return with the evening shadows from the four winds, their horses loaded with bloody pelts and dead ostriches in bunches; the muzzles of the dogs are red. Stretched out on their saddle gear, squatted around the fire, seated on the skulls of steers, they pass the long night as if in conversation with the stars. The *payador*,[6] his fingers playing lightly across the guitar, sings of his misfortunes, of the sad death of the gaucho Santos Vega, of the *china* he loved but who was stolen from him, of the sadness that filled him when a rival *payador* sang better than he, of the battle between the gauchos and the Indians, of the tenderness a man feels within when he sees the starlit heavens at night.

When they reach the *pulpería*, they boast of their exploits in song, sit in the shadows on the benches that run the length of the wall carving the brands of the region in the wall with their knives or stand elbow to elbow at the bar, chatting with the keeper who serves them from behind the sturdy counter. And then, their pockets filled with the money the *pulpero* gave them for the pelts and ostrich feathers, they all go outside as the racers begin to gather from near and far, on their silver-studded saddles. The clearing has been carefully prepared as if for a big race. The horses that are going to race are led past the public by their leather halters. Some observe them closely, comment, and bet; others are more interested in the *chinas* who have come in their Sunday dresses and yellow or violet shawls. They wear gold and glass earrings, and their hair is carefully combed,

6. A traveling country singer in South America who sings while playing the guitar.

drawn back, and caught in a ribbon. Look, there are the riders in white shirts, and brightly colored headbands! Everybody stands back now, for the race is about to begin. From the waist down, there are no holds barred. A rider can catch his opponent's horse at the withers with his knee to break his stride, or hook his rival's leg with his own and suddenly unseat him, or lead him toward a hidden gopher hole. They are off in a tangled, straining pack! Now they return and thunder back at a breakneck speed, a mêlée, horse against horse!

The *chinas* gossip about the expedition that passed through the week on the road to Juárez. They drove an impressive herd of reserve horses and there were more women than ever, for the expedition is not to return until the last Indian has been cleared from the frontier. Many old women went with the troop, those who make the tarts the soldier likes, and many a new born babe, too. All the women rode good horses, loaded with stoves, pots, baskets, bundles, and irons, with which to earn pin money doing the officer's wash, so their man "will see that he is loved for his courage and merits, and not for what he can give on payday, because if he has nothing to give, the industrious woman finds a way to buy her handkerchiefs, pins, and perfumes." That is the way of the women who follow the troop in the field, of whom there are not so many now with the railroad and organized troops. The soldier does not fare well in the lonely desert without his woman. He leaves her behind, and then he must send for her. The dog is loyal to the battalion; but the woman is more so. If tempers are quick after the rum has flowed too freely and there are blows, a tasty tart comes on the heels of the whipping as the bread of peace. If there is fighting, she puts on a spare uniform and guards the horses, driving off the Indians.

The betting, the conversation, the cock fights are suddenly cut short. With a swing of the axe, the losing gaucho lops off the head of the bastard cock that crowed. The riders rein their horses off to one side. The stagecoach thunders in. The postilions, one for each pair of horses, spring from their exhausted beasts. Down from his seat atop the coach clambers the stage driver who is the hero there and who has left his mark on many an insolent face. His beard is black and his shoulders broad above a flat, tapering waist. His legs are thin and long-striding. He is curt of speech and a stranger to laughter. While the horses are changed in the bustling corral filled with dust and shouting, chairs and *mate* are brought out for the ladies traveling on the stage; the ladies are fashionably dressed, but they talk easily with the common folk. The keeper of the *pulpería* outdoes himself in his attentions toward the owner of the *estancia*, who wears patent leather boots and a fine-spun poncho. Among the passengers there is a gaucho wearing a fancy *chiripá* and a curly haired Italian with a valise filled with the jewelry and trinkets that are the delight of the *chinas*. There is also a gaucho in irons guarded by two policemen, an "unfortunate" who killed his friend "because he ran too hard against his knife and the wound festered." For him there is a double portion of *mate* and the good rum; he is given a silk handkerchief so that he will remember in his sorrow that there is a compassionate *china* somewhere. There is singing and dancing, and the *payador* sings of the sufferings of men of honor pursued by the law, and of the caution the stagecoach should take on the road to Juárez because the frontier is aflame, and there is a scalped white man's skull bleaching out there for every steer's skull; the women listen and sip their *mate*. The stage driver and the *pulpero* throw a box of rifles into the back of the stagecoach that is about to proceed on its journey.

The stagecoach is taking a road of no return! The Indians, the last savages, will attack, leaping on the galloping stage horses; the driver will tumble from his seat, killed by the first shot; the Indians will carry off the women on their horses, leaving the naked corpses scattered around the stagecoach. But out there on the frontier there is now an Indian chief who is the son of a Frenchman and lives among the huts of his Indians in a brick house with his Spanish wife; he sports a pair of trousers like those the Argentine top sergeants wear, with gold braid down the side. Beyond, in the sandy hills of Patagonia covered with wind-tortured shrubs, the remotest city in the world, Our

Lady of Carmen, there are now bankers, farmers and loving husbands and fathers where only short years ago there were highwaymen, forgers, and murderers, sent there by the government to start life anew with women whose sin was to have loved without measure.

The America of José Martí,
trans. Juan de Onís (New York, 1968), pp. 198–212

Flaubert's Last Work

The death of the fearless writer, Gustave Flaubert,[1] who knew how to tell the truth, still occupies the world of letters.

The Parisian journals still speak of his plain house at Croisset. Prussian soldiers, fancying that they had found the retreat of a butterfly of the Empire fond of fine dishes and rich old red wines, discovered only a clean and quiet home where a bronze statue of the Hindu Buddha stood facing the figure of the Lydian Bacchus, the god with the curly beard, the calm forehead, and the golden crown.

French papers have been filled with recollections of Flaubert. Their readers see the athletic writer, a Greek in strength, in elegance, in grace, moving along like a mighty shade. He is seen upon the green grass in profound thought, searching the depths of the soul. And despising the miserable bourgeois, whom in sonorous voice he called Philistines, and who use the noble gift of life only as an instrument for making money, buying white cravats for Sunday wear, and carping at all who dare to love, to suffer, and to think.

It is not of Flaubert, but of his last work, the one that killed him and the one that he finished a few hours before his death, that we wish to speak—*Bouvard and Pécuchet*. It is a strange

1. Gustave Flaubert (1821–1880), novelist regarded as the pioneer of the Realist school of French literature whose masterpiece *Madame Bovary* (1857) was a realistic portrayal of bourgeois life.

book. Pages written with the grand eloquence of a Cervantes,[2] or a Rabelais,[3] and the solid symplicity of Homeric times are extracted from it. We speak of this in no petty enthusiasm. We have studied those crucified lions of *Salambo*, the wedding among the Bretons of *Madame Bovary*, and the frightful "Nebuchadnezzar," who wipes with his arm the perfumes from his face, who eats in sacred vessels, then breaks them, and inwardly takes the census of his fleets, his armies, and his people. His is tired of captures and exterminations, and the notion of rushing into degradation seizes him. When a man writes in this style pure, and solemn, and vibratory, he is certainly a great writer.

It has always been the style of the master hand, and it is the style in *Bouvard and Pécuchet*. Flaubert hated adjectives. He supplied their places with words so plain that they needed nothing to make them clear. Between two words he always took a long puff of his cigar. He did not walk, because he thought it beneath the dignity of a philosopher. He was wont to say that "repose is strength." Seated like a Turk, he examined his phrases, turning, analyzing, and pruning them. There was no obscurity. From truth vigor came forth, and from severity beauty. He did not write his first work thus. The work was not, as has been said, *Madame Bovary* but the *Chateau des Couers*. *Bovary* is a novel that smells of blood. *Salambo* is a book so solid that it seems formed of marble and colored with the purple that made so famous the countries he describes. In *Bouvard and Pécuchet*, a résumé of a life learned, independent, and original—we recognize a pen which carves, chisels, and models: a pen which cuts, scourges, and wounds in order the better to cure. It is a good father who is correcting his child.

Bouvard and Pécuchet is to be published in the *Revue Nouvelle* of Mme. Edmond Adam, a modern Mme. Récamier, but with

2. Miguel de Cervantes (1547–1616), novelist, playwright, and poet, famous as the creator of *Don Quixote*.

3. François Rabelais (1483–1553), French writer, author of the satirical masterpiece, *Gargantua and Pantagruel*, an attack on sham and superstition of the Middle Ages.

no tinge of Chateaubriand.[4] The book is awaited with anxiety. It will doubtless prove successful, quite as much as *Nana*, which is certainly far below the other works of Zola.

It may soon be translated and the public will be obliged to us for noticing it beforehand.

This is the age of writers, actors, and painters. Bouvard and Pécuchet are two old men who, loving chocolate, quietly take their seats regularly every evening upon the same bench. As they remove their hats they discovered that each has his name painted in the crown.

This simple identity of thought and action calls out the friendship of their souls. They say that since there are so many thieves in the Ministry, citizens ought to look out for their hats. The satire is not bad for a beginning. The two faces softened by sudden friendship, display their wrinkles. Bouvard says to Pécuchet that his life as a ministerial employee has become tiresome. He drifts into memories of the past. In broken accents he recalls his misfortunes in love—the sentiment that always remains young even in old hearts. Pécuchet tells Bouvard that he, also an employee in a government office, sighs for an active life. He detests the horrible existence that bends him over stamped paper, forcing him, a man, to perform the duty of a silk worm. They love the country: they detest Paris; they have saved some money; they quit the bench upon which their mutual confidence was created, and, arm in arm, the two old men start off like two children in search of happiness, far away from the sphere where happiness certainly does not exist.

Then follows a promenade through modern life, in which nothing escapes the penetrating eye of Flaubert.

He has not seen fit to judge what is called the march of progress like a writer filled with prejudice.

This existence of ours is artificial.

4. Vicomte François René de Châteaubriand (1768–1848), diplomat and author, and one of the first Romantic writers in France who had a profound influence on the youth of his day with his exotic accounts of America and its Indians.

After discarding old absurdities, we perhaps only substitute new ones.

Flaubert endeavours to put in front of this imposed and conventional life the simple and plain life of nature.

He has created two artless old men whose impressions are genuine.

He wished to create two fools; he really makes two men simple and pitiable.

The two resigned employees, always credulous, always deceived, crushed and broken against the sharp corners of real life, oppress the heart, and awaken profounds sympathy. They reach for everything, they get nothing. In seeking happiness they find a vacuum. They leave the Ministry with hearts full of joy, with hearty laughter, and with brilliant hopes.

They pass through life falling at every step, bruising their flesh and breaking their bones, and they at length return to the Ministry with sick hearts, pinched lips, and dead hopes. Poor old men! Whether Flaubert intended it or not, it is a magnificent allegory of unrealized idealism.

These two men, with wrinkled foreheads, and shrivelled faces, exhibit something of the eternal man, always in pursuit of that which is beyond his reach, stretching forth his hands towards an ever fleeting phantom.

They do not represent men, they represent man—possibly the bourgeois Don Quixote. The hero of La Mancha crossed the desolate plains with lance under his arm, helmet on his head, and a hand gloved in iron, seeking wrongs to right, widows to defend, and the unfortunate to aid. Bouvard and Pécuchet pass through the life of the nineteenth century, by no means a plain, seeking that repose of soul, and that happiness which cannot exist in great cities. Alas! happiness is not the fruit of time! They return, bruised and torn, and die like Quixote.

But what have the old men done on their travels? They have tried everything, science, poetry, love. Why force them to so much travel? To make them talk about everything. It is after seeing that they speak. They judge of things as they find them, and their judgment in this romance is the judgment of Flaubert in a notebook. They try everything: politics, which fatigues: science, which deceives; criticism, which is venomous and jealous; purchasable poetry, the illegitimate, the false art, the murderer of art.

Thiers left an unfinished work in the form of a romance which he called his "monument" and in it he gives a résumé of the discoveries, aspirations, superstitions, greatness and smallness of the modern world. Bouvard and Pécuchet abandon the cultivation of fields for that of letters, a rocky field if there ever was one.

They write plays, novels, and works of a high order of literature. Flaubert takes advantage of this to punish, and for cause, the classic tragedy, the affected criticism, and the absurd romances of adventures, unworthy of sensible people.

Bouvard and Pécuchet fail to find in literature the happiness that they expected. They take to politics. The people must be taught morality. But politics gives no return for their expenses. Upon politics men waste and lose the best blood in their veins. The two old men study all systems. Neither divine right nor the absolute right of the people can suit them, and they come out of politics, as from everything else, deceived and disappointed.

Woman's love may possibly console them after so many disasters. Their foreheads are wrinkled, their cheeks are hollow, and although their faces are sallow and like parchment, they cherish the hope that the grandeur and freshness of their minds may be attractive. But love is always the son of eros. He deceives the good old men. Flowers do not grow in the winter: or if they do they must be forced, and purchased at too dear a price. And here the author becomes both profound and charming.

Where then are the old men to find happiness? The miseries of the world cannot satisfy their sincere souls. They turn their eyes toward heaven. Heaven in the form of the priest does not please them. The liberty of reason leaves them with an empty soul, which the dictation of the church cannot fill. Since happiness is not found in the sickly conceptions of men, perhaps it is to be found in the innocence of children. They have already lost the right to hope for children of their own. The selfishness of old bachelors must be punished. They adopt the children of others. Here again the blue sky becomes black and stormy. The children are careless and ungrateful. They cause the last tears that flow from the eyes of unfortunate old men.

On their return from their voyage through modern life, we finally find the two old fellows again seated upon their bench eating chocolate cakes, looking at each other tenderly and pointing to the names in their hats: Bouvard and Pécuchet. They have traveled through the world and suffered from its errors, they have been close observers, and from their long pilgrimage have saved one grand sentiment, which after all is sufficient: the friendship of men. They are warm friends. They were Frenchmen: they are citizens of the whole world.

The work will last because, as Flaubert said, "it is a cordial book."

New York Sun, July 8, 1880[5]

5. According to a notice in José Martí, *Obras Completas*, vol. XV (La Habana, 1964), pp. 205–09, the article was written in English. However, Alejo Carpentier, the famous Cuban novelist, in the article "Flaubert and the Hispanic World," published in the French magazine *Le Nouvel Observateur* in 1980, points out that the article was written by Martí in French and was translated into English. At any rate, Carpentier notes that the publication of the article, exactly two months after Flaubert's death, was evidence of the dissemination of Flaubert's work in the Spanish-speaking world.

The article by Carpentier was the last one he published. He turned it in to the French magazine the morning of his death.

Pushkin

Moscow has had her festival in the erection of a monument to Pushkin,[1] the Russian apostle and poet. A due tribute has been paid with solemn éclat, great orators have spoken, and memorable verses have been read, but ominous voices were heard. Do the people both adore and detest him? Is the East shaken to her very vitals, preparing, with more firmness and practical common sense than its prototype, its terrible '89? If the monarchy will not make a revolution, the revolution will unmake the monarchy. A prudent chieftain will make himself the leader of forces that cannot be held back.

The recent festival at Moscow was a political agitation, marked with terrible accusations and popular bitterness. The people knew Pushkin by heart, but they wanted to punish his lack of character. It was a merciless chastisement. In becoming the historiographer of the Czar, he was no longer the outspoken friend of the people. He had kissed the ship that he had tried to break. Russians insist that the actions of genius must correspond with the promises of its songs. The hand must follow the inspiration of the intellect. It is not enough to write a patriotic strophe: you must live it. In the sombre politics of Russia there are only two parties, the whipped serfs, and their masters. He who has not the courage to be honest in Russian politics cannot

1. Alexander Pushkin (1799–1837), Russian poet, novelist, dramatist, and short-story writer, considered Russia's greatest poet and founder of the modern Russian literature.

be regarded as an honest man. After weeping over the wrongs of his countrymen, Pushkin finally caressed and lauded the hand that inflicted them.

The poet's talent was fresh, rich, and powerful. Prosper Mérimée,[2] who translated his works into elegant French, speaks of him as "the first poet of his time," Mérimée, the connoisseur of all literature, spoke these words in the days of Alfred de Musset and Victor Hugo. With a sad smile Alfred had plunged his heart into a glass of absinthe after it had been wounded by a woman. A sea of new poetry, fresh and sparkling, was pouring from Hugo's boundless imagination.

Byron had died with his sword across his lyre. As a poet, Pushkin was his superior, but not as a man. True, he did not reach the mysterious magnificent heights in which the Englishman soared. Byron saw injustice and lashed it. Pushkin raised his voice against it, and then became its chamberlain and historian. He was more humane, more fluent, more imaginative, more spontaneous, and more national than Byron, but less brave, and totally undesirous of dying in the cause of liberty. Pushkin might have lived to an old age; Byron could not. Death is a right belonging to lives devoted to the rights of man—lives full of passion, resigned, and proud. Pushkin has been compared to Victor Hugo. It is not an apt comparison. Both were essayists at an early age. At fifteen, the Russian wrote verses in French as charming as the lines of La Fontaine,[3] and as cutting as those of Molière.[4] The two styles were especially adapted to the Russian character. That of La Fontaine was primitive good sense, and that of Molière marked by hatred of the privileged classes. At the age of fifteen Victor Hugo abandoned the student's promenade, rushed up the steps of the Academie Française, and with trembling hands placed on the Secretary's table

2. Prosper Mérimée (1803–1870), French dramatist and archeologist, master of the short story.

3. Jean de La Fontaine (1621–1695), French poet, author of the famous *Fables*.

4. Molière, stage name of Jean-Baptiste Poquelin (1622–1673), great French comic dramatist.

his ode on "Les Plaisirs de l'Etude" which won an accessit [*sic*]. Beyond this there was no similarity between the poets, except in the power of imagination. With romance Hugo vindicated murdered liberty.

Pushkin aroused a people, lifted a Nation, and put life into a corpse. The people whom he aroused have indeed become a people. The advanced parties owing him their existence, are breathing and growing, because he did not do all that he allowed them to see that he could do. The French revolution owes its existence to Mirabeau, despite the stains on his brilliant career; the approaching Russian revolution owes its existence to Pushkin, despite his relations with the Court.

"Away with darkness! Hail to the sunlight!" cried the poet fifty years ago, when his liberal ideas had buried him in the Caucasus, when nobody but he dared with such a cry. Today, anybody stands in the path that he opened, and cries "Hail to the sunlight! Away with darkness!"

But the people whose applause is sought assume the right to punish. It would have been better not to think of the weakness of the man on the day of his glorification. It was hardly proper to cross swords over his cold body. It was a strange festival. The masters whom he flattered in the waning of life, and the people, whose songs and aspirations vibrated in the chords of his lyre, both claimed the dead man's shroud as their battle flag.

It is impossible to say how far this man would have gone. He died in time to prevent the effacement of all the glories of his early life. His generous soul, had he lived, might have begun to hate and to lash the Court that he had served. And then again, aristocrat that he was, living a fast life and accustomed to all its prodigal and luxurious surroundings and its pecuniary demands, he might have become still more strongly attached to his imperial tempter. His life was the career of a race horse. He had all the impulses and vagaries of nervous creatures. Like all geniuses, he was extreme—extreme in boldness and extreme in weakness. He allowed his reason at times to be guided by his impulse. Poets are like seas, they ebb and flow. When almost a boy, Pushkin reigned in drawing rooms. He was adored by women, and honored and feared by men. His imagination perfumed the palace. His wonderful flow of wit warmed all hearts. True men are always true, despite the surroundings of a capricious life. If perchance they fall away from truth or virtue, it is only for a short time. They are sure to again return. Love of justice and the hatred ignited by hatred and tyranny, forced young Pushkin to write biting satires.

Forbidden to be printed, they found their way into the hands of the people in manuscript form. These satires were a rumbling in distant clouds that forecast a tempest. The people began to murmur. The cup of souls in distress indicated a moral revolt. Farseeing poets are always ahead of the times. Pushkin wrote in the generous language of youth, and with all the freshness that characterizes political pamphlets forced to the surface by the oppression of tyranny. Monarchy unites itself with religion. When one is struck the other staggers. Pushkin wrote the "Gabriellade," in which libertine gods, marshalled by the archangel Gabriel, did deeds that were anything but divine. He tickled the public ear with a Voltairean sneer that greatly amused the philosopher Bielinski.

The poet was banished; but when nourished with the bitter bread of exile, his sarcasm became more poweful. His verses cracked like whips over the head of Prince Vorontzov. He was driven to the forests, where he could sing his strophes afar from men. The monarchists did not want him to put life into the dead masses.

The universities were the intellectual valets of the Czar. The possession of a foreign book was a crime.

How blessed was Pushkin's enforced solitude! Beautiful are the songs of poets who suffer. To make them suffer is to make them sing more sweetly. It was in exile.that Pushkin wrote his "Prisoner of the Caucasus." His "Fountains of Bajchisarai" and his "Freies Brigands." Then also he wrote the superb and rich popular tragedy "Boris Godunov" in which a genius proud and free, with no power to flatter, no school to follow, and no success to strive for, enlarged by solemn solitude, poured out in full the great passions and inmortal sentiments by which it was inspired. Liberty, the mother of genius being absolute, the child was healthy. Pushkin himself said that "Boris" was his best work.

Nicholas ascended the throne. With the hand that opened the universities to the people, and the frontier to books, he signed the pardon of Pushkin. The fierce yearnings that torment a poetic soul in exile, were limitless when the unexpected hour of happiness arrived. Pushkin again embraced old friends. He drank the good old wines, and again paid homage to beauty. He feverishly drained the cup of pleasure. Talent like a pretty woman is sought, flattered and caressed. It is crushed when it rebels: it is adored when it submits. Nicholas praised his poet and lavished money upon him, after appointing him historiographer of the Court. He promenaded with him, and paid his debts, but in assuaging his grief he broke his lyre. His friendship debased the poet. Time abruptly broke the degrading association. A duel with one said to be the lover of Pushkin's wife, stretched the poet dead upon the ground—dead at the age of 37!

But what a work was the work of that stormy life! True, Pushkin's odes and epistles, like the first works of all men of letters, were imitations of the earlier masters, but they were very happy imitations. Byronic outcries with Shakespeare profundity. When the true sorrows of life took the seat usurped by artificial grief absorbed from foreign literature a new epoch was opened for the talent of the poet. Abandoning individual sufferings, and romantic reminiscences laden with traits of his genius, he produced "Ruslan and Liudmila" and astonishing legends, popular stories, and Russian tragedy. Man is a magnificent unity, composed of individual varieties. The Eternal Man was revealed to Pushkin in his ardent study of the cruelties and misfortunes of humanity. The poet, for the time being, was the creature tormented and the creator of torments.

By the divine power of his poetry he created magnificent human types.

He took his "Convidado de Piedra" from the Spaniard Tirso

de Molina.[5] His "Mozart" from the German and his "Chevalier Avare" and his "Scènes du Temps de la Chevalerie" from the good old times when men rode on saddled horses, with swords in their hands, beneath moonlit gothic windows filled with pretty ladies. Nationalities passed before his eyes like clouds in the sky. He was a man of all times and all countries—the intrinsic man—the universe in a single breast.

Russian newspapers have described the splendid monument and great processions at Moscow. They have sketched the decorations and enumerated those who were present at the inauguration of the memorial, but they have not mentioned the magnificent literary congress that honored the occasion. All that Russia has not yet exiled, and all that the fermenting country still possesses among the famous and illustrious, were there to consecrate Pushkin as the National poet. We must throw aside the bitterness against the dead cherished by the Russian Liberals. It is like the bitterness of the Poles against Michiewicz.[6] All of the literary coteries, except that of the humorist Salykov,[7] representatives of all political parties, and all Russian men of letters were seated there, like good sons, to honor their father. The debris of the polite Occidentals and of the ferocious Slavophiles, who on the one hand made so much noise after Pushkin's death by their sympathy with the revolution of '48, and on the other made Moscow the impregnable fortress of the genius of Russia, were among them. The Congress lasted two days, Turgenev,[8] so well known in Paris, so

5. Tirso de Molina, pseudonym of Gabriel Tellez (1571–1648), Spanish dramatist.

6. Adam Berman Michiewicz (1798–1855), greatest poet of Poland, and Apostle of Polish national freedom.

7. Fyodor Stepanovich Salykov (1826–1889), pen name Schedrinn, novelist, author of satirical sketches of life of the upper classes in provincial Russia.

8. Ivan Sergeyevich Turgenev (1818–1883), Russian novelist and poet, author of *Fathers and Sons* (1862).

dear to his country, and so famous through his "Mes de Gentilhommes" and his sweet "Liza" was a member.

There also was Count Tolstoy,[9] the deposed Minister of Public Instruction. At the side of Ostroski,[10] the most celebrated among the sorry modern dramatists of Russia. Potiekhine, the charming novelist, and the genial Dostoyevsky,[11] who handles a pen with a steel point, and who has the eye of an eagle and the heart of a dove, sat on the same bench. Yuriev, Katkhov[12] and Aksakov[13] of historic fame, all editors of powerful journals were not absent and the list included Polonski,[14] a poet in love with humanity, and Maykow,[15] a poet devoted to old Russian manners and customs.

This Congress did not discuss the merits of Pushkin. While paying tribute to the poet, they sifted his claims as the maternal bard of Russia. Potiekhine asserted that great as was Pushkin, he did not, like Gogol,[16] study and denounce the evils of society.

His assertion was controverted by quotations showing that the intuitive foresight of Pushkin had outlined the footpath leading to Russian freedom. Yuriev, the journalist, asked the

9. Count Pyotov Andreyevich Tolstoy (1645–1729), Russian diplomat and statesman, influential in the time of Peter the Great.

10. Alexander Nicolayevich Ostrovsky (1823–1886), Russian dramatist who is generally considered the greatest representative of the Russian realistic period.

11. Fyodor Mikhailovich Dostoyevsky (1821–1881), famous Russian novelist, author of *The Idiot*, *Crime and Punishment*, and *The Brothers Karamazov*.

12. Mikhail Mikiforovich Katkhov (1818–1887), Russian reactionary journalist.

13. Sergei Timofeyevich Aksakov (1791–1859), Russian writer of the realist school, author of four noted autobiographical works.

14. Yakov Petrovich Polonsky (1819–1898), Russian poet, author of the allegorical poem *The Cricket-Musician* (1859).

15. Apollon Nikolayevich Maykow (1821–1897), Russian poet, influenced by Greek and Roman mythology.

16. *See above* pp. 237.

convention to honor the extraordinary genius, who although a Russian, was the poet of the world. He added that Pushkin personified the one thing lacking in Russia—the solidarity of the people. Katkhov, a journalist famed for intellectuality, and a vindictive spirit, made a conciliatory speech. He besought both parties, separated through his agency, to forgive and unite. He forgot that there can be no pardon, when there has been no justice. Aksakov, the fiery Slavophile, praised Pushkin for rescuing the Russian spirit from the current that was bearing it towards France. He is still the warrior who fought from 1838 to 1848, the battle signalled by the death of Pushkin. He flourishes the sabre and poises the lance of the pregnant Russian idea, but he does not attack Bielinsky[17] with the old-time fury. He is the man-at-arms as Koniekov[18] is the book, and Kvojivsky[19] the incarnation of the Russian idea.

Ostroski, the dramatist, glorified Pushkin for his love of sincerity and his hatred of exaggeration. He said that his romances were as clear as the blue sky in a cold wind. Presemsky extolled the dead author as the true master of the greatest Russian prose writers.

Turgenev speaks with the neatness of a Frenchman. His sentences are ornate, and he has the style of an academician intensified by the sharpness which so well becomes Russian talent. He would not pronounce Pushkin as great a poet for Russia as Dante for Italy, Shakespeare for England, or Molière for France, because he did not have the time nor the opportunity to do what those poets did. The unfortunate period in which he wrote was barricaded with insurmountable difficulties and obstructions.

17. Vissarion Grigorievich Belinski (Bielinsky) (1811–1848), Russian literary critic. His writings (12 vols., 1859–1862) provide a firm foundation for Russian literary criticism.

18. Serg Timof Konekov (1874–?) Russian sculptor, whose subjects were Slavic and Greek mythology.

19. Iukov Gerasimovich Kvaskov, a Russian author, whose first work was published in Moscow.

In response to Turgenev another romancer delivered a speech so eloquent and brilliant that it won for him, by a unanimous vote, an honorary membership in the Russian Society of the Friends of Literature. It is an honor highly prized in Russia. This orator, however, was no parvenu. He did not come then, like Castelar when he made his maiden speech at the Teatro de Oriente, after timidly threading his way through a crowd, absolutely unknown to those whom he was about to dazzle and astonish. Dostoyevsky came to Moscow with fresh laurels won in the Assembly of Nobles. He came there loaded with his literary effects.

After writing books so severe as *Crime and Punishment*, so rich in imagination as *Demons*, so sweet as the *Brothers Karamazov*, he had acquired the right to judge Pushkin. He put in bold relief the genuine character, the virginal freshness, the absolute originality, and the exquisite literary polish of the works of this great writer. He spoke of Titiana as the most thorough Russian woman created by Russian poets, and of Eugene Oneguin as a sad hero, a Russian Cavalier containing all the germs of vice and virtue, hating wrong and still traveling with it arm in arm. In speaking of that splendid poem, the "Tzigane," he pointed out Aleko as a Russian type of good alloy. He warmly praised the tragedy of "Boris Godunov" in which was portrayed all the sorrow, the pride, the strength, and all the weakness of Oriental character. He closed amid a whirlwind of applause by asserting that Pushkin was the creator and guardian of the new intellectual life of Russia.

Dostoyevsky was the mouthpiece for all who appreciate Pushkin. The great poet is so thoroughly Russian, so truly the son of that proud land so little known, and has come so naked from the bosom of Nature, that on reading his "Ode to God" you would imagine that its writer was lying in the frozen snow beneath the northern sky, wrapped in a bearskin, pouring out his wild notes far from the habitations of man. His is the poetry of Nature in a new country, where the breath of a long life, and the poison of cities have not yet polluted hearts, blasted forests and wilted fields. In this "Ode to God" you hear the moaning of the sea, the rumbling of the earthquake, the roaring of the tempest, and the thunder of man's rebellion.

In it you see the living East. It is whitened with the foam of the sea, and it sparkles like Persian gems.

Nobody accused Pushkin's antagonist of a crime for killing him in a duel.

The people said that he had previously been killed by the court of the Czar.

Its seductions had destroyed the rich source of his inspirations. Love of justice and of truth was regarded as a crime by the society that had perverted his nature. His life was a battle. A battle follows his apotheosis. But the praise of the poet cannot be excessive. He is not universally known because he wrote in Russian; but once known he can never be forgotten. He had extreme eloquence, a surprising literary fecundity, a precise intuition, a healthy love of truth, and the unalloyed sentiment of Nature. His faults, both of life and of poetry, came from the extreme feminine sensibility which almost invariably weakens the natural energy of genius.

New York Sun, August 28, 1880
[written in English]

Oscar Wilde[1]

All of us speakers of Spanish live lives that are steeped in Horace and Virgil, and the frontiers of our spirit would seem to be the frontiers of our language. Why must the literature of other lands be virtually forbidden fruit for us, rich as it now is in that natural background, honest strength, and contemporary spirit so lacking in modern Spanish literature? Byron's influence upon Núñez de Arce, the German poets' sway over Campoamor[2] and Bécquer,[3] and the occasional pallid translation of some German or English work, would hardly give us any idea of the Slavic, German or English literature whose poetry contains white swans, castle ruins, lusty young girls upon flower-strewn balconies, and the calm and mystical light of the aurora borealis, all at once. Knowing various literatures is the best way to free us from being oppressed by some, just as there is no way to avoid blindly following a single philosophical system unless we feed upon them all. Thus we find that all systems pulse with one spirit, subject to the same hazards—violent or cowardly, according to the climate—no matter how the human

1. Oscar Wilde (1854–1900), English wit, poet, and dramatist. Wilde made a lecture tour of the United States and Canada in 1882.

2. Ramón de Campoamor y Camposorio (1817–1901), Spanish poet who attained wide popularity for his epigrammatic poetry and who became known as a leading poet in Spain.

3. Gustavo Adolfo Bécquer (1836–1870), Spanish lyric poet and author of popular prose tales.

imagination may have clothed that faith in the infinite and that yearning to escape from itself, and regardless of that noble nonconformity with one's own existence engendered by all the schools of philosophy.

Take Oscar Wilde, the young Anglo-Saxon who writes some excellent poetry, a dissenter in the arts who accuses English art of having been a divisive factor in the temple of beautiful universal art. An elegant apostle, filled with faith in his message and scornful of those who criticize it, he is travelling over the United States at this very moment, telling smoothly and discreetly how much he abominates the people who make a cult of material well-being to the detriment of spiritual well-being, unmindful that the latter would so lighten their shoulders of life's burdens and make all kinds of effort and endeavor more pleasant. To embellish life is to give it purpose. To escape from oneself is an irrepressible human desire, and whoever tries to beautify men's existence does them a favor, for he makes them satisfied to be as they are. It is like damaging the beak of the vulture that devoured Prometheus.[4] These are the things that the rebel says, although he may not succeed in being so precise or seeing such a broad panorama. He wants to shake from his attire of a cultivated man the coal dust and oily soot that blackens the sky of English cities upon which the sun shines like an opaque reddish sphere struggling through the thick fog to send its life-giving heat to the harsh, rude-limbed, stiff-necked northerners. So the poet born on those shores strengthens his living faith in the neglected and disregarded things of the spirit. To hate tyranny one need only live under it, and nothing so kindles the poetic fire than to live among those in whom it is missing. But poets suffocate unless they have kindred souls into whom they can pour out their overflowing spirit.

Look at Oscar Wilde! He is in spacious Chickering Hall where the New York public goes to hear lectures. This place is a

4. In Greek religion one of the Titans, God of fire. After Prometheus was chained Zeus sent an eagle to eat his immortal liver which constantly replenished itself.

mecca for popular lecturers of established fame and fortune who foregather there to woo it brazenly. Christian dogma is attacked and defended there, the old retained and the new explained. Travelers describe their voyages with the aid of lantern slides and chalk drawings upon a large blackboard. A critic studies a poet. A lady holds forth upon the suitability or unsuitability of this or that type of dress. A philosopher expounds the laws of philology. In one of the halls in this building Wilde will read his lecture about the great English renaissance in art, of which he is regarded as the authority when in reality he is no more than a spirited connoisseur and an active and fervent disciple. He is spreading his faith. There were others who died for it, but more of that later. The hall is crowded with elegant ladies and distinguished gentlemen. Great poets there are none, as if afraid of being taken for accomplices of the innovator. Secretly, men love the dangerous truths, and their fear of defending them before they have won acceptance is equaled only by the tenacity and enthusiasm they show in supporting them once the risk has ended.

Oscar Wilde has a distinguished Irish heritage, and being independently wealthy he could purchase the right to independent thought. This is one of the diseases that kill men of genius; it often happens that their poverty prevents them from defending the truth which consumes and enlightens them, a truth too new and revolutionary for general acceptance. So their very existence depends upon withholding the revealing truth they bring to the world, and it is from the pain of this that they perish.

The carriages crowd about the wide doors of the imposing lecture hall. A lady is carrying a lily, emblem of the reformers. Everybody has taken great pains to dress with elaborate elegance. Like the esthetes who are renovating art in England, they strive for perfect harmony in the combination of colors in both dress and accessories. The stage is simple and uncluttered. A high-backed chair with heavy arms, like our choir stalls, awaits the poet. The chair is made of a dark wood with a dark morocco seat and back. The backdrop is a curtain of the most delicate shade of chestnut. Beside the armchair stands an elegant table with an artistic pitcher in which the pure water sparkles like imprisoned light. Here comes Oscar Wilde! He is not dressed like the rest of us, but in quite an individual fashion. His attire announces the flaw in his doctrine, which is not so much to create the new, something he feels incapable of doing, as to resurrect the old. His hair is meticulously parted down the center, and falls to his shoulders in the manner of Elizabethan cavaliers. He is wearing a black dress coat, a white silk vest, comfortable knee breeches, long black silk stockings and buckled shoes. His shirt collar is open like Byron's, and held together by a carelessly tied white silk cravat. A diamond stud shines from his resplendent shirt front, and from his vest pocket hangs an artistic watch fob. A man must dress handsomely and he sets the example. But art demands a unity of time in all its works, and it offends the eye to see a spruce young man with a Cromwellian hair style wearing this year's waistcoat, old-fashioned breeches, and a foppish, turn-of-the-century watch chain. A noble sincerity radiates from the young poet's face. He is circumspect in displaying his extravagant garb. He respects the sublimity of his views, and they command respect for him. He is smiling with self-assurance. The illustrious audience is beginning to whisper. What can the poet be saying?

He says that beauty needs no definition after Goethe's, that the great English renaissance of this century combines a love for Grecian beauty with a passion for the Italian renaissance and with the desire to avail itself of all the beauty put into its works of art by the modern spirit. He says that the new school has sprung up like a harmony of love in Faust[5] and in Helen of Troy, from the close bond between the spirit of Greece, where all was beautiful, and the burning, inquiring and rebellious individualism of the modern romantics. Homer came before Phidias;[6] Dante came before the marvelous renewal of the arts in Italy; the poets invariably lead the way. The pre-Raphaelites, painters who loved a genuine, natural and unadorned beauty,

5. The famous dramatic poem in two parts by Goëthe.
6. Phidias (490–430 B.C.), famous Athenian sculptor.

preceded the esthetes, men who love beauty in the art and culture of every age. And the exuberant and adaptable Keats came before the pre-Raphaelites.[7] These partisans of the painting techniques used by the predecessors of the lyrical Raphael wanted those painters to put aside all they knew about art, and devote themselves to teaching the old masters; with a palette covered with colors they set about copying objects directly from Nature. They were honest to the point of brutality. Because they hated convention in others, they commenced to work under conventions of their own. Because they scorned an overabundance of rules, they ended by scorning them all. Improvement cannot be achieved by a turning back; but if the pre-Raphaelites were incapable of building, at least they demolished some dusty idols. After them, and largely because of them, people in England camė to appreciate truth and freedom in art. "Don't ask the English who those worthy pre-Raphaelites were," said Oscar Wilde. "One of the prerequisites of education in England is to know nothing about her great men. Back in 1847 the admirers of our Keats gathered to see him arouse poetry and painting from their stony bed of slumber. But doing this in England means losing all one's rights as citizens. They had youth, strength and enthusiasm, qualities the English can never forgive. They were satirized, because satire is the tribute which jealous mediocrity always pays to genius. This must have made the reformers quite pleased with themselves, for to be in total disagreement with three quarters of the English people is one of the most legitimate reasons for self-satisfaction, and in moments of spiritual dejection this must be a great source of comfort."

Now hear Wilde talk about another most harmonious poet, William Morris,[8] author of *The Earthly Paradise*, a man who gloried in his personal beauty and in the lyricism of his poetry,

7. A name adopted by a group of young British artists, led by Dante Gabriel Rossetti, who reacted against the dominant art of the Royal Academy in the mid-nineteenth century.

8. William Morris (1834–1896), British socialist and poet, famous as a designer and craftsman.

vibrant and transparent as Japanese porcelain. Hear Wilde expound Morris's belief that to copy Nature very closely is to deprive her of one of her loveliest qualities: that mist that surrounds her creations like a luminous halo. Hear him say that English literature owes to Morris that precise manner of inscribing the images of fantasy upon the mind and poetry so skillfully that Wilde knows of no English poet who has surpassed Morris in the lucid phrase and the pure image. Hear him recommend that practice of Theophile Gautier[9] who considered no book more worthy of being read by a poet than the dictionary. "Those reformers," said Wilde, "came singing praises to all the beautiful, whether of their own time or of any other." They wanted to state it all, as long as they stated it beautifully. Beauty was the only restraint they put upon freedom. They were guided by a profound love for perfection.

They did not strangle inspiration but clothed it in beautiful garments. They wanted it to go through the streets dressed decently, not shabbily or in poor taste. "We do not want to clip the poet's wings," said Wilde, "but we have grown used to counting their endless flapping, to calculate their unlimited strength, to control their uncontrollable freedom. Let the bard sing of everything, if what he sings is worthy of his poetry. The poet's scope is limitless. He lives from spirit, which is imperishable. He finds no forms worthless, no subjects sterile. But with the serenity of one who feels he possesses the secret of beauty, the poet should accept whatever he considers undeniably beautiful from every age, and reject whatever fails to fit his consummate idea of beauty. Swinburne,[10] also a great English poet, whose imagination floods his lyrical lines with countless riches, claims that art is life itself, knowing nothing of death. Let us not reject the ancient, for it happens that the ancient is a perfect reflection of the present. Life in all its various forms is

9. Théophile Gautier (1811–1872), French poet, novelist, critic, and journalist.

10. Algernon Charles Swinburne (1837–1909), English poet and critic, who was the symbol of the mid-Victorian poetic revolt.

essentially eternal, and seen in the past it has none of that 'aura of familiarity' or concern that obscures it for the living. Choosing a proper subject, however, is not enough to exalt men's souls. It is not the subject painted upon canvas which attracts the eye; it is the emanation of the spirit which comes from the skillful use of color. Therefore the poet who wants his poetry to be noble and enduring must acquire the merely technical craftsmanship that lends his songs that spiritual fragrance which is so captivating. Who cares if the critics grumble! The true artist does not restrict himself to being a critic, and artists who stand the test of time are fully understood only by other artists. Our Keats[11] used to say that he revered only God, the memory of great men, and beauty. This is why we esthetes came: to show men the utility of loving beauty, to encourage the study of those who have cultivated it, to stimulate the desire for perfection and the abhorrence of all ugliness, and to bring back the fashion of admiring, knowing and practicing all that mankind has admired as beautiful. But what is the use of our desiring to perfect the dramatic form attempted by our poet Shelley, sick with love for the sky in a land where it is not loved? What is the use of our zealously pursuing improvement in our conventional poetry and pallid arts, in the embellishment of our homes, in the grace and quality of our dress? There can be no great art without a beautiful national life, and England's spirit of commercialism has killed it. There can be no great drama without a noble national life, and this too has been killed by the commercial spirit of the English." Warm applause encouraged the excellent speaker at these strong words, and he had obviously won the affectionate curiosity of his audience.

And then Wilde addressed the North American: "Children of a new nation, perhaps you may be able to achieve here what costs us such effort to achieve over there in Britain. Blessed be your lack of ancient institutions, for this is tantamount to a lack of obstacles; you are not bound by tradition, and your critics are

11. John Keats (1795–1821), one of the greatest of nineteenth century English lyric poets.

not armed with hypocritical and mundane conventions with which to belabor you. Starving generations have never trampled upon you. You are not compelled to constantly imitate a type of beauty whose elements are dead. The splendor of a new imagination and the wonder of some new freedom could originate with you, but now your cities as well as your literature lack the grace and flexibility that endows sensitivity with beauty. Love all that is beautiful merely for the pleasure of loving it. All repose and happiness stem from this. A devotion to beauty and the creation of beautiful things is the best part of all civilizations; it makes every man's life a sacrament rather than a number in a ledger. Beauty is the only thing that time cannot kill. Philosophies die, religious creeds vanish, but the beautiful lives forever. It is the gift of all the ages, the sustenance of all peoples everywhere, and an eternal treasure. Wars will be of little account when all men love the same things with equal intensity, when a common intellectual climate unites them. England is still a powerful sovereign by virtue of her military might; and our renaissance would give her a sovereignty to endure long after her yellow leopards tire of the roar of battle, and the rose upon her shield is no longer tinged with the blood of combat. And you also, Americans, by planting the heart of this great nation with the aesthetic spirit that makes life better and alleviates its hardships, will amass such riches for yourselves that they will make you forget, for being so trivial, those you now enjoy from having made your land a network of railroads and your harbors a haven for all the ships that sail all the seas known to man."

Those were the wise and noble words the Chickering Hall audience heard from the young English poet with the long hair and the short trousers. But what is in this gospel to raise such a protest from his disciples? These thoughts are shared by all of us: we look upon the wonders of art with this same reverence. We also have less of the commercial spirit rather than too much. Then what peculiar greatness lies in these beautiful but commonplace and self-evident truths that Oscar Wilde is parading throughout England and the United States? Can it be that what we take for granted is for others a miracle? Is this bold young man to be respected or ridiculed? He is to be respected! True, for fear of appearing presumptuous or taking more delight in the contemplation of beautiful things than in the moral power and transcendental purpose of beauty, this lecture we are summarizing did not reflect the profound design and extensive scope that would please a thinker. There is certainly a childish aspect to anyone preaching such vast reforms, and dressed in clothes that add not a vestige of grace or nobility to the human form—an affectation that is nothing but a timid sign of his hatred for present-day conventions.

Surely the esthetes are wrong in trying, with a strange kind of love, to find the secret of spiritual well-being in the future by means of an adoration for the past and for the extraordinary times gone by. There is no doubt that the vigorous reformers should pursue the wrong in the source that spawned it—an excessive love for physical well-being—instead of in the disaffection for art, which is its result. True, in our fragrant and luminous lands we hold to be highly important those truths that are now preached to the Anglo-Saxons as bold and startling reforms. Yet with what bitterness this young man is seen, and with what indifference the children of his own country seem to respond to that fervent cult of the beautiful, a consolation for the greatest afflictions and a source of ineffable pleasure! And what sorrow he must feel to see his native land worshiping perishable idols and lost to life eternal. Think of the effort needed to combat the criticism of the cartoonists and satirists who live by catering to the taste of a public that dislikes anyone who exposes its defects! Think of the strength and energy needed to defy the fearful anger and vengeful scorn of a cold, hypocritical and calculating nation! What praise is too great, in spite of his long hair and short trousers, for this gallant youth who tries to change that dim reddish sphere that sheds its light upon the melancholy English into a sun whose shining rays will suffuse the air with gold! Love of art purifies the soul and inspires it; a beautiful painting, a luminous statue, a tastefully made toy, a modest flower in a pretty vase, brings a smile to the face that moments before may have been streaked by tears. Greater than the pleasure of knowing the beautiful, a strengthening and improving experience in itself, is the pleasure of possessing the beautiful—something that gives us self-satisfaction. Decorating one's home, hanging the walls with paintings, enjoying them, praising their merits and discussing their beauties, are noble delights which give value to life, diversion to the mind, and lofty employment to the spirit. A new sap seems to flow through the veins when one contemplates a new work of art. It is like having the future in one's presence. It is like drinking the ideal life out of a Cellini[12] goblet.

How brutal the nation that killed Byron! And how foolish and as if made of stone the nation that silenced the poetry from the youthful lips of the prolific Keats! English scorn congeals just as the cold mountain air freezes the English lakes and rivers. Disdain springs like an arrow from cold and bloodless lips. It delights in wit, which is pleasing; not in genius, which consumes. Since too much light is damaging, it delights in half-light. It enjoys the fashionable poet who makes one smile, not the poet of genius who makes one meditate and suffer. Like an iron shield it always opposes custom to any spirited voice that comes to disturb the sleep of its soul. The young esthetes hurl their war clubs at that shield, and with that shield the critics try to smother the noble words of those burning lips, just as it sealed Keats' lips even before his death. From Keats comes that vigorous poetic breath demanding music and spirit for verse, and the cult of art for the ennoblement of life. From Keats the English poets derive that subtle and jealous love of form which he gave to simple Greek thoughts. In a nation that rejects everything offensive and neither praises nor lulls the senses, it is Keats who gives birth to that painful struggle of the English poets who fight as if against an invincible army to awaken a love for impalpable beauty and the pleasing spiritual intangibles. Where can a poet turn in that land except to his inner self? What

12. Benvenuto Cellini (1500–1571), famous Florentine sculptor and goldsmith.

is he to do but fold up within his soul like a violet trampled by a horse's hoof? Keats' ideas overflow his winged and lyrical stanzas like the water of a virgin sea. His images tumble over one another as in Shakespeare, only Shakespeare subdues and plays with them, while Keats is sometimes carried away by his. An inner fire consumes his body. Adoring beauty, Keats goes to Rome—his shrine—to die. May his fervent disciple—whose defiance of the critics gives proof of great integrity, and whose noble poetry bids his soul abandon the market place of virtues and cultivate itself in tragic silence—quicken his scornful and busy nation's love for art, the source of all true happiness and the consolation that heals the spirit crushed by life's sorrows!

La Nación (Buenos Aires), December 10, 1882

Literary Matters[1]

. . . America will not produce a single immortal writer, such as a Dante, Luther, Shakespeare, or Cervantes[2] of the Americas, unless he reflects within himself the multiple and confused conditions of this age: concise, poetic, pithy, and shaped by supreme artistic genius. A language formed by the mother tongue itself, and by the language now influencing America, may bring to bear that necessary influence with sufficient fore-judgment to impress upon us what must remain fixed from this age of genesis, and to scorn that part of it which lacks stability and fails to accomodate itself to the essential nature of our mother tongue. It is a language plentifully endowed with beauty, and therefore powerful because of its solid structure. After the process of purification, it will finally have supreme dominion. Such must be the language that our Dante speaks.

Since it is a continental matter or a historic wellspring, and a monument visible from afar, his work will stand as a two-fold statement of the country whose literature is starting to be creative, through the form and spirit of this language. Because we can boast a rudimentary native literature and the raw materials for it, and hear its newborn cry and brag about some disconnected, but vibrant and very powerful ways of writing. However, we have no literature of our own. There can be no

1. This notebook was written in 1881.

2. Miguel de Cervantes (1547–1616), celebrated Spanish author of *Don Quixote*.

literature, which is expression, unless there is substance to express in it. And there will be no Spanish-American literature unless there is a Spanish America. We live in times of upheaval, not of condensation; in times of a mixture of elements, not of energetic labors of united elements. The species is struggling for dominion in the unity of a method. An exalted attachment to the past is barring the way to an apostolic desire for the future. Patricians and neopatricians object to the fact that plebeians and freedmen are enjoying their right to unity. They are afraid that their natural preponderance may trample them underfoot, or that they may not recognize the plebeians' legitimate part in the government. The Indians are too ardently attached to their government. Wise practice prevails over superficial theory. Institutions originating in the country's native elements—the only durable ones—are gradually being established, with difficulty, with certainty, upon the imported institutions that could topple at the slightest gust of wind. It takes centuries to create that which must last for centuries. Great works of literature have always been the expression of great ages in history. To an irresolute nation, irresolute literature! But as soon as the elements of a people approach some unity, the elements of its literature draw nearer together and condense into a great prophetic work. Let us now bemoan the fact that we lack this great work, not because we lack it but because it is a sign that we are not yet the great people of which it must be a reflection; for it must reflect, it must be the reflection. Will there be an essential and blessed merging, in urgent and mutual affection, of the ancient and related peoples of America? Or will there be a division, because of belly greed and petty jealousies, into spineless, misguided, marginal, and dialectical countries?

Words are wrapped in a cloak of usage; one must go directly to their substance. In this survey there is a sense that something is breaking, and that one can see the bottom. Words must be used as they are seen in depth, in their true and etymological and primitive meaning, which is the only vigorous meaning that

3. Miguel Antonio Caro (1843–1909), Colombian politician, poet, and author, president (1874–1898) of Colombia.

The Poem of Niagara[1]

Stop traveler! This man I bring by the hand is not a concocter of rhymes, nor a plagiarizer of the old masters—who are such because they never imitated anyone—nor a fluent teller of love tales like those who changed the dark hulls of treacherous Italian gondolas into magical citharas, nor a professional complainer like so many who force honest men to hide their sorrows as if they were sins, and their sacred laments as if they were childish frivolities! This man coming with me is great even if he is not from Spain, and he comes in disguise. He is Juan Antonio Pérez Bonalde, author of *The Poem of Niagara*. And if you should ask me any more about him, curious traveler, I will tell you that he was compared with a giant and did not come out wanting, but with the lyre securely hung over his shoulder—for he is one of those good contenders who fight with the lyre—and a laurel wreath upon his brow. And do not question me further, for it is sufficient proof of greatness to dare to be measured against giants; because a man's worth does not lie in the success of the attack, although this man did come out of the contest well, but in the courage of attacking.

Infamous times, when the only prevailing skill is that of having a well-stocked larder in the house, and sitting in a golden

1. This work appeared as a prologue to the *Poem of Niagara* by Juan Antonio Pérez Bonalde, published in New York in 1882, and later reprinted in the *Revista de Cuba*, vol. XIV, 1883.

chair, and living a gilded life, not realizing that human nature must stay as it is; and if one puts all the gold on the outside, one can only be left without any gold within! Infamous times, when the love and practice of greatness is a superior but obsolete virtue! In these days men are like certain young women who become very fond of virtue when they see it praised by others, or exalted in ringing prose or winged poetry, but no sooner do they embrace it than it takes the form of a cross; they cast it off in horror as if it were a consuming shroud, feasting upon the roses in their cheeks, and the pleasure of kisses, and that necklace of many-colored butterflies that women so enjoy wearing around their necks! Infamous times, when priests no longer deserve the veneration of poets, and poets have not yet commenced to be priests!

Infamous times!—not for man in the mass, who, like the insects, spins from his own substance the magnificent web in which space must later ride; but for those eternal youths; for those excitable and sensitive discoverers and visionaries—sons of peace and fathers of it; for those vehement believers—hungry for tenderness, devourers of love, not made for walking and for cultivating the land, filled with memories of clouds and wings, seekers of their broken wings—in short, the poor poets! It is their natural task to drive out of their breasts the eagles constantly being born there—the way a rose pours out fragrance, the sea gives shells, and the sun sheds light—and to sit down, as with mysterious sounds they accompany the voyagers upon their lyres, to see the eagles soar; but now the poet's work has changed, and he is strangling the eagles. What gyrations will they take if today their gyrations are obscured by the dust of battle that began to rise a century ago and still has not subsided? And who will follow them in their flight if present day men scarcely have time to drink the gold from their glasses, and cover their women with it, and take it out of the mines?

Since for a greater exercise of reason there appears in contradictory Nature all that is logical, it is coming to pass that this age of splendid elaboration and change—in which man is preparing, among the obstacles preceding all greatness, to enter the enjoyment of himself, and to be king of kings—belongs to the poets. And the age belongs to these great men because of the confusion that causes changes of condition, of faith, and of governments—an age of tumult and affliction in which the din of battle deadens the melodious prophecies of better times ahead, and the overthrow of the combatants leaves the rose bush without roses, and the mists of battle dim the soft brilliance of the stars. But in the structure of the universe there is nothing so small that it does not contain within itself all the germs of great things, and the sky revolves and moves with its storms through the days and nights, and man is changeable and moves with his passions, faith, and bitterness. And when his eyes can no longer see the stars in the sky, he turns them to the stars of his soul. Hence these pale and complaining poets; hence this dolorous and tormented poetry; hence this intimate, confidential and personal poetry, a necessary consequence of the times—ingenuous and useful, like a song of brothers, when it springs from a strong and healthy nature; colorless and absurd when an insensitive person, endowed, like the peacock of brilliant plumage, with a gift for song, tries to pluck its strings.

Nowadays, men would look like females—weak females—as if under the protection of Alexander and Cebetes, and crowned with garlands of roses, they devoted themselves to purifying the honeylike wine of ancient Rome that seasoned the banquets of Horace. Pagan lyrical poetry is out of style because of its sensuality, and Christian lyrical poetry, which was beautiful, because of humans having changed the ideal of Christ—yesterday regarded as the least important of the gods and today loved as perhaps the greatest of men. Poets today can be neither lyrical nor epic with any naturalness or calm; nor is there any lyric poetry other than that which each one takes out of himself, as if his own being were the only thing whose existence he did not doubt, or as if the problem of human life had been challenged with such courage, and investigated with such eagerness, that there is no better objective—nor more stimulating nor more moved by profundity and greatness—than the study of oneself. Today nobody holds his faith secure. The believers themselves are deceived. The very ones who put their beliefs in writing, harassed by handsome inner beasts, bite the fists with which they write. There is no painter who succeeds in coloring, with the novelty and transparency of bygone days, the luminous aureolas of virgins, nor is there a preacher or religious singer who puts any fervor or words of conviction into his phrases and imprecations. All are soldiers of the army on the march. The same priestesses kissed them all. New blood is boiling in all of them. Although their entrails may be torn to shreds, Restlessness, Insecurity, Vague Hope, and Secret Vision are enraged and famished in their quietest corner. A huge pale man, dressed in black, with a thin face, tear-filled eyes, and a dry mouth, treads heavily over all the earth, never resting or sleeping—and he has sat down in every home, and laid his trembling hand upon the headboard of every bed! What a blow to the brain! What a shock to the heart! How to demand what does not come! How to know what one desires! How to feel both nausea and delight in one's spirit—nausea from the dying day, delight from dawn!

There is no such thing as a permanent work, for works of the times of reform and of once again putting things upon a stable basis are essentially anxious and changeable. There are no constant paths, and one can barely discern any new altars, great and open as forests. The mind solicits different ideas from everywhere, and ideas are like octopuses and starlight and waves of the sea. One longs incessantly to know something that confirms present-day beliefs, or is afraid of knowing something that may change them. Forming a new social state makes the battle for personal existence uncertain, and makes it more difficult to carry out the daily duties which, finding no broad paths and shaken by the right caused by the probability or nearness of misery, change form and direction at every instant. The spirit thus divided into contradictory and uneasy objects of one's affection; literary concept alarmed at every turn by a new gospel; all previously revered images divested of value and robbed of their prestige; future images as yet unknown—a well-defined character in this confused state of mind and in this restless life without a true course, appears impossible. Nor does a certain objective seem likely in this severe dread of household poverty, and in the various kinds of faint-hearted effort we put into avoiding it, into producing those lengthy and patient works, those long drawn-out histories in verse, those zealous imitations of the Latin peoples who wrote slowly and deliberately, year after year, in the repose of their cells, or in the pleasant idleness of the pretender at court, or in the spacious armchair upholstered with richly worked cordovan leather studded with gold, or in the beatific calm put into the spirit by the certainty that the good Indian was making the bread, the good king giving the laws, and the Mother Church providing protection and a grave. Only in an age of constant elements, of a general and definite literary type, of possible individual tranquility, of fixed and well-known channels, is it easy to produce those massive and imposing works of genius that inevitably require so many favorable conditions. Perhaps a cumulative and concentrated hatred can still give rise to such a genre of writings naturally, but love abounds and spreads; and this is the time of love, even for those who hate. Love sings brief songs, but it does not create—through vehement and culminating feelings whose tension tires and oppresses—any works of peaceful strength and laborious development.

And today there is something like a tearing asunder of the human mind. The times for raising obstacles are past; these are the times for demolishing them. Now men are beginning to walk the entire earth without stumbling; before, they had scarcely started walking when they struck against the wall of a nobleman's mansion or the bastion of a monastery. One loves a God who penetrates and pervades everything. It seems blasphemous to give to the creator of all beings, and of all that is still to come, the form of only one of His creatures. Since in the human realm perhaps all progress consists in returning to the point of departure, one keeps returning to Christ—to the crucified Christ who pardons and captivates, He of the naked feet and the outstretched arms; not a nefarious, satanic, malevolent, hating, inflamatory, scourging, death-dealing, impious Christ. And these new objects of affection do not incubate slowly, as they formerly did, in silent cells where a sublime and venerable solitude hatched radiant and gigantic ideas. And nowadays they do not carry these ideas in the mind for long days and long years, fructifying and nourishing, growing with the analogous impressions and judgments that hurried to cluster around the mother idea, like wartime standard bearers, to the little hill where the flag is to be raised. Today this prolonged mental pregnancy does not give birth to those Cyclopean and disturbed children—a natural outcome of an age of silence and retreat in which ideas were to turn into the timbrels of the king's jester, or into the clapper of a church bell, or into the fruit of the gallows; and in which the only way of expressing human wisdom was by some witty gossip in bad settings for romantic plays caught among the handguards of a sword, and the bounding and leaping farthingales of the town's handsome women, and their suitors. Now the trees in the forest have no more leaves than the cities have languages; ideas take shape in the plaza where they are taught, going from hand to hand and from foot to foot. Talking is not a sin, but a privilege. Listening is not heresy, it is a pleasure and a habit, and fashionable. The ear is alert to everything. No sooner do thoughts germinate than they are laden with flowers and fruit, and leaping onto paper, and entering every mind like a fine, subtle dust. Railroads are knocking down the forests; newspapers are knocking down the human forest. The sun is penetrating the cracks of old trees. All is expansion, communication, flowering, contagion, dissemination. The newspapers are deflowering grandiose ideas. Ideas do not produce a family in the mind, or a house, or a long life, as they once did. They are born on horseback, and ride the lightning with wings. They do not believe in one mind alone, but in commerce among them all. They do not take long, after a difficult start, in benefiting a small number of readers, but exert their beneficial influence immediately. They crush them, elevate them, wear them as a crown, nail them to a post, set them up as idols, overturn them, mistreat them. Even if poor ideas began by shining like superior ones, they cannot endure the traffic, floggings, undercurrents of unrest, and harsh treatment.

Superior ideas appear at last—somewhat mangled and bruised—but whole, concise, and with the virtue of spontaneous maturing. We get out of bed with one problem and go to sleep with another. Images devour each other in the mind. There is too little time for giving shape to what one thinks. In the mental sea some ideas are lost in others, as when a stone skips along the blue water and some of the widening circles are lost in others. Formerly, ideas would silently stand erect in the mind like strong towers, visible from afar. Today they leave the lips in a shower, like golden seeds that fall upon actively fertile soil. They burst, take root, evaporate, come to nothing—oh beautiful sacrifice for the one creating them!—and vanish in burning sparks, disintegrated. Hence those splendid small works, hence the absence of those great works of culminating, sustained, majestic and concentrated power.

And it also happens that—with man's great common labor and the healthful habit of self-examination, and the demanding of accounts of each other's lives, and the glorious necessity of kneading by themselves the bread to be served upon their tables—the age neither encourages nor accidentally permits the isolated appearance of superhuman beings gathered together in a unique labor of a kind considered marvelous and supreme. A great mountain seems less important when it is surrounded by hills. And these are times when the hills rise higher than the mountains; when the peaks are wearing themselves down into plains, and all the plains will become mountain peaks. With the descent of the heights, the plains are climbing to their level, thus facilitating communication throughout the world. Individual geniuses are less distinguished, because the smallness of the environs that once made their stature so prominent is beginning to fail them. And since all of them are learning how to harvest the fruits of Nature and to appreciate its flowers, the old masters show less concern for flower and fruit, and the new people—once a mere cohort of the worshipers of good reapers—show more. One is present at a kind of decentralization of the intelligence. It has come to be the beautiful domain of everyone. It stops the number of good second-class poets, and the shortage of isolated important ones. Genius is becoming less individual and more collective. Man is losing for the benefit of men. The qualities of the privileged classes are expanding and being diluted for the masses, which fact will not please the mean-spirited upper classes, but will please those of a gallant and generous heart who know that there is nothing on earth, no matter how great a creature it is, but the golden sands that will return to the beautiful golden spring, and light from the eyes of the Creator.

And since the man from Auvergne dies happily in Paris from the wrongs of the country rather than from bewilderment, and everyone who stops to look at himself is sick with the pleasant malady of heaven, today's poets—the simple residents of Auvergne in sumptuous and agitated Lutetia—are nostalgic for heroic deeds. War, formerly a source of glory, is falling into disuse, and what appeared to be grandeur is beginning to be a crime. The royal court, once the inn of hired bards, views with dismay the modern bards who, although sometimes hiring the lyre, no longer do so forever, and are still not in the habit of hiring it. God is confused, woman perplexed and exasperated, but Nature always rekindles the solemn sun in the center of space. The gods of the forest still speak the language no longer spoken by the divinities of the altar, man hurls into the sea his serpents with talking heads which on the one hand seize the wild and rugged thorny terrain of England, and on the other the smiling coasts of America; and he bottles up the starlight in a crystal toy, and tosses over the waters and mountain ranges his dark and fuming tritons. And when the suns that have been lighting the earth for tens of centuries grow cold in the human soul, the sun has not. There is no East for man's spirit; there is only North, crowned with light. The mountain ends in a peak; the towering wave, formed and thrown to the sky by the storm, ends in a crest; the tree ends in a mass of leaves; and human life must end in a summit. In this change of axis which we are witnessing, and in this remedy for the world of men in which new life gallops along the road like spirited chargers pursued by barking dogs; in this blindness of the fountainheads and in this obscurity of the gods—Nature, human effort, and man's spirit open to the thirsty lips of poets like pure and inexhaustible springs. Take your goblets set with precious stones, empty them of the sour old wine, and fill them with the sun's rays, with echoes of one's labors, with good simple pearls taken from the depths of the soul—and before the eyes of startled men let your feverish hands lift the sounding goblet!

Thus the lyrical poet re-enters himself, eyes burning and feet sore from walking through the still smoking ruins. He was always, to a greater or lesser degree, a personal poet, and the one who had been an epic poet in courtly, monastic, or bloody times, now looks to the battles and solemnities of Nature. The battle is in the workshops, the glory in peace, the church throughout the earth, the poem in Nature. When life agrees, the Dante of the future will appear, not because of greater strength of his own over the Dantesque men of the present, but because of the greater strength of the times. What is arrogant man but a spokesman for the unknown, an echo of the supernatural, a mirror of eternal enlightenment, a more or less perfect copy of the world in which he lives? Today Dante lives in and of himself. Ugolino[2] nibbled away at his son, but he at his very self; today there is no crust of bread more chewed than the soul of a poet. If poets view themselves with the eyes of the soul, their raw fists and the hollows of their torn-out wings ooze blood.

Historical life, then, suddenly arrested in its course; emerging institutions still too new and too confused to have been able to give of themselves any poetic elements—for fragrance develops with the years as in peoples or wines; the disintegrating roots of seasoned poetry brought out into the open air and exposed to critical pressure; one's personal life filled with doubt, alarmed, questioning, restless, and satanic; one's intimate life feverish, unstable, competitive and clamorous—all this has become the principal factor, and with Nature the only legitimate factor, in modern poetry.

But how much effort it costs to discover oneself! No sooner

2. The original name of Pope Gregory IX.

does man enter the enjoyment of reason that has been hidden to him from the cradle, than he must wear himself out to truly enter himself. It is a herculean lashing out at the obstacles raised against him by his own nature, and the obstacles accumulated by the conventional ideas with which—in cowardly times and because of imperious advice and sinful arrogance—he is fed. No task is more difficult in our existence than that of distinguishing the parasitic and latterly acquired life from the spontaneous and inherent: what is intrinsic in man from what was added to him by his predecessors with their lessons, legacies, and laws. On the pretext of perfecting the human being, they inhibit him. As soon as he is born, the various philosophies, religions, passions of his parents, and political systems are already standing by his cradle with great strong bandages ready in their hands. And they bind him and swaddle him, and for his entire life on earth man is a bridled horse. Therefore the earth is now a vast dwelling place of masqueraders. We enter life as wax, and destiny pours us into ready-made molds. Created conventions deform true existence, and true life becomes a silent current that glides away invisibly underneath apparent life, at times not experienced by the same one in whom it does its cautious work, the way the mysterious Guadiana flows its long and silent course beneath the lands of Andalusia. To insure human free will, to leave to the demons their own seductive form, not to dull the luster of virgin natures by the imposition of another's prejudices, to enable those natures to take for themselves what is useful, without clouding them or driving them down a prescribed path—this is the only way of peopling the earth with the vigorous and creative generation it needs! Salvation has turned out to be formal and theoretical; it must be effective and essential. Neither literary originality nor political freedom can exist as long as there is no assurance of spiritual freedom. Man's most important task is to reconquer himself. It is urgent to return men to themselves; it is urgent to rescue them from the bad discipline of a conformity that stifles or poisons their feelings, speeds the awakening of their senses, and overloads their intelligence with a pernicious, alien, cold, and false arsenal of ideas. Only the genuine bears fruit. Only the direct has power. What is bequeathed to us by another is like warmed-over food. It behooves every man to reconstruct his life: as soon as he looks into himself, he does reconstruct it. The one who, on the pretext of guiding the new generations, teaches them an absolute and isolated heap of doctrines, and fills their ears with sermons on the barbarous gospel of hate rather than with gentle lectures of love, is a treacherous murderer, ungrateful to God, and an enemy of men! Guilty of treason against Nature is the one who prevents, in one way or another, and in any way at all, the free use, the direct application, and the spontaneous employment of the magnificent faculties of man! There is now coming to us the fearless one, the good lancer, the mighty jouster, the knight of human liberty—which is the grand order of knighthood; he who arrives at himself directly, without the violent desires of Valbueno or the leavings of Ojeda, through the epic poetry of our times; he who held out his generous hands to Heaven in an attitude of supplication, and took them from prayer like a deep-toned amphora, filled with opulent and vibrant stanzas, caressed by Olympic reflections! The poem is within man, determined to enjoy all the apples, to dry all the sap of the tree of Paradise, and to change into a comforting bonfire the flames in which in other days God forged the exterminating sword! The poem is in Nature, a mother provided with breasts, a wife who never hates, an oracle who always answers, a poet of a thousand tongues, a priestess who makes known what she does not say, a comforter who strengthens and perfumes the air! Now comes the good bard of Niagara, who has written a splendid and extraordinary song about the everlasting poem of Nature!

The poem of Niagara! What Niagara has to say; the voices of the Falls; the groans of the human soul; the majesty of the universal soul; the titanic dialogue between impatient man and contemptuous nature; the desperate cry of the son of a great unknown father demanding of his mute mother the secret of his birth; the cry of all mankind in a single breast; the tumult of the heart responding to the savage waves; the divine warmth inflaming with passion the brow of man in the face of the grandiose; the prophetic and most gently pervasive penetration of rebellious and unknowing man, and of a revealing and inevitable Nature; the tender betrothal to the eternal, and the delightful effusion in creation from which man—drunk on power and merrymaking, strong as a well-loved monarch, anointed king of Nature—is returning to himself!

The poem of Niagara! The spiritual halo that encircles the halo of prismatic waters; the battle of their heart, less thundering than the human battle; the simultaneous surge of all that lives, rearing and wheeling, impelled by the unseen, to end there in the unknown; the law of existence, logical because of being incomprehensible, that devastates without apparent agreement both martyrs and scoundrels, and like a ravenous ogre, swallows with a single breath a group of evangelists, while it leaves alive upon the earth, like red-mouthed predators that divert it, a gang of criminals; the ready way in which men and thundering waterfalls collide, explode, rebel, leap to the skies, and crash to the depths; the outcries and angelic struggles of man snatched away by the sweeping law which, even as it submits and dies, yet curses, shakes, and bellows like a titan shaking worlds; the hoarse voice of the Falls that actuates an equal law, and striking sea or grotto howls and rages; and after all of this the tears that now envelop everything, and the heart-rending groans of the lonely soul—here is the imposing poem which this man of his times saw in Niagara.

This entire treatise deals with that poem. Since the poem is a representative work, to talk about it is to talk about the age it represents. Good flints make big sparks. The relative that fails to awaken thought of the absolute is faulty. All must move in such a way that it leads thought to the enormous and the grand. Philosophy is no more than the secret of the relationship between the various forms of existence. This poet's soul is moved by the anxieties, loneliness, bitterness, and inspiration of singing genius. He appears armed with every kind of weapon in an arena where he sees neither combatants nor rows of seats enlivened by an enormous public, nor does he see a reward.

Weighed down by all his arms, he runs in search of opponents. What he finds is a mountain of water come out to meet him, and since his heart is full of fight, he challenges that mountain of water!

No sooner had Pérez Bonalde begun looking into himself than he in turn, living in disturbing times and in a very cold land, found himself alone—an eager convert to a new religion, his spirit ripe for worship, but his reason averse to reverence; a believer by instinct, but a nonbeliever by intellect. In vain he sought dust worthy of his manly brow to touch when prostrate in homage; in vain he tried to find his place in this age when not a country exists that has not turned everyone around in the confused and fast-paced struggle of the living; in vain—since to his misfortune he was created for heroic purposes, and armed with the study of an analysis that represses them when it is not ridiculing or prohibiting them—he resolutely followed the great deeds of men who now consider it an honor, and proof of a strong spirit, not to undertake anything major, but instead something quite easy, productive, and feasible. Forceful poetry poured from his lips; perhaps the sword of freedom vibrated in his hand—for surely he should never have carried a sword; his spirit held the sharp anguish of living with too many mental powers unused, which is like putting the sap of a tree into the tiny body of an ant. The blowing winds beat against his temples; the thirst of our times constricted his throat. As for the past, all is a lonely castle and an empty shell! As for the present, all is question, denial, rage, the blasphemy of defeat, the cry of triumph! As for the future, all is obscured by the dust and smoke of battle! Weary of vainly searching for heroic deeds in men, the poet went to hail the feats of nature.

And they understood each other. The Falls lent its voice to the poet, the poet his groans of pain to the roaring marvel. From the sudden encounter of an ingenuous spirit with an astounding spectacle emerged this throbbing, exuberant, uninhibited, magnificent poem. In places it falters, because the words cut through the ideas instead of giving them form. In places it rises to great heights, for it contains ideas that pass above the words as above a valley of ditch grass. The poem has Pindaric vanity, Heredian sweep, rebellious curves, a proud exuberance, magnificent uprisings, heroic rages. The poet loves, invokes, is not astonished. He knows no fear, sheds all the tears of his heart. He rebukes, deals blows, implores. He sets straight all the arrogance of the mind. He would fearlessly clutch the scepter of darkness. He seizes the mist, tears it apart, goes into it. He coaxes God from the cavern, sinks into the slimy cave, chills the air around him, and reappears crowned with light, and singing hosannas! Light is the supreme joy of men. He depicts the sounding, turbulent, down-crashing river, broken into silver dust, vaporized into many-colored mists. His stanzas are tableaus—at times snow flurries, at times columns of fire, at times lightning. Now Lucifer, now Prometheus, now Icarus. He is our day, facing our Nature. To be all this is granted to few. He told Nature the sorrows of contemporary man. And he was powerful because he was sincere. He mounted a golden coach.

This poem is an impression, an impact, a beating of wings, a genuine work, an unexpected delight. Occasionally one still sees a very studious reader who is behind the times in these clashes of man with nature; but gallant and daring, man fortunately leaps above him. The grumbler begins to appear, but the passionately perceptive one is the victor. The Falls tells him nothing even if it is telling him everything; but soon he sharpens his ear, and in spite of the skeptical books that build walls around him, he hears it all. Powerful ideas rise high, plunge low, conceal themselves, knock against each other, intertwine. Sometimes the rhyming word mangles them, as rhyming words always do; sometimes it prolongs them, which is harmful; but generally, the fertile and inspired idea nobly fits into the sparkling poem. The entire poet overflows from these verses; he elicits majesty and sets upon its feet all that is majestic. This time his lines are like waves born from the turbulent sea, and growing as they join the other waves, and towering and twisting and spreading noisily, and starting to die in crashing surf and rebellious irregular circles not amenable to form or extension; here riding roughshod and spreading over the sand like a conqueror throwing his cloak over the lady whom he takes prisoner, there gently kissing the chiselled edges of capricious sea stones, elsewhere breaking into sheaves of dust against the lofty rims of rocks. His unevenness comes from his strength. Perfection of form is nearly always obtained at the cost of perfection of idea. For lightning obeys a precise course on its journey, does it not? When was a jackass handsomer than a colt in the pasture? A storm is more beautiful than a locomotive. Works that spring straight from the depths of great souls excel because of their turbulence and the free rein of their passions.

And Pérez Bonalde loves his language, both caressing and punishing it; for there is no pleasure like that of knowing the origin of each word one uses, and how far it reaches; nor is there anything better to enlarge and strengthen the mind than the meticulous study and appropriate application of language. After writing, one feels the pride of a painter or sculptor. The style of this poem is forthright and beautiful, the form full, the canvas spacious, the colors sun-proof. The phrase reaches high, inasmuch as it comes from far below, and falls broken into many hues, or majestically folded, or thundering like the waters it depicts. In haste to overtake the fleeting image, the line is left unfinished at times, or finished under pressure. But the sublimity is constant. There is wave and wing. Pérez Bonalde pampers what he writes; but he is not, nor has he any desire to be, a stone-cutting poet. As a matter of course he likes to have his lines flow sonorously from his pen, well formed and polished. But he will never become like another poet, attacking poetry with a golden hammer and a silver engraving tool, with cutting and incising instruments, to notch an ending here, to strengthen a connection there, to brighten and perfect the jewel, without seeing that if the diamond suffers from cutting the pearl dies from it. The poem is a pearl. Lines of poetry must not be like a rose that is top-heavy with petals, but like Malabar jasmine filled with fragrance. The leaf must be neat, sweet-smelling, compact, glossy. Every one of its cells must be a reservoir of aromas. No matter where the poem is broken, it must shed light and fragrance. All the sickly or yellowish or malformed suckers must be pruned from poetic language as from a tree, and only the healthy, strong, and vigorous suckers left, so that with fewer leaves the branch will grow with finer bearing, the breeze will blow over it more freely, and it will produce better fruit. Polishing is a good thing, but within the mind and before bringing the poem to paper. Poems seethe in the mind the way grape juice ferments in the vat. But after the wine is made, it does not improve by the addition of alcohol and tannin; nor does one weigh the merits of a poem, after it is started, by dressing it up with added paraphernalia and finery. It must be made of a piece, and of one inspiration only, for it is not the work of an artisan turning out articles in mass production, but of a man in whose breast condors nest, and who must make use of the flapping of the condors' wings. And that is how this poem burst from Bonalde and is one of his virtues: it was made of a piece.

Oh, that task of paring and trimming, that mutilation of our creations, that replacing of the poet's inspiration with the dissector's knife! Polished poetry is deformed and dead. Since each verse has to be charged with its own spirit and bring its own wealth to the poem, to erase words is to erase spirit, and to change them is to reheat grape juice which, like coffee, must not be reheated. The soul of the poem, as if mistreated, complains about those chisel blows. And it looks more like a Pompeian mosaic than a painting by da Vinci.[3] A trotting horse never wins battles. The ills of matrimony are never cured by divorce, but by wisely choosing the lady and not being unduly blind to the real reasons for the marriage. Nor does the poem's merit lie in the polishing, but rather in its having come into being already winged and singing. Nor may the poem be considered finished in hopes of finishing it later, when it is not yet finished; for later it may be given the appearance of a finished work, but will not actually be so, nor will it have that virginal charm of a poem that has not been trimmed or tampered with or mutilated. For wheat is less fragile than poetry, and it breaks and spoils when

3. Leonardo da Vinci (1452–1519), Italian painter, architect, sculptor, and engineer, one of the titans of the Italian Renaissance.

its granary is changed too often. When the poem is complete it must be armed with all the weapons, with a solid resounding cuirass, and with a white plume crest crowning a sturdy helmet of shining steel.

For even with all of this—like the stray straw that, in the delight of the fragrance itself, one did not take the trouble to pick up when the box from the perfume shop was opened—there are still some loose ends which could well have been finished: here one too many epithets, there an inappropriate assonance, in another place a bold antepenultimate displaying its capricious volute. For an occasional line of poetry does turn out to have a short wing, which is really not very important in this conjunction of verses overendowed with long wings. And, as a natural result of the times, there appears in this or that stanza, like St. Elmo's fire in a star-strewn sky, groans of contamination and memorized despair. Come now, it may well be, but all this meticulousness is a task for pedants. The one in quest of mountains does not stop to pick up stones in the road. He salutes the sun and worships the mountain. These are after-dinner confidences, things to be whispered into the ear. For who does not know that language is the horseman of thought, and not its horse? The inadequacy of human language to express man's judgments, emotions, and purposes precisely, is perfect and absolute proof of the need of a future existence.

And at this point it is fitting for me to comfort the sometimes perplexed and downcast soul of this most gallant poet, to assure him of what he so anxiously desires to know, to fill him with the knowledge given to me by the glances of children—glances as angry as those of the one who enters a miserable hovel after having come from a palace, choleric as the final glance of the dying, which is an appointment and not a farewell. Bonalde himself does not deny, but he does inquire. He has no absolute faith in the life to come, but neither has he absolute doubt. When he desperately wonders what is to become of him, he remains calm, as if he had heard what he fails to say. He derives faith in the eternal from those conversations in which he bravely questions it. In vain he is afraid to die when he finally lays his head upon that pillow of earth. In vain the echo that juggles words—for Nature, like the Creator himself, seems jealous of her finest creatures, and takes pleasure in clouding the wisdom she gave them—answers him that nothing survives the hour that is apparently our last. The echo in the soul says more meaningful things than the echo of the Falls. There are no falls like our own soul. No, human life is not the whole of life! The grave is a means and not an end. The mind would not be able to conceive of what it could not accomplish; existence cannot be an abominable plaything of an evil lunatic. Man leaves this life like a length of folded cloth, anxious to display his colors and in search of a frame; like a gallant ship anxious to roam the world, that finally puts to sea. Death is a rejoicing, a resumption, a new task. Human life would be a barbarous and repugnant invention if it were limited to life on earth. For what is our brain, a seedbed of heroic acts, if not a forerunner of the certain country where they are to grow to fruition? A tree sprouts in the earth, and finds air in which to spread its branches; and water finds the deep river bed, and a trench to send its springs. And the ideas of justice, the joyous desires of unfulfilled sacrifices, the finished plans of spiritual feats, the delights accompanying the imagination of a pure and honest life, impossible to attain upon earth, will all be born in the mind—and will this golden grove find no space in which to spread its mass of foliage? No matter how hard a man may have toiled in this life, what is he when he dies but a giant who has lived condemned to weave monks' baskets and build little nests for linnets? What is to become of the gentle and overflowing spirit which, lacking in fruitful employment, takes refuge within itself and goes out of the world whole and unused? This fortunate poet has not yet entered the bitter heart of life. He has not suffered enough. Like a halo of light, faith in a future existence springs from suffering. He has lived with the mind, which beclouds; and with love, which sometimes disabuses. He still needs to live with the sorrow that strengthens, purifies and enlightens. For what is the poet but living fuel for the flame with which he lights the way? He flings his body into the bonfire, and the smoke climbs to the sky, and the light from the wonderful fire reaches out like a gentle warmth over all the earth!

You do right, sincere and honest poet, to feed upon yourself. Here is a lyre that vibrates! Here is a poet who can touch and feel his own heart, who fights with his hand turned to the sky, and who proudly faces the living winds! Here is a man, a marvel of high art and a rare fruit in this world of men! Here is a lively, high-stepping trotting horse who puts his sure foot, his greedy mind, and his calm and eager eyes upon that pile of church debris, and propped-up walls, and gilded corpses, and wings made of chains which, with sinister zeal, so many artful fighters of today use to remake fetters for modern man. He does not pursue a poetry—transient foam of the deep sea—that comes to the surface only when there is a deep sea and a voluble coquette who neither looks out for her admirers nor dispenses her whims to the unsuitable. He waited for the difficult time when the body grows huge, and the eyes are flooded with tears and the breast with rapture, and the sail of life swells with unknown winds, like the sail of a ship, and one moves naturally at the pace of a mountain. The stormy winds are his, and he sees lights in them, and fire-spangled chasms opening, and mystical promises. In this poem he bared his tormented breast to the pure air, his trembling arms to the pious oracle, his passionate brow to the calming caresses of sacred Nature. He was free, ingenuous, humble, questioning, self-controlled, a knight of the spirit. Who are the high and mighty who usurp the right to curb what is born free, to snuff out the flame that Nature lights, to prevent a creature as noble as the human being from exercising his faculties naturally? Who are those owls that watch over the cradle of the newborn, and drink out of his golden lamp the oil of life? Who are those wardens of the mind who keep the soul, that gallant Spanish language, imprisoned behind double bars? Can there be a greater blasphemer than he who, on the pretext of understanding God, ventures to correct the divine work? Oh Liberty, never stain your white robes, so that the newborn will not fear you! You do well, Poet of the Falls, to dare to be free in an age of pretentious slaves, for men are so accustomed to slavery that when they have ceased to be slaves of the monarchy, they are now beginning, with greater humiliation, to be slaves of Liberty! You do well, illustrious minstrel, and see how well aware I am of the value of these words I say to you! You do well, knight of the flaming sword, rider of the winged horse, rhapsodist of the oaken lyre, man who bares his breast to Nature! Cultivate the great, since it was you who brought to the land all the tools of cultivation. Let us leave the other trifles to the children. Let us be always stirred by these solemn winds. Let us lay aside those usual empty rhymes strung with pearls and adorned with artificial flowers, for they are generally more of a juggling feat and a diversion for idle skill than a sudden blaze from the soul and a feat worthy of the magnates of the mind. Let us bind together in a tall sheaf the contagious sorrows, Latin tepidity, borrowed rhymes, the doubts of others, the harm in books, a prescribed faith, and cast them into the flames. And warm yourself from the cold of these grievous times beside the healthful fires in which, since the drowsy creature in the mind is now awakened, all men have both feet firmly planted upon the ground, lips compressed, courageous breast bared, and fist to the sky, demanding of life its secret.

Nuestra América
(Buenos Aires, 1937), pp. 110–48

III
José Martí's Literary Will and Testament

Letter to Gonzalo de Quesada

Montecristi, April 1, 1895

Dear Gonzalo:

I have not spoken to you of my books. Keep them, since you will always need the office, and the more so now, in order to sell them for Cuba at some propitious occasion. Keep all of them except those on American history or having to do with America—geography, literature, etc.—which you will give to Carmita for safekeeping, in case I come out alive or am thrown out and return to earn my livelihood with them. Sell all the others at some propitious time. You probably know how. Send the paintings to Carmita and she will collect all the papers. You still have no permanent home, and she will add them to those she is already keeping for me. Do not put the papers in order or try to take any literature out of them; all of that is dead and buried and there is nothing here worthy of publication, either in prose or poetry: they are merely notes. In case of necessity, from the material in print—including collections from *La Opinión Nacional*, *La Nación*, *El Partido Liberal* and *La América*, until they fell into Pérez' hands, and even later from *El Economista Americano*—you can be selecting material from the six main volumes. And one or two from lectures and articles on Cuba. Do not tear up that poor *Lalla Rookh* which was left upon your desk. Antonio Batres from Guatemala has a play of mine, or a dramatic sketch on Guatemalan independence, which the government had me write in two week's time. *The Age of Gold*, or some of it, would bear reprinting. I have many writings lost in countless periodicals: in Mexico from '75 to '77—in *Revista Venezolana*, where the arts are featured, I have articles on Cecilio Acosta and Miguel Peña; namely in newspapers of Honduras, Uruguay, and Chile in I do not know how many prefaces. If I fail to return and you insist upon putting my papers together, make up the volumes as we have planned:

I. North American
II. North American
III. Spanish American
IV. North American Panoramas
V. Books on America
VI. Literature, Education, and Painting

And you could make another volume of poetry: *Ismaelillo*, *Simple Verse*, and the more painstaking or significant of some of the *Free Verse* that Carmita has. Do not confuse them with any other rough and less characteristic drafts.

Regarding the portraits hanging in my office, you choose two and let Benjamín[1] choose two others. And to Estrada,[2] Wendell Phillips.[3]

You will find material for other volumes in the aforementioned sources: you could double volumes IV and VI.

Concerning my poetry, do not publish any written before *Ismaelillo;* none is worth a fig. Those written later, after all, have unity and sincerity.

My Views, a nucleus of plays which could have been published or performed in that form—and there are a good number of them—are so scribbled on the backs of letters and scraps of paper, and in such shorthand, that it would be impossible to publish them.

1. Benjamín Guerra, treasurer of the Cuban Revolutionary Party.

2. Tómas Estrada Palma, head of the Cuban junta in New York.

3. Wendell Phillips (1811–1884), great American abolitionist and labor reformer whom Martí enormously admired. For Martí's evaluation of Phillips, *see* his essay in *Inside the Monster*, pp. 55–66.

And if, like a model son, you do all this work for me after my death, and you should have some money left over—which would be a wonder—what will you do with it? Half should go to my son Pepe, and the other half to Carmita and María.

Now I think that perhaps another volume could be made of *Lalla Rookh*.[4] The introduction at least could go into volume VI. You will take care not to make more than one volume out of the material from volume VI. *El Dorador* might be one of its articles, *Vereshchagin* another, and a review of the *Impressionist* painters and the Munkacsy *Christ*. The Sellén preface and the Bonalde, although it is so violent, and that prose had not yet solidified and was like unmellowed wine. Of course you will select none but the durable and essential.

Concerning what would amount to a kind of *spirit*, as this sort of book used to be called, you could take from the more picturesque and important starts you might find in my occasional articles. What will I have written without blood, or depicted without first having seen with my own eyes? The *En Casa* writings have been kept here in a thin notebook; they are expressive and useful.

Concerning our Spanish Americans I recall *San Martín*, *Bolívar*, *Páez*, *Peña*, *Heredia*, *Cecilio Acosta*, *Juan Carlos Gómez*, *Antonio Bachiller*.

Concerning the North Americans: *Emerson*, *Beecher*, *Cooper*, *W. Phillips*, *Grant*, *Sheridan*, *Whitman*. And as lesser although perhaps more useful studies you will find among my correspondence *Arthur*, *Hendricks*, *Hancock*, *Conkling*, *Alcott* and many others.

Concerning Garfield I wrote about the burial emotions, but

4. The *Lalla Rookh* was a poem by Thomas Moore Martí translated from English. However, the manuscript of the translation was not found among Martí's papers. In a letter to Martí, Boston, March 7, 1888, the publishing firm of Estes & Lauriat wrote: "We are pleased to receive the completion of the 'Lalla Rookh' translation." However, thus far efforts to locate the translation in the archives of the publishing firms which acquired Estes & Lauriat have been unsuccessful.

one cannot see the man nor did I meet him, so that the highly praised description is nothing but a paragraph from a gossip column. And you will find much on *Longfellow*, *Lanier*, *Edison*, and *Blaine*, and on some minor poets and politicians and artists and generals. Enter the forest but do not burden yourself with branches that may not bear fruit.

Concerning Cuba, what have I failed to write? And not one page do I consider worthy of her; I consider worthy only what we are going to do. But neither will you find a word without a pure idea and a very yearning and hankering for good. You can put the men into one group, and into another those carefully considered lectures relative to the early years of edification, which are worthwhile only if one bases them upon reality and sees with what literary sacrifice they were adapted to it. You know that my best way of talking is to serve. This is the list and a diversion from the anguish possessing us at these moments. Will we also be found wanting in today's hope, with everything within our reach? In order to suffer less, I am thinking of you and of what I never think—my pile of papers.

On that day, March 25, hope was found wanting. Today, April 1, I think it will not be. I have great affection for Gonzalo, but I am surprised he is coming, as I now feel he is, to the point of moving me to write my personal emotions to him against my nature and habits. If these were mine alone, I would write them down for the pleasure of paying him the fondness I owe him; but they would have to include the emotions of others, and of those I am not the owner. Sometimes they are magnificent, but most often they are unutterably and predictably bitter. A man once died upon the cross, but one must learn to die upon the cross every day. Martí neither tires nor talks. So then, does he have a cicerone for a few of his papers?

Regarding the sale of my books, as soon as you learn that Cuba has decided against my return, or when enthusiasm might produce some needed money for their sale—this still undecided—you and brother Benjamín may dispose of my writings on history, literature, and art, which will furnish my immediate needs if I return, or if we remain alive, saving only the books on our America. And let the entire proceeds go to Cuba, after my $220 debt to Carmita has been paid. These books have been my vice and my luxury—these poor occasional and laborious books. I never had the ones I wanted, nor did I think I had the right to buy any that were not needed for the task. You could put together and sell a curious catalogue announcing the sale and its promotion. I should prefer not to lift my hand from this paper, as if your hand were in mine; but I shall end, fearful of being tempted to put into words the things which do not fit into them.

Your

J. Martí

IV
Chronology of the Life of José Martí

1853, January 28: José Martí y Pérez is born in Havana, Cuba.

1865, March 19: Begins to attend the Municipal School for boys.

1868, October 10: Beginning of Ten Years' War.

1869, January 23: Date of first issue of *La Patria Libre (The Free Homeland)*, a newspaper in which Martí collaborates and in which his drama *Abdala* is published.

October 21: Accused of treason, he is arrested and confined in the Havana City Jail.

1870, March 4: A court martial sentences him to six years in prison.

April 4: Sent to prison.

October 13: Sentence commuted and transferred to the Isle of Pines.

1871, January 15: Deported to Spain, leaves for Cádiz on the mail ship *Guipúzcoa*.

January: His *El Presidio en Cuba (Political Prison in Cuba)* is published by the Ramón Ramírez printing shop.

May 31: Enrolls at the Central University of Madrid.

1873, February: Publishes *La República Española ante la Revolución Cubana (The Spanish Republic Before the Cuban Revolution)*.

1874, January: Fall of the Spanish Republic. Delivers speech at public meeting organized to raise funds for the widows and orphans of the fallen Republicans.

June 30: Receives the degree of Bachelor of Civil and Canon Law.

August 31: Enrolls in all the subjects of the Faculty of Philosophy and Humanities.

October 24: Passes graduating examinations for the degree of Doctor of Philosophy and Humanities with outstanding grades.

December: Leaves Spain for Paris.

1875, January: Sails from Southhampton for Mexico.

February 8: Arrives in Vera Cruz.

March 7: Work published in *Revista Universal* magazine in Mexico.

April 7: Participates in debate on materialism and spiritualism at Hidalgo Lyceum.

May 5: Assumes publication of the "Bulletin" of *Revista Universal*, dealing with national affairs.

November 30: Last of his "Bulletins" appears.

December 19: Play *Amor con amor se paga* (Love is Returned with Love) presented at the Teatro Principal in Mexico City. Represents Chihuahua workers at a workers' congress.

1876, November 19: Last issue of *Revista Universal* appears.

November 23: Entrance of Porfirio Díaz in the capital of Mexico, marking defeat of Lerdo regime.

December: Collaborates in *El Federalista*.

December 29: Sails for Havana.

1877, January 6: Arrives in Havana, using his middle name and second family name: Julián Pérez.

February 24: Sails for Vera Cruz using the same name, and from Mexico leaves for Guatemala, stopping at Belize, capital of British Honduras, and at Livingstone.

May 29: Appointed professor of French, English, Italian, and German literature and History of Philosophy at the Central School of Guatemala.

July: Gains recognition for speech at literary meeting at the Central Normal School.

September 15: Writes drama *Morazán*, to commemorate Independence Day. Work appears to be lost.

December: Authorized to move to Mexico.

December 20: Marries Cuban Carmen Zayas Bazán.

1878, January: Returns to Guatemala after leaving manuscript of booklet, *Guatemala*, to be published in Mexico.

April 6: Resigns post at the Central School. Booklet *Guatemala* published in Mexico.

May: End of Ten Years' War for Cuban Independence.

July 6: Leaves Guatemala for Honduras.

August: Sails for port of Trujillo.

September 3: Arrives in Havana with his wife.

September 16: Asks permission to practice law. Request denied. Teaches in private schools.

November 12: José Martí Zayas Bazán, is born.

1879, January 12: Appointed Secretary of Literary Section of the Guanabacoa Lyceum.

April 21: Speaks at reception in honor of the journalist Adolfo Marquez Sterling, and voices opposition to Autonomist policy.

April 27: Delivers eulogy of the violinist Diás Albertini at the Guanabacoa Lyceum.

August 26: Outbreak of Little War for Independence.

September 25: Accused of conspiracy and deported.

December: Leaves Spain for Paris.

1880, January 3: Arrives in New York.

January 24: Delivers lecture at Steck Hall, later published under the title, "Cuban Affairs," New York, 1880.

February 21: Publishes first article on art in *The Hour*, weekly magazine in New York, and writes article in English.

May 13: Writes Proclamation of New York Revolutionary Committee in connection with arrival in Cuba of General Calixto García to assume leadership of the Little War.

October: Capitulation of General Emilio Núñez, last leader to give up arms, ends Little War. Writes for New York *Sun*.

1881, March 21: Appointed professor in Caracas.

July 1: First issue of *Revista Venezolana*, edited by Martí, appears.

July: Dispute with Dictator Guzman Blanco forces him to leave Venezuela.

July 28: Departs for New York.

August 20: Begins sending articles from New York to newspaper *La Opinión Nacional* of Caracas.

1882, April: Book of poems *Ismaelillo* published. Writes most of *Versos Libres* (*Free Verse*) which remains unpublished.

July 15: Sends first article to *La Nación* of Buenos Aires, published September 13.

1883, March: Begins to collaborate in *La América* of New York.

July: Delivers speech on occasion of Bolívar centennial at Delmonico Hall.

October: Edits *La América*.

1884, January: Appointed New York correspondent of *La Sociedad Amigos del Saber* of Caracas.

October 10: Delivers first speech commemorating Grito de Yara, October 10, 1868.

October 20: Writes letter to Máximo Gómez excluding himself from revolutionary plans of Gómez and Antonio Maceo.

1885: Publishes novel *Amistad Funesta* under pseudonym, "Adelaida Real" in *El Latino-Americano* of New York.

1886: Becomes correspondent of *La República*, of Honduras.

1887, April 16: Appointed Uruguayan Consul. Mother visits New York.

1888, February: Works on translation of poem "Lalla Rookh" by Thomas Moore. Appointed corresponding member of Academy of Sciences and Arts of San Salvador.

October 12: Becomes representative in the United States and Canada of association of "La Prensa" of Buenos Aires.

1889, March 21: New York *Evening Post* publishes his letter "Vindication of Cuba," later printed in booklet, *Cuba and the United States*. Invited to become correspondent of *El Partido Liberal of Mexico*.

April 18: Sends first article to *La Opinión Pública*, of Uruguay.

July: Appearance of first issue of *La Edad de Oro* (*The Golden Age*) monthly publication dedicated to the children of America.

November 2: Writes articles, published in *La Nación* (Buenos Aires), warning Latin America that Pan-American Congress represents a move by expansionist forces in the United States to dominate Latin America economically and politically.

November 20: Speaks at meeting in Hardman Hall, in honor of the poet José María Heredia.

December 19: Speaks at meeting of Spanish-American Literary Society of New York in honor of delegates to the International American Conference (Pan-American Congress).

1890, January 22: Inauguration of The League, a society for the promotion of education, in New York. Becomes a teacher of the League for Negro Workers.

June 16: Appointed Argentine Consul in New York.

July 24: Appointed Paraguayan Consul in New York.

December 23: Appointed Uruguayan representative to International Monetary Conference in Washington.

December: Appointed chairman of the Spanish-American Literary Society of New York.

1891, March 30: Report read in English and Spanish at the Monetary Conference in Washington.

April: Speaks at meeting at Spanish-American Literary Society in honor of Mexico.

May: Publishes article on Monetary Conference warning Latin America of United States designs.

June: Speaks at meeting organized by the Spanish-American Literary Society, in honor of the Central American Republics. Publishes *Versos Sencillos*.

October 11: Resigns posts as consul of Argentina and Uruguay.

October 30: Resigns post as chairman of the Spanish-American Literary Society.

November 25: Visits Tampa at the invitation of the "Ignacio Agramonte Club."

November 27: Speaks at "Convención Cubana de Tampa." Founds the League for Education in Tampa, similar to The League in New York, and joins Patriotic Cuban League.

November 28: His "Resolutions taken by the Cuban Emigrés in Tampa," considered as the preamble to the bases of the Cuban Revolutionary Party, approved.

December 25: Visits Key West at invitation of group of Cuban workers.

1892, January 3: Speaks at meeting organized by the "San Carlos Club."

January 4: Attends meeting of club "Patria y Libertad" (Homeland and Freedom). Tours tobacco factories of Key West and addresses Cuban tobacco workers.

January 5: Presides over meetings of club presidents where agreement is reached to organize Cuban Revolutionary Party. Writes bases and statutes of Cuban Revolutionary Party.

January 8: Submits program of the Cuban Revolutionary party to the Tampa Patriotic League. Program unanimously approved.

January 21: League of New York holds meeting protesting letter in which Collazo and Roa slander Martí.

February 17: Makes report at meeting in Hardman Hall on his tour of Tampa and Key West.

March 14: Appearance of first issue of *Patria*.

April 18: Elected delegate of Cuban Revolutionary Party.

July: Tours Florida to organize support for Cuban Revolutionary Party.

August 4: Gives instructions to Major Gerardo Castellanos, first commissioner of Cuban Revolutionary Party, who is leaving for Cuba.

September 4: Leaves for Santo Domingo.

September 11: Meets with Máximo Gómez at La Reforma, Santo Domingo. Invites him to join new revolutionary movement for independence of Cuba.

September 24–October 13: Visits Haiti and Jamaica.

October 23: Reports on his tour at meeting of The League in New York.

November: Visits Tampa and Key West. In Tampa life endangered by plot to poison him.

December: Speaks at meeting of Spanish-American Literary Society of New York, in honor of Venezuela.

1893, January 31: At meeting in Hardman Hall Cuban Revolutionary Party publicly rejects autonomist policy.

February 1: Invites Antonio Maceo to assume leading position in liberation movement.

February–March: Tours Florida for Cuban Revolutionary Party.

April 10: Re-elected delegate of Cuban Revolutionary Party.

April: Visits Philadelphia for Cuban Revolutionary Party.

May 24: Delivers speech at Hardman Hall, giving an account of events in Cuba, and introduces Rubén Darío to meeting.

May 24: Issues communiqué in name of Cuban Revolutionary Party on events in Cuba.

May 26: Leaves for Santo Domingo.

June 3: Meets again with Máximo Gómez.

June 7: Delivers lecture at School of Law at Costa Rica, at the invitation of the Association of Students.

July 8: Visits Panama, en route to New York.

September: Tours Florida again for Cuban Revolutionary Party.

October 28: Speaks at meeting of the Spanish-American Literary Society in New York in honor of Bolívar.

December: Visits Philadelphia, Tampa, and Key West for Cuban Revolutionary Party. Publicly thanked by clubs in Key West for "zeal, activity and good judgment" with which he has discharged duties as delegate.

1894, January 2: Intervenes in conflict in Key West resulting from introduction of Spanish workers from Cuba to break strike of Cuban tobacco workers in "La Rosa Española" factory, and brings about return of Spanish workers to Cuba.

April 8: General Máximo Gómez arrives in New York for discussion with Martí.

April 10: Re-elected delegate of Cuban Revolutionary Party.

May 4: Accompanied by Francisco Gómez, son of Máximo Gómez, leaves for tour of Philadelphia, Key West, Tampa, Jacksonville, and other cities.

May 30: Visits New Orleans.

June: Travels to Costa Rica, Panama, and Jamaica.

July 22: Visits Mexico and is greeted by *El Universal*.

December 25: Organizes Fernandina plan calling for expeditionary force to leave for Cuba from Fernandina, Florida, picks up Maceo in Costa Rica, and begin the War for Independence.

1895, January 10–14: Fernandina plan betrayed and exposed. U.S. authorities detain three vessels and confiscate weapons of war.

January 29: Order for uprising in Cuba signed in New York.

January 31: Leaves for Santo Domingo.

February 24: "Grito de Baire," outbreak of the Second War for Independence.

March 24: Writes letter to Frederick Henríquez Carvajal from Montecristi, Santo Domingo.

March 25: Writes *Manifesto of Montecristi*. Signed by Martí and General Máximo Gómez.

April 1: Writes letter to Gonzalo de Quesada from Montecristi, Santo Domingo, considered his literary will and testament. Leaves on schooner from Montecristi for Cuba.

April 5: With assistance of Haitian consul obtains passage on German fruit ship, *Nordstrand*, for Cape Haitian.

April 9: Leaves Cape Haitian.

April 11: Arrives at Inagua at dawn. Sets sail for Cuba at 2 p.m. At 8 p.m. ship stops three miles off coast of Cuba. Boards little boat with five companions and at about 11 p.m. lands on Playitas.

April 16: Proclaimed Major General before the Liberating Army. Marches through the mountains of Baracoa in search of Antonio Maceo.

May 2: Writes letter to editor of *New York Herald* explaining aims and methods of the Cuban War for Independence.

May 6: Meets at La Mejorana with Generals Máximo Gómez and Antonio Maceo. They agree on the strategy of the War.

May 18: Standing between Generals Gómez and Maceo, speaks to thousands of Cuban patriots in the Maceo encampment near Jagua.

May 18: Writes last letter—unfinished—to Manuel Mercado.

May 19: Killed in action at Dos Rios, Oriente Province, Cuba.

Index

Aboriginal American Authors, 202-04
Ackerman, Louisa, 233
Acuña, Manuel, 39
Adam, Edmond, 279
Adventures of Huckleberry Finn, The, 198
Age of Gold, The, 30
Agassiz, Louis, 189
Aguado y Madrago, José, 77
Agüero, Juan Miguel, 214
Alcott, Amos Bronson, 18, 151, 197
Alcott, Louisa May, 18, 197-200
Alegu, Antonio, 67
Alvarez, Manuel, 77
Amazons, 178
America, La, 20
American Artists, 80-82
American Indians, 29, 186, 201-04, 271
Ane, Hartmann von, 228
Angelica, Fra, 64
Anti-slavery, 186
Aranda, José Jiménes, 78
Arce, Gaspar Núñez de, 262
Argentina, 266-77
Aristophanes, 69
Arnim, Ludwig Achim von, 228
Arras, Jacquet d', 89
Art, ancient, 113-17; as a form of harmony, 44-48; Barbizon school, 77; baroque, 77; Flemish School, 74; Impressionists, 118-24; in France, 83-86, 90-91, 95-105, 118-24; in Italy, 66-68, 77-79; in Mexico, 13-63, 92-93; in Spain, 76-77, 120-23; of painting, 81; in United States, 74-79, 80-82
Ayuntamiento, 93

Baer, Karl Ernst von, 247
Balzac, Honoré de, 206
Barbier, Auguste, 260
Barbizon school of Romantic landscape painting, 77, 87
Baron, Michel, 104
Baroque, 35, 77
Barreiro, Elena, 43
Battle of Waterloo, 207
Baudelaire, Charles, 112, 233, 260
Baz, Juan José, 42
Beaumont, Claudio-Francesco de, 104
Becquer, Gustave Adolfo, 294
Belinsky, Vissarion Grigorievich, 291
Benavides, Juan, 214
Bierstadt, Albert, 76
Blumenthal, Oskar, 226
Bodenstadt, Friedrich Martin von, 228
Boldoni, Giovanni, 89
Bolívar, Simón, 212
Bonalde, Juan Antonio Perez, 308-27
Bonheur, Rosa, 78
Borrais de Coll, Palmira, 42
Boucher, François, 104
Bougereau, Adolph William, 78
Brinton, Daniel Garrison, 203
Brooklyn Eagle, 32
Browning, Robert, 257
Brutus, Marcus Junius, 211
Buchanan, Robert Williams, 170
Byron, George Gordon, 219, 258, 263, 285

Caesar, Julius, 61
"Calamus," 23

Calderón, Pedro de la Barca, 165
Campero, Francisca, 48
Campoamor, Ramón Don, 264
Campoamor y Camposorio Ramón de, 294
Canova, Antonio, 67
Carbó, José V., 63-65
Carducci, Bartolomeo, 234
Carlyle, Thomas, 151
Carpentier, Alejo, 283
Casal, Julian de, 242-44
Casarín, Alejandro, 41-42
Caus, Lucretius, 210
Cellini, Benvenuto, 242, 303
Cervantes, Miguel de, 27, 278-79, 305
Chase, William Merritt, 75
Châteaubriand, Vicomte François de, 28
Chavez, Manuel, 40
Chelmmonski, Josef, 79
"Children of Adam," 23
Cicero, Marcus Tullius, 210
Civil War, 198-99
Clemens, Samuel L. *See* Twain, Mark.
Collazo, Guillermo, 29
Colonna, Vittoria, 64
Connecticut Yankee in King Arthur's Court, A, 25, 26-27, 33, 194-96
Conquistadores, 39
"Corregio," 67
Cooper, Thomas Sidney, 79
Corday, Charlotte, 54-62
Cordero, 51-53
Corot, Jean-Baptiste-Camille, 87, 120
Cortés, Hernán, 39, 93
Courbet, Gustave, 16, 120
Curtis, George William, 189
Cuba, Ten Years' War, 214
Cuvier, Georges Leopold Frederick Dagobert, 247
Cybele, 234

Dante Alighieri, 305, 316
Darío, Rubén, 22
Darwin, Charles, 21, 245-56, 269
Daubigny, Charles-François, 87
Daudet, Alphonse, 205-06
Day, Clarence, 25
Degas, Edgar, 16, 118
Delacroix, Eugene Ferdinand-Victor, 83
Delaroche, Paul, 64
Delille, Abbé Jacques, 219
Descamps, Jean Baptiste, 83
Detaille, Edouard, 97-100
Dewey, John, 20
"Divinity School Address," 20
Don Quixote, 27, 28, 195, 278-79, 305
Doré, Gustave, 77, 105
Dostoyevsky, Fyodor Mikhalovich, 290
Duke of Wellington, 207
Durmaine, Francisco, 66-68
Dupré, Jules, 87

Echegaray y Eisaguirre, José, 262
Echeverría, Esteban, 267
Emerson, Ralph Waldo, 18-25, 146-67
Estrada Palma, Tómas, 330
Estrampes, José de, 244
Etienne, Louis, 22
Euripides, 69

Fabre, Ferdinand, 207
Fergusson, D. David, 63-64
Fernández, María, 109
"Fifty-Fifth Exhibition in the National Academy of Design," 16
Firduso, 237
Flaccus, Aulus Persuus, 197
Flaubert, Gustave, 278-83
Flemish School of Art, 74
Fontaine, Jean de la, 285
Fortuny, José María Bernardo Mariano, 78, 94-96, 114, 119
Fouquier-Tinville, Antoine Quentin, 210
Français, François, Louis, 101
France, art in, 63-69, 77-79, 83-86, 87, 88, 90-91, 95-105, 116, 118-24
Franklin, Benjamin, 166
Freiligrath, Hermann Ferdinand, 228
French art, 62-64, 77-79, 83-86, 87, 90-91, 95-105, 118-24
French novelists, 205-07
French Revolution, 54-62, 210
French Water Color Society, 101
Friend of the People, 57
Fromentín, Eugéne, 83-86

Garfield, James B., 28
García, Rafael, 41
Gaucho, 266-77
Gauls, 61
Gautier, Théophile, 299
Geibel, Emmanuel, 228
Gerícault, Théodore, 98

Gérôme, Jean León, 78
Gifford, Sanford Robinson, 75
Girondins, 55
Gladstone, William Ewart, 23, 169
Goethe, Johann Wolfgang von, 297
Gogol, Nicolai Vasilievich, 237, 290
Gómez, Juan, 36, 37
Gonzales, Manuel Pedro, 30
Gonzalbo, Pablo, 14
Goya, Francisco de G. y Lucientes, 14, 76, 106-12, 122-24
Grant, Ulysses S., 80
Gray, Henry Peters, 79
Greek independence, 219
Greek mythology, 122, 178, 234
Greeley, Horace, 32
Grito de Dolores, 47
Grito de Yara, 214
Guatemala, 28, 200
Guatemalan Review, 33
Guerra, Benjamin, 330
Gutiérrez, Felipe, 15, 35-37, 40

Haeckel, Ernst Heinrich, 269
Hall, George Henry, 82
Halleck, Fritz-Greene, 18
Hawthorne, Nathaniel, 198
Haymarket Affair, 29
Herzen, Alexander Ivanovich, 140
Heine, Heinrich, 228, 258
Hellenism, 234
Henner, Jean-Jacques, 102
Heredia, José María, 208-24
Hiawatha, 28, 186
Hidalgo y Costillo, Miguel, 47
Hispanic America, 22
Holmes, Oliver Wendell, 189
Homer, 203
Homer, Winslow, 75, 81, 82
Horace, 210, 226
Hour, The, 13, 29
Howells, William Dean, 18, 29, 189
Hugo, Victor, 170, 239, 257, 285
Huguet, Jaimes, 123
Humboldt, Alexander von, 207, 216
Hungarian Revolution, 127
Hungary, 237
Hunt, William Holman, 79
Hunt, William Morris, 79

Ibsen, Henrik, 226
Iduarte, Andrés, 18
Impressionists, 16, 118-24
India, 137
Innocents Abroad, The, 75, 194
Ireland, 23, 169
Irving, Washington, 18
Isabey, Jean-Baptiste, 104
Italy, art in, 64, 67-68, 77-79
Italian art, 64, 67-68, 77-79

Jackson, Helen Hunt, 18, 19
Jaipur, 137
Jacobins, 55
Jacquemart, Hesden de, 101
Jesus, 125, 128-35, 140-47
Johnson, Jonathan Eastman, 75, 81
Jourdain, Francis, 103-04

Kallmeyer, Hans Julius, 79
Katkohov, Mikhail Makiforovich, 290
Kaulbach, Wilhelm von, 76
Keats, John, 300
Kerner, Justinus Andreas, 228
Knaus, Friedrich von, 77
Konekov, Serg Timof, 291
Kossuth, Louis, 127
Kvaskov, Inkov Gerasimovich, 291

La Forgue, Jules, 22
Lalla Rookh, 331
Leaves of Grass, 22, 168-85
Le Brun, Charles, 104
Leloir, Louis, 103
Leloir, Maurice, 78, 103-04
Leopardi, Gracomo, 263
Lieb, Michael, 84, 125–34
Lisle, Leconte de, 233
Literature, Martí on purpose of, 28
Little Men, 280
Little Woman, 200
Lizaso, Félix, 18, 19, 30, 33
Lizst, Franz, 127
Longfellow, Henry Wadsworth, 18, 27-28, 186-89
Louis XIV, 55
Lowell, James Russell, 29
Lucanus, Marcus Annacus, 210
Luther, Martin, 264, 305
Lyell, Charles, 247

McPherson, James, 211
Madrago y Kuntz, Federico de, 77
Maja, La, 106-12

Malory, Sir Thomas, 27
Malot, Henri Hector, 206
Manet, Edouard, 16, 118, 122
Mantilla, Carmita, 29
Marat, Jean-Paul, 54-62, 216
Marat's Death, 54-62
Marten, Robert K., 31
Martínez, José María, 39
Martínez, José Robles, 79
Mata y Ocampo, Josefina, 39
Maykov, Appolon Nikoeayenich, 290
Medea, 58
Meissonier Jean-Louis-Ernest, 41, 84, 97, 119
Mejía Ignacio, 40
Mendelson, Maurice, 31, 32
Mendive, Rafael María de, 27
Mendoza, Francisco, 42
Mérillat, Louis, 83
Mérimée, Prosper, 285
Metropolitan Museum of Art, 13, 74-79
Mexico, art in, 14-16, 35-73, 92-93; conquest by Spain, 39; war against, 32; war for independence in, 215
Mexican art, 14-16, 35-73, 92-93
Mexican School of Painting, 38
Mexican Revolution, 47
Michelet, Jules, 262
Michiewicz, Adam Berman, 289
Millet, Jean-François, 88
Millevoye, Charles Hubert, 219
Milton, John, 198
Miranda, Primitivo, 41
Molière, 69, 285
Molina, Tirso de, 289
Monet, Claude, 16, 118
Monroy, Petronilo, 42
Montaigne, Michael Eyquem, 154
Montezuma, 93
Moore, Thomas, 331
Morales, Salvador, 50
Moran, Thomas, 76
Morris, William, 298
Morte d'Arthur, 27
Müller, Friedrich, 78
Munkacsy, Michael, 84, 125-34
Munkacsy Christ, The, 125-34
Murillo, Bartolomé Esteban, 36
Musset, Alfred de, 26, 259

Nación, La, 21, 22, 26
Nature, 21, 158
Narcisse-Virgile, Dias de La Peña, 77
Neuville, Alphonse-Marie, 84
New York Sun, 13-14
New York Tribune, 32
Nicol, Père, 79
Nouvel Observateur, 283

Obligado, Rafael, 267
Ocaranza, Manuel, 14
Ode to Niagara, 219
Opinión Nacional, La, 28
On the Origin of Species, 247, 251
O'Rell, Max, 17
Orphans, The, 66, 68
Ossian, 211
Ostrovsky, Alexander Nicolayevich, 290
Overbeck, Johann Friedrich, 64
"Over-Soul, The," 259

Páez, José Antonio, 212
Paleolithic art, 113-17
Palestine, 138
Pampa, The, 266-77
Parnassians, 233
Partido Liberal, El, 17, 30
Passini, Ludwig, 78
Pedroza, Gómez, 40
Peloponnesian War, 69
Pérez Sierra, Francisco, 78
Peter the Great, 290
Petofi, Sandor, 127, 237
Phidias, 297
Phillips, Wendell, 330
"Philosopher of Democracy, The," 20
Pietro, Guido di. *See* Angelica, Fra.
Pilate, Pontius, 130
Pindar, 166, 216
Pissarro, Camille, 16, 118
Placido, 214
Plato, 155, 165-66
Platonism, 155
Plotinus, 154
Poe, Edgar Allan, 18, 24, 31, 173, 237
"Poem of Niagara," 308-27
Poets of America, 25
Polonsky, Yakov Petrovich, 290
Pope, Gregory, 14, 316
Poquelin, Jean-Baptiste. *See* Molière.
Portillo, Miguel, 39
Portuondo, José Antonio, 18, 25, 32
Pre-Raphaelite Brotherhood, 79
Pre-Raphaelites, 298

Prieto, Guillermo, 47
Prometheus, 295
Pushkin, Alexander, 148, 284-93
Puebla, 36, 40

Quartley, Arthur, 76, 81
Quesada, Gonzolo de, 17, 26, 27, 329-33
Quiroga, Juan Facundo, 267
Quetzal, The, 48

Rabelais, François, 279
"Raven, The," 24, 173
Rebull, Santiago, 54-62
Renaissance, 35
Renoir, Pierre-Auguste, 16, 118, 123
Revista Universal, 14
Rivera, Josepe (José) de, 35
Robusti, Jacopo. *See* Tintoretto.
Roll, Alfred Phillippe, 122
Rosas, Concêpción, 46
Rosetti, Dante Gabriel, 298
Roughing It, 25
Rousseau, Theodore, 77
Rubens, Peter Paul, 77, 103

Saint Anthony, 36
Saint Augustine, 70
Salykov, Fyoda Stepanovich, 289
San Carlos Academy, 38, 49-53, 66
Sánchez Solís, Felipe, 40
San Martín, José de, 212
San Martín, Juan Zorilla de, 257
Sappho, 178, 220
Sarmiento, Domingo Faustino, 267
Sartain, Samuel, 82
Sartain, William, 82
Schreyer, Gabriel, 79
Schulman, Ivan, 25, 27
Sculpture, 66-68
Sellén, Francisco, 225-41
Seneca, Lucius Annaeus, 210
Shakespeare, William, 304, 305
Shelley, Percy Bysshe, 263
Shuler, Esther Elise, 18, 30
Spain, art in, 20-23, 35, 77-79, 120-23
Spanish America, Martí spreads knowledge of Emerson to, 22
Spanish art, 20-23, 77-79, 120-23
Spanish poets, 257-65
Spencer, Herbert, 258
Stedman, Edmund Clarence, 32, 151
Stowe, Harriet Beecher, 18, 29
Struggles of Love and Honor, 69-73
Suchet, Joseph François, 90
Swedenborg, Emanuel, 154, 159
Swinburne, Algernon Charles, 299

Talleyrand, Charles Maurice de, 207
Tapiro y Buro, José, 79
Tellez, Gabriel, 289
Tennyson, Alfred, 170
Ten Years' War, 204
Thompson, Count, 82
Thoreau, Henry David, 17, 18, 198
Tiffany, Louis Comfort, 79
Tintoretto, 15, 35
Titian, 106
Tolstoy, Count Pyotov Andreyevich, 290
Torres, Jesús, 39
Tramp Abroad, A, 25
Transcendentalism, 155
Trojan Wars, 211
Turgenev, Ivan Sergeyevich, 289
Turner, J. M. W., 88
Twain, Mark, 18, 25-27, 190-96
Tyndall, John, 165

Uhland, Ludwig, 228
Uncle Tom's Cabin, 29

Valdés, Gabriel de la Concepción, 214
Valley of Mexico, 43
Vargas, José, 40
Vargas, Romero, 40, 41
Vecellio, Tiziano. *See* Titian.
Velasio, José María, 43, 77
Velásquez, Diego, 120
Vercingetorix, 61
Vereshchagin, Vasily, 105, 135-47
Vergniaud, Pierre-Victurnien, 55
Verne, Jules, 27
Vernet, Claude-Joseph, 98
Vetella, 61
Viandi, Miguel, 13
Victoria, Felix Juan Manuel Fernández, 215
Villegas, Esteban Manuel de, 79
Vinci, Leonardo da, 323
Volney, Constantin François de, 216

Warner, Charles Dudley, 30
Watteau, Jean-Antoine, 104

Weir, John Alden, 80
"When Lilacs Last in the Dooryard Bloom'd," 24
Whitman, Walt, 17, 22-25, 132, 151, 168-85
Wilde, Oscar, 294-304
Whittridge, Washington, 76
Wood, Francis Derwent, 82

Zamacois y Zabala, Eduardo, 76
Zola, Emile, 205-06